全国英语专业博雅系列教材/总主编　丁建新

口 译 教 程

主编：李　茜
编者：严小庆　周　泉　佟佳琳　罗巾如
　　　招晓杏　叶　青　张　嘉

中山大学出版社
SUN YAT-SEN UNIVERSITY PRESS
·广州·

版权所有　翻印必究

图书在版编目（CIP）数据

口译教程/李茜主编．—广州：中山大学出版社，2014.6
（全国英语专业博雅系列教材/总主编　丁建新）
ISBN 978-7-306-04832-5

Ⅰ.①口…　Ⅱ.①李…　Ⅲ.①英语—口译—高等学校—教材　Ⅳ.①H315.9

中国版本图书馆 CIP 数据核字（2014）第 021936 号

出版人：	徐　劲
策划编辑：	熊锡源
责任编辑：	熊锡源
封面设计：	曾　斌
责任校对：	刘学谦
责任技编：	何雅涛
出版发行：	中山大学出版社
电　　话：	编辑部 020-84111996，84113349，84111997，84110779
	发行部 020-84111998，84111981，84111160
地　　址：	广州市新港西路135号
邮　　编：	510275　　　传　真：020-84036565
网　　址：	http://www.zsup.com.cn　E-mail:zdcbs@mail.sysu.edu.cn
印刷者：	广州中大印刷有限公司
规　　格：	787mm×960mm　1/16　12.5 印张　245 千字
版次印次：	2014 年 6 月第 1 版　2014 年 6 月第 1 次印刷
印　　数：	1～4000 册　　定　价：33.00 元

如发现本书因印装质量影响阅读，请与出版社发行部联系调换

全国英语专业博雅系列教材编委会

总主编　丁建新（中山大学）

编　委　会

李洪儒（黑龙江大学）
司显柱（北京交通大学）
赵彦春（天津外国语大学）
田海龙（天津外国语大学）
夏慧言（天津科技大学）
李会民（河南科技学院）
刘承宇（西南大学）
施　旭（浙江大学）
辛　斌（南京师范大学）
杨信彰（厦门大学）
徐畅贤（湖南城市学院）
李玉英（江西师范大学）
李发根（江西师范大学）
肖坤学（广州大学）
宫　齐（暨南大学）
张广奎（广东财经大学）
温宾利（广东外语外贸大学）
杜金榜（广东外语外贸大学）
阮　炜（深圳大学）
张晓红（深圳大学）

博雅之辩（代序）

大学精神陷入前所未有的危机，许多人在寻找出路。

我们的坚持是，提倡博雅教育（Liberal Education）。因为大凡提倡什么，关键在于审视问题的症结何在，对症下药。而当下之困局，根源在于功利，在于忘掉了教育之根本。

博雅教育之理念，可以追溯至古罗马人提倡的"七艺"：文法、修辞、辩证法、音乐、算术、几何、天文学。其目的在于培养人格完美的自由思考者。在中国教育史上，博雅的思想，古已有之。中国儒家教育的传统，强调以培养学生人格为核心。儒家"六艺"，礼、乐、射、御、书、数，体现的正是我们所讲的博雅理念。"学识广博，生活高雅"，在这一点上，中国与西方，现代与传统，并无二致。

在古罗马，博雅教育在于培育自由的人格与社会精英。在启蒙时代，博雅教育意指解放思想，破除成见。"什么都知道一点，有些事情知道得多一点"，这是19世纪英国的思想家约翰·斯图亚特·密尔（John Stuart Mill）对博雅的诠释。同一时期，另外一位思想家，曾任都柏林大学校长的约翰·亨利·纽曼（John Henry Newman）在《大学理念》一书中，也曾这样表述博雅的培养目标："如果必须给大学课程一个实际目标，那么，我说它就是训练社会的良好成员。它的艺术是社会生活的艺术，它的目的是对世界的适应……大学训练旨在提高社会的精神格调，培养公众的智慧，纯洁一个民族的趣味"。

博雅教育包括科学与人文，目标在于培养人的自由和理性的精神，而不是迎合市场与风俗。教育的目标在于让学生学会尊重人类生活固有的内在价值：生命的价值、尊严的价值、求知的价值、爱的价值、相互尊重的价值、自我超越的价值、创新的价值。提倡博雅教育，就是要担当这些价值守护者的角色。博雅教育对于我们来说，是一种素质教育、人文教育。人文教育关心人类的终极目标，不是以"有用"为标准。它不是"万金油"，也无关乎"风花雪月"。

在美国，专注于博雅教育的大学称为"文理学院"，拒绝职业性的教育。在中国香港，以博雅教育为宗旨的就有岭南大学，提倡"全人教育"；在台湾大学，博雅教育是大学教育的基础，课程涉及文学与艺术、历史思维、世界文明、道德与哲学、公民意识与社会分析、量化分析与数学素养、物质科学、生命科学等八大领域。在欧洲，博雅教育历史中的七大范畴被分为"三道"（初级）与"四道"（高级）。前者包括语法、修辞与辩证法，后者包括算术、几何、天文与音乐。在中国大陆的中山大学，许多有识之士也提倡博雅之理念，让最好的教授开设通识课程，涉及现代学科之环境、生物、地理等各门。同时设立"博雅学院"，学拉丁，读古典，开风气之先。

外语作为一门人文性很强的学科，尤其有必要落实博雅之理念。对于我们来说，最好的"应用型"教育在于博雅。早在20世纪20～40年代，在水木清华的外文系，吴宓先生提倡"语""文"并重，"中""西"兼修，教学上提倡自主学习与互动研究。在《西洋文学系学程总则》中，吴宓明确了"博雅之士"的培养目标：

> 本系课程编写的目的为使学生：（甲）成为博雅之士；（乙）了解西洋文明之精神；（丙）熟读西方文学之名著，谙悉西方思想之潮流，因而在国内教授英、德、法各国语言文字及文学，足以胜任愉快；（丁）创造今日之中国文学；（戊）汇通东西方之精神而互为介绍传布。

博雅之于我们，不仅仅是理念，更重要的是课程体系，是教材，是教法，是实践，是反应试教育，是将通识与专业熔于一炉。基于这样的理念，我们编写了这套丛书。希望通过这样的教育，让我们的学生知道人之为人是有他内在的生活意义，告诉我们的学生去求知，去阅读，去思考，去创造，去理解世界，去适应社会，去爱，去相互尊重，去审美，去找回精神的家园。

无需辩驳，也不怕非议。这是我们的坚守。

中山大学外国语学院　教授、博士生导师
中山大学语言研究所　所长
丁建新
2013年春天

前　　言

《口译教程》作为"全国英语专业博雅系列教材"之一，是一部适用于高校英语专业口译教学的特色教材，以完成专业基础课的本科英语专业学生为教学对象，也适用于翻译专业本科学生及具有一定英语水平的社会人士。

《口译教程》由"口译概述"、"口译技能"、"口译实战"、"口译培训"与"口译职业"组成，共五章。"口译概述"主要介绍口译的概念、特点、类型、标准以及口译员的素质要求；"口译技能"共六节，每节分为"技能讲解"与"技能训练"两部分，"技能讲解"侧重口译基本技能的详细阐述，"技能训练"以前者为基础，通过提供相应的配套练习，进一步巩固提升学生的口译能力；"口译实战"以话题为线索，内容涵盖了礼仪致辞、旅游、教育文化、能源环境、信息科技、体育、经贸等主题，共八节，每节内容都包含"背景阅读"、"口译精讲"、"实战演练"、"词语拓展"与"厚积薄发"五大模块，每一模块特点鲜明，各有侧重；"口译培训"围绕国内外设有口译专业的著名高校以及国内主要口译资格水平考试展开介绍；"口译职业"着眼于行业与市场，不仅对国内口译行业现状进行分析讲解，同时也为有志于成为专业译员的口译学习者提供切实可行的宝贵意见。

《口译教程》不同于市面上大多数教材，仅局限于口译课堂的教与学，而是以"新手入门—学习演练—培训深造—面向行业"为全新思路，为学习者提供全方位的口译知识。教材所选材料以国内外大型会议发言人的演讲稿为主，力求内容真实，具有学习价值，且所选材料难度适中，配套练习形式多样，题材广泛多元，兼具时代性与典型性。

《口译教程》是较为系统的口译教材，各章节的先后顺序体现了编者对口译教学活动安排的看法和主张。教师在使用时，宜灵活处理，因材施教，既可按照教材内容的编排顺序组织教学活动，也可根据教学大纲及学生的实际水平自行安排讲解顺序，同时结合当下时事热点，充分利用杂志、报纸、互联网等渠道，对书中内容进行适当补充。

由于编者自身的能力有限，教材中难免有疏漏错误之处，请业内专家及广大师生不吝赐教。本书相应听力材料，请从中山大学出版社网站（www.zsup.com.cn）"下载分区—课件下载"中下载。

编　者

2013 年 12 月

目 录

第1章 口译概述 ... 1
- 1.1 口译概念 ... 1
- 1.2 口译特点 ... 2
- 1.3 口译类型 ... 3
- 1.4 口译标准 ... 4
- 1.5 译员素质 ... 4

第2章 口译技能 ... 7
- 2.1 听取信息 ... 7
- 2.2 逻辑分析 ... 9
- 2.3 口译记忆 ... 12
- 2.4 公众演讲 ... 14
- 2.5 口译笔记 ... 18
- 2.6 应对技巧 ... 24

第3章 口译实战 ... 35
- 3.1 礼仪致辞 ... 35
- 3.2 旅游观光 ... 54
- 3.3 文化教育 ... 74
- 3.4 能源环境 ... 93
- 3.5 体坛聚焦 ... 113
- 3.6 信息科技 ... 130
- 3.7 经贸往来 ... 147
- 3.8 政治外交 ... 164

第4章 口译培训 ... 181

2 口译教程

第 5 章 口译职业 ··· 186
    5.1 初识口译职业真面目 ··· 186
    5.2 口译新人入行锦囊 ·· 187

参考文献 ··· 188

第1章 口译概述

1.1 口译概念

口译（interpreting）是一种古老的实践活动。自从人类开始使用语言作为沟通交流的工具，口语交际便成为最直接、最便捷、最普遍的交际手段。而与此同时，也出现了因语言不通而无法沟通的困境，因此人类最早的翻译形式——口译也就随之产生了。

古代的口译与现代的口译有较大的差别，更准确而言，早期的口译只能称作带有口译性质的口语交往。尽管口译有着悠久的历史，纵观整个翻译史，对于口译的研究却少之又少，这极可能是由于口头表达的内容不易进行书面记录而造成的。严格意义上的口译是到了不同民族、不同国家有了正式的贸易和外交往来之后才出现的。

口译真正开始步入现代社会，是在第一次世界大战后的巴黎和会上。当时，英语与法语首次成为正式的工作语言，不懂法语的与会者只能通过口译员进行交流，这让交替传译成为当时会上的亮点。紧接着第二次世界大战后，纽伦堡审判第一次大规模使用同声传译，实现了多语种的接力，令人耳目一新，这大大缩短了会议时间。此后经过一段时间磨合，交替传译和同声传译最终都成为了被认可的模式，并且也确立了口译作为一种专门职业的国际地位。

现在，众多高校已纷纷开设口译的相关培训课程，职业译员也频繁现身于各种场合，口译的使用范围变得更广，规模也更大了。

那么，口译员所从事的口译工作到底是一种什么样的活动？从事口译工作的人，被称为"译员"，在英语中是 interpreter，来自于拉丁词"interpres"，意思是"详述者，解释晦涩难懂之事的人"。因此可以说，"做口译"的人，就是把难以理解的事物解释给他人听。相应地，可以认为口译就是解释的过程，是一种以口头表达的形式在源语（source language）和目的语（target language）之间做转换的活动，是在源语一次性表达的基础上向其他语言所做的一次性翻译。口译的过程就应该是这样的：口译员在对源语进行听辨和理解之后，以口头语的方式向听众传递发言人的内容和意思，让语言上无法沟通的人能够进行交流。

1.2 口译特点

许多口译学习者都有笔译的经验，这里不妨拿笔译与口译做对比，以便更好地了解口译的特点以及对译员素质的要求。

译者在进行笔译过程中如果遇到难题，可以反复阅读揣摩文字，如果仍有疑惑，可以将整个段落或者篇章重新阅读一遍。译者可以有时间查阅字典、手册和专业书籍，可以请教身边的专家。如果问题仍然没有得到解决，可以先搁置一边，完成后面的部分再回过头思考。与笔译相比，口译员面临的问题就比较特殊了。译员接收到信息之后，几乎没有时间去反复斟酌，就必须立刻作出判断。如果当下没有解决问题，那过后也基本没有补救的机会。译员无论遇到多么棘手的问题，也只有短暂的时间解决，因此要求译员有快速的反应能力，同时译员的知识积累、语言功底、心理素质和技巧等等都会在这短暂的时间里暴露无遗。

可以看到，口译与其他形式的翻译活动最明显的不同在于它的即时性。从根本上说，口译是给想要跨越语言和文化障碍进行交际的人们提供即时即地的便利。因此，口译活动有以下两个显著特点：源语语篇只会完整呈现一次，一瞬即逝，一旦错过就很难重听；目的语语篇在较紧张的时间内产出，译员在输出译文后，几乎没有更正和修改的机会。

当然，口译还具有其他特点。首先，口译具有不可预测性。译员可以事先对可能出现的内容进行准备和预测，但是任何的估计都不可能充分。口译的话题千变万化，涉及的专题外知识更是包罗万象，临时抱佛脚准备的内容是远远不够的，还需要平时有意识地进行积累。因此坐在口译现场的译员，不仅应该是一名具备相关专题知识的专家，还应是一名具备丰富百科知识的杂家。其次，口译现场带来的压迫感是另外一个特点。上文提到口译的时间极其紧迫，除此之外，口译的场合有时也会非常严肃，例如国际会议或者商务谈判等，会场的气氛会给译员带来极大的心理压力，从而影响译员的表现。即便是较为轻松的环境，译员仍然是全场的焦点，沟通顺利与否都看口译的效果，重大的责任也会给译员带来巨大的心理负担。最后，译员的工作大多存在个体性。在同声传译中会有两人或三人搭档，但每个译员在整个口译过程中大多还是孤立无援的，能得到外界的帮助少之又少，更不必说其他形式的口译。译员基本处于单打独斗的状态，要独立处理碰到的任何问题，无论是专题知识的难题，还是语言知识的空缺，都只能硬着头皮上，无法回避。在口译过程中，译员也几乎没有时间查阅工具书和参考资料。也正因为如此，在口译过程中的任何差错，都只能由译员一人承担。

1.3 口译类型

根据工作形式的不同，口译主要可以分为交替传译和同声传译两种形式。交替传译的目的语语篇产出是在源语之后进行，而同声传译的目的语语篇是在源语表达的过程中同时表达。

交替传译通常被认为是对较长的整个语篇，或者对其较长的一个部分进行口译，期间译员需要借助笔记减轻其记忆负荷，这是经典的"长交传"。由于交替传译并没有规定源语语篇的长度，所以也会有不需要借助笔记进行的"短交传"存在，也就是语篇很短，能一口气进行翻译，不超过译员的记忆负荷。在"短交传"中往往包含着口译场合中存在的一种特殊的口译形式"联络口译"。"联络口译"可看作一种短的"交替传译"形式，因为语篇较短，不必做笔记。

同声传译通常是指"在有隔音效果的同传箱子中使用同传设备做口头语的口译"。由于科技发达，很多大型的会议场合都配有同声传译的设备。同声传译由于发言人讲话和译员翻译是同时进行，可以节省会议的时间，因此广泛受到欢迎。同声传译主要可以分为"无稿同传"、"有稿同传（视译）"、"耳语传译"和"同声传读"。在同声传译中，通常需要使用设备接收源语，以降低外部环境对译员的干扰，但是当设备不许可，或者只有少数人需要口译服务时，便会采取"耳语传译"的形式，也叫做"咬耳朵"，在服务对象的耳边进行口译。译员在进行"视译"时，其目的语的产出，并不是与源语的语篇表达同步，而是跟他所看到的目标文本同步。如果视译进行的场合并不是实时的环境，也就是说没有源语语篇的同步表达，那么视译就会变成一种类似"口头笔译"的形式。在很多时候，译员在进行同声传译时，能事先拿到目标文本，但是由于实时环境中演讲者会有即兴发挥或者为节省时间删减稿件的情况存在，所以这种"有稿同传"不应当被当成纯粹的视译对待，而是一种包含了视译且较为复杂的同传形式。

除了根据工作形式进行分类之外，口译还可以根据工作场合和内容进行分类，主要包括商务口译、外交口译（军事口译）、法律口译（司法口译与法庭口译）、教育口译、社区口译、卫生保健口译（医疗口译，医院口译）、媒体口译和广播口译、科技口译等等。商务口译应该是最原始的口译类型，最初的口译就是广泛应用于贸易和物物交换之中。随着族群、国家和团体的出现，一旦发生分歧和争端，就需要借助外交口译。社会的发展让人们的交流越来越频繁，各种场合对于口译的需求也越来越高，近些年来最常见的就是对法律口译和教育口译的需求。移民政策的出现，也促使了社区口译的兴起。口译员如果根据自己的爱好，在某个专业方面深入钻研，成为某个领域的专家，不但可以提高自己的口译水平，也会为自己的职业发展开辟更大的空间。

1.4 口译标准

提到翻译的标准，很多人会自然而然地想起严复的"信"、"达"、"雅"翻译三标准。且不论业界对于这条标准的认可程度如何，此标准更适用于衡量笔译作品的优劣。口译跟笔译存在较大程度的不同，口译自身的性质决定了其标准应该有别于笔译的标准。

而关于口译的标准，不同译员和学者提出的看法不尽相同，但经过多年探讨也已达成一些共识。具体可以总结为四点：准确、完整、流畅、及时。

"准确"是指译员要把说话人的内容、思想、情感和意图等等准确地传递给听众。有学者曾细致地将口译的准确性分为主题准确、精神准确、论点准确、风格准确、术语准确、数字准确、表达准确、语速准确以及口吻准确等方面。归根结底，准确的译语应该同时保持源语的意义和风格。

"完整"要求译员要把讲话人发出的信息完整地传译给听众，不能遗漏任何内容和细节。

"流畅"是指译员在保证"准确"的前提下，迅速流利地将信息传译，并且能做到层次分明，掌握节奏。

"及时"在交替传译中体现为译员在讲话人停止说话后2～3秒之内就开始进行口译，并且不间断地译出所有内容；在同声传译中表现在译员的目标语产出尽量与源语产出保持同步，不能延迟过久，且避免出现太多的空白和停顿。

1.5 译员素质

最初的译员都被披上了神秘的面纱。人们认为译员是极具天赋的人，而这类人数量极少，又由于人们对口译的翻译过程缺乏了解，这更强化了译员的神秘色彩。随着人们对口译工作的深入了解，以及在社会发展过程中口译逐渐深入到社会的各个方面，人们开始意识到，除了有一定的天赋之外，译员的很多素质是可以在后天的学习过程中培养出来的。一名优秀的译员至少应该具备以下素质及条件：

(1) 语言功底和口头表达。

成为一名合格的译员，首先需要具有深厚的语言功底，这个语言功底指的是对源语，也是对目的语的熟练掌握。我们说的熟练掌握，并不仅仅是指掌握词汇与语法，还要去了解相关语言的文化背景，理解一些各个阶层可能出现的地道表达和文化用语。深厚的语言功底可以帮助译员在短时间内准确地理解源语的含义、感情色彩，并在迅速组织目的语语言后立即传递给听众。

口头表达也是对译员的一个要求，对于"靠嘴巴"吃饭的译员而言，这一点显得至关重要。试问一个口头表达能力差的人，即便能够百分百理解源语的意思，但是无法充分地传递听到的内容，又怎能顺利完成口译任务？一名合格的译员，也应该是一位优秀的演讲者，擅长表达自己的观点，能够做到言之有物、词能达意。并且，译员的谈吐也会影响译文的质量，说话必须要吐字清晰、干脆利落。

(2) 专题知识和百科知识。

专题知识和百科知识，我们可以合并称之为言外知识。由于翻译本身就是一种文化和知识交流的手段，那么口译作为翻译的一种形式，必然也涉及很多不同的领域。现在国际社会的合作日益增多，口译的话题也愈加多样化，并且呈现一种复杂的趋势。即便是在专业性特别强的会议上，演讲者仍然会提到很多非本专业的话题，因此对于译员的知识要求也不断提高。

专题知识的准备，是可以临时抱佛脚的。在接到相应的口译任务之后，译员应该大量阅读相关的资料和文件，熟悉要讨论的专题以及可能遇到的专业词汇，对服务对象的立场和态度也要有相应的了解。这种准备对于完成口译任务而言是非常重要的。而百科知识则与专题知识不同，口译任务中可能出现的百科知识是不可预测的，只能在日常生活中有意识地进行积累。译员应注重平日生活中的积累，对一般性的话题有所认识，要有最基本的"常识"，并且要关注和了解当今世界的热点问题。如果译员的知识储备不够，就跟"巧妇难为无米之炊"一样，纵使有高超的口译技巧也难以充分发挥。

(3) 口译技能。

现在仍然有很多人存在这样一种观念：懂双语的人就能做翻译。其实不然，很多例子都说明口译是一门技术活，要从事口译工作就必须掌握相应的技术。即便有深厚的语言功底和丰富的知识底蕴，如果没有口译技巧，不懂得如何去处理信息和产出信息，仍然无法成为一名出色的译员。技能的学习不是一蹴而就的，必须分阶段进行训练，而且要在日常的刻苦练习和实践中反复磨练。

(4) 心理和身体素质。

有时一个口译任务是否能够顺利完成，很大程度上取决于译员的心理素质。前面提到口译时面临的紧迫性，因此译员在口译过程中会承受巨大的心理压力，精神也时刻处于紧张状态。很多人在做演讲时会有怯场的情况出现，但是作为一名交替传译译员，工作的一部分就是公共演说，并且译员的任务不仅仅是说，要在听辨理解后去向观众解释。如果心理素质不佳，一上台就怯场，不仅语言表达受影响，恐怕连内容都没有办法听懂。同声传译虽不必直面观众，但译员进行同声传译时精神本来就十分紧张，当两名译员共处狭小的同传箱子中时，可能会给彼此带来心理上的不适。译员在口译时应该从容自信，而这一切都建立于平时的刻苦练习和大量积累的基础上。因此，心理素质的培养要靠平时的锻炼。

身体素质也是不可忽视的一个原因。身体状况会影响到译员的记忆力、注意力以及反应能力，这些都与口译质量息息相关。口译任务对译员的体力也有一定的要求，例如在进行陪同口译的时候，有时译员需要在陪同客户四处辗转的同时还要进行翻译工作；又有时候口译工作是在车上进行的，对于会晕车的译员是一个大的挑战；由于口译场合的要求，译员需要经常短期出行，也会让身体十分疲劳。

（5）职业道德素养。

译员在进行口译任务的时候，会接触到很多不公开或是尚未公开的内容。有时在翻译一些较敏感的话题时，会有记者紧追着译员，希望能得到一些"内部消息"，这种情况时有发生。但是作为译员，应该恪守职业道德，不能够向外界透露不应透露的内容。

在口译过程中，始终保持自己中立的立场也是职业道德的一种体现。在两种文化的交流中，不同的价值观、意识形态、国家立场、民族文化等都可能造成说话人的观点与译员本身保持的观点相悖，甚至让译员的情绪出现波动。即便如此，译员也应该保持中立，如实地将自己听到的内容传递给听众，不能有所改动。

当然，一个译员的职业素养，更多是体现在一些工作细节之中。例如，准时到达任务地点，因为一个活动可能会因为缺少译员而无法继续进行；在有麦克风的现场要注意麦克风的开关，以及使用麦克风的礼仪；养成良好的说话习惯，不能把平时的口头禅带到工作之中；等等。

第2章 口译技能

2.1 听取信息

2.1.1 技能讲解

听取信息是完成口译任务的大前提，因而也是口译过程中最为关键的步骤之一。对于交替传译来说，正确地听取信息要比记笔记更为重要。

"听"大概应该是我们日常生活中最熟悉的一种活动，我们在课堂上听老师讲课，在考试中做听力题目，在日常生活中和朋友交谈。但是，由于聆听的目的不同，听取信息的方法也不尽相同。口译员是很特别的听众，他们听取信息的目的不仅是为了要听懂，而更重要的是为了将原话中的信息原原本本地翻译成另外一门语言，因此口译员采取的听力策略是"积极聆听"（active listening）。这种听力策略要求口译员在听的过程中透彻地了解信息，在转瞬即逝的时间里迅速地捕捉到说话者的意思和逻辑。在这一个过程中，口译员不仅要听懂原语的信息，更重要的是要对信息的逻辑进行梳理和分析，将信息的整体结构有机地串连，从而有效地以译入语清晰、完整地表达信息内容。

要做到积极聆听，可以采用一些听取信息的具体策略。第一，使用"视觉化"的听力方法，即用想象的方法，将注意力集中在说话人所描绘的信息上，而不是放在字词上，从而将语言信息转化为脑海中的画面。这种策略对于信息的理解和记忆非常有效。第二，译员在听的过程中要尤其做到"心无旁骛"，即避免因外界因素如空调的声音、旁人的说话声和其他噪音等分散自己的注意力。第三，译员应做到将个人偏见放置一边，不要评论发言人的立场和观点，不要在翻译过程中分心去判断发言人的口音或者对发言内容挑刺，这些都会影响译员聆听信息的效率。第四，正确的姿势也将有助于我们更好地投入倾听，如身体坐直并稍微靠近发言人。这样的姿势也是向发言人发出积极的信号，表示你在认真听他说话。

除此之外，译员对源语信息背景所掌握的知识在这里也尤为重要。我们往往更容易听懂我们所熟悉的内容和题材。因此在语言学习的过程中，也应该注意百科知识的积累,拓宽知识面,并在聆听的过程中积极地将发言人的说话内容与自己的经验和背景知识联系起来。

要提高听取信息的能力,除了平时要下苦功进行大量的练习以外,正确的训练方式也是不可或缺的。口译员在工作中光听懂是不够的,因为他们听取信息的目的是为了准确、完整地表达信息。在练习中,听完语音材料后,可采用复述的方法。这项练习虽然看似简单,其实不然,复述过程中可能会暴露出现如信息混乱、逻辑不清等问题,但造成这些问题的原因并非都是因为语言表达能力不好,可能是在听力过程中没有注意逻辑分析。复述练习能够很好地锻炼逻辑分析能力、口头语言表达能力及听、说和记忆的精力平衡分配。在进行复述练习时,不应死记硬背原文的遣词造句,而应从整体上把握语音材料的逻辑顺序,抓住关键信息。

2.1.2 技能训练

1. 原语复述

Three Ways of Improving Time Management

Why do we have to work so hard to learn Time Management, to master it? Shouldn't we be born with the ability to work efficiently? The problem is that we have the tendency to want to take the easy way, the short way, and as many have said before me, "A shortcut can often lead to long delays."

Even though multi-tasking, relaxing and other shortcuts might feel as though they save time, working focused on one task at a time and obeying the rules of Time Management, is the real time saver. Here are three ways of making you a better time manager.

1. Batching Tasks

Each time you start a new task it takes time to "warm up", you have to gather all the materials you need and it takes a while before you find a flow. Once you are done, you need to put everything away, which wastes several minutes as well. By spending longer time on each task you decrease the amount of time you spend "Warming up" and "Cooling down" every day.

2. Planning Your Weeks

By organizing your weeks to streamline processes and batch tasks you will save a lot of time.

It also grants you the calm to know that you will be doing all your tasks during the week. I have noticed in myself and others, that it is easy to feel as though I should be doing more each day, but once I started using a weekly schedule I didn't need to feel this way, since I knew the tasks would be handled at the right time.

3. Prioritizing Your Day

Most of us fail to start with the most important (and often most time consuming) task. Instead we hide and do simple tasks such as checking our email.

The problem with that approach is that it leaves the most difficult tasks to the end of the day. If you instead organize your day to have the most difficult tasks first and then have them getting easier and easier, it will motivate you to work faster since your day will be over once you have finished the final simple task.

It will take time to learn and require a lot of discipline, but if you put your mind to it you will quickly start saving 5 minutes here and 5 minutes there.

2. 原语复述

皮尤研究中心周三发布一项针对3000人的电子书阅读调查。调查发现，过去一年里每5个美国人中有一个阅读电子书。在这1/5的人群中，有42%的人表示他们是在电脑上阅读电子书，这使得电脑成为最热门的阅读电子书设备。

这项调查结果令人惊讶。一方面，对于阅读电子书来说，电脑既不舒适也不方便；另一方面，因为大多数电子书出版商或零售商都优先考虑手机、电子书阅读器和平板电脑的阅读体验。例如，亚马逊已经推出了两代的Kindle电子书阅读器，并且还发布了针对智能手机和平板电脑的应用。

排在个人电脑之后，最流行的设备是电子书阅读器（41%），其次是手机（29%）和平板电脑（23%）。

阅读电子书的都是哪些人呢？首先，他们更加喜欢阅读。阅读电子书的人群过去一年内平均读了24本书，非电子书读者只有15本。电子书阅读人群也没有放弃传统纸质书：他们中有88%的人称过去一年内也在阅读纸质书。调查发现，这些人选择电子书是喜欢它的快速和可移植性；选择纸质书是为了读给儿童听或与他人分享。

总体来说，阅读电子书的人群正在上升。根据皮尤的调查，相比两年前，现在每天阅读电子书的人群是当时的4倍。

2.2 逻辑分析

2.2.1 技能讲解

20世纪六七十年代，法国的著名口译专家塞莱斯科维奇提出了释意学派理论，认为口译的实质就是"释意"，即"脱离原语语言外壳"，用另外一种语言复述原文的意义而非字词。这种理论认为，口译员之所以能够记住一篇几分钟的讲话，并凭借记忆自如地用译入语将译出语内容完整、清晰地表达出来，并非因为他们记忆力超群，而是因为他们对原语信息的理解远远不止认识字词那么简单。译员在理解过程中"摆脱了原语言的形式"，口译员接受的是由字词的聚合传递的"意义"。口译员不仅是信息的接受者，同时也是信息的发布者。而为了更好地接收并发布信息，对意义的逻辑分析能力便显得尤为重要。

口译员的听是积极的听，分析也是积极主动的分析，在听的过程中不是被动机械地接收信息，而是要努力地理解说话人的意图。说话人是怀着交际沟通的目的向听众发表讲话的，这就要求译员要善于把握交际双方，即说话人和听众的交际目的。说话人在其所使用的字词背后往往怀着特定的意图，希望达到特定的效果。译员要准确理解讲话的逻辑思想，对讲话内容的整体进行有效的把握。而要做到这一点，译员可以在听讲话的过程中搞清楚 5 个 W 元素，即"What happened? When did it happen? Who was involved? Where did it happen? Why did it happened?"这几个问题也有助于译员把精力集中在信息上而不是发言人所使用的字词上。

除了把握讲话的整体中心思想以外，理清句子间的前后逻辑关系尤为重要。译员在听的过程中要尤其注意表示句子中的逻辑关系词。如表示先后次序关系的词组有 first, to start with, to begin with, next, last but not least 等；表示因果关系的词组有 as a result, hence, consequently, therefore, so that, on account of 等；表示转折关系的词组有 even though, but, nonetheless, despite that, regardless, yet, however 等；表示并列关系的词组有 and, also, as well as 等；表示递进关系的词组有 moreover, furthermore, accordingly, in addition, at the same time, in other words 等；表示举例关系的词组有 for instance, namely, for example, notably, such as 等；表示条件关系的词组有 unless, if necessary, if it is the case, provided that, lest 等。

2.2.2 技能训练

1. 原语复述

患感冒之后，就会出现鼻塞、呼吸不畅、说话瓮声瓮气、流清鼻涕等症状。如果患上比较严重的感冒，那么体温将会升高，全身都会因此而感到不适。

引起感冒的真正原因是病毒。当病毒入侵体内时，为了抵御这些肉眼看不见的敌人，人体会自发地采取各种各样的措施，鼻塞、流涕、打喷嚏和发热等症状，是人体的一种本能的自我保护反应。

鼻子塞住可防止病毒入侵；不停地流鼻涕和打喷嚏，有助于把已经入侵的病毒赶走；发热也就是体温升高，能够刺激白细胞的吞噬功能，促进抗体形成，而且大部分感冒病毒是怕热的,发热可以阻挠病毒的繁殖。

2. 原语复述

If you've just got back from holidays and can't settle into work again, you're probably suffering from a case of the holiday blues. If it goes on for a few days, you may even have Post Holiday Syndrome, a general feeling of discomfort on having to get back to work, with sufferers experiencing symptoms like tiredness, lack of appetite, muscle ache and anxiety. But never fear — there are ways to get back into a routine and boost your spirits after your break.

First, don't go straight back to work. It's difficult to go from relaxing days straight into full-on meeting mode. So it's advised to build in a period of "re-adaptation" between holiday and work.

Second, work out what you have to do. No doubt you'll have an inbox crammed of emails and have dozens of voicemails to return. But don't get overwhelmed by the work that's built up in your absence. If you don't manage it properly, you will run the risk of undoing all the relaxing effects of your holiday. So spending half an hour planning out what you have to do before actually getting back into your work. And don't be shy about letting people know that you're just back from a break and that you will respond to them in due course, in an organized fashion.

Third, keep up your exercise habit. When we reflect on what we enjoyed about our holidays, one thing that often comes up is that we tend to go for lots of walks and we exercise more when we're away. It's important to incorporate that into our daily life when we get back.

Fourth, book your next break. Having another holiday to look forward can ease the effects of Post Holiday Syndrome. If you know that you're going away in a few weeks' time, it can help keep you motivated.

Fifth, re-evaluate your priorities. Some people like to veg out while on holidays but others take time to figure out what they're doing in life and what makes them happy. If you're one of the latter, getting back from a break may bring all these issues into focus. If you're coming back to something you really love, you won't have the holiday blues.

However, if you have these negative feelings for a few days, then you should pay attention to them. Often they are a prompt for change in your life.

2.3 口译记忆

2.3.1 技能讲解

总地来说，记忆分为存储和提取两个阶段。而口译的记忆主要分为以下三种：

第一种：瞬时记忆。这种记忆只能维持 0.25 秒左右，主要是通过视觉获得图像或通过听觉获得声音所产生的记忆。因为声音转瞬即逝，所以瞬时记忆非常短。而提高语言能力基础将有助于译员从声音辨别意义，从而增强瞬时记忆。

第二种：短时记忆。这种记忆的时间维持在 15～20 秒之间，通常包括 5～9 个信息单位。短时记忆是口译中最活跃的记忆，译员可以通过这几个信息单位的清晰记忆进行逻辑分析与信息关联，从而达成信息的解码，并最终实现原语与译入语的转化。除此之外，短时记忆还能激活长时记忆。

第三种：长时记忆。此种记忆主要包括译员过去的经历、常识以及专业知识。长时记忆的信息容量比前两种都要大很多，因此在口译过程中被激活的长时记忆配合短时记忆成为工作记忆。由于长时记忆都是经验性的，比如过去看过、听过、经历过的事情，所以在口译工作中提取出来的与正在听的信息相结合，可以有助于译员更好地理解分析。

这三种记忆机制在口译过程中各司其职。瞬时记忆的前提是良好的听辨能力，从而能从转瞬即逝的声音中捕捉到有意义的信息，短时记忆不断地将信息单位进行串联和解码，而长时记忆的信息量最大，持续时间最长，这与译员平时的语言知识和言外知识积累有关。如果译员经验丰富，或者正在听的是自己熟悉的内容，能大量激活长时记忆，这样就能减轻瞬时记忆和短时记忆的负担。这就是为什么译员平时除了口译训练以外，还要在拓展百科知识、了解国内外时事方面做大量工作。

著名的口译专家 Daniel Gile 在他的口译"认知负荷模型"中指出，口译分输入和输出两个阶段。其中交替传译在输入阶段的认知负荷为 L + N + M + C，即听辨 + 笔记 + 短时记忆 + 协调。没有记忆，则译员对信息的解码和转化无从谈起。由前文可知，听辨和逻辑分析能力与短时记忆是密不可分的，听辨能力和逻辑分析能力越强，则短时记忆越活跃，时间跨度越长。

为了提高记忆效率，可以采取信息组织法，即按照信息的逻辑顺序，如时间顺序、总分关系、方向方位等进行记忆。另外，也可以采取信息视觉化法，将听到的内容想象成静态或动态的画面，这和听力理解的视觉化方法很相似，能有效帮助记忆。如果正在听的内容和自己的经验和背景知识有联系，那么调动长时记忆与听到的信息联系起来，也可以有效地提高记忆效率。

为了提高短时记忆的能力，译员在平时训练中应进行大量的复述练习，一开始可以先从原语复述做起，慢慢过渡到目的语复述。口译员超群的工作记忆并不是天生的，而是要通过正确的训练方法以及长期不懈的训练来实现的。

2.3.2 技能训练

1. 原语复述

栖息在井里的青蛙在井边碰上一只从东海而来的海龟，便对它吹嘘自己的惬意："你瞧我住在这儿多么快乐呀！我从井栏上蹦进浅井，可以在井壁的缝隙里小憩。在井水里游耍，水面就托住我的胳肢和下巴。在软绵绵的泥地上漫步，淤泥就漫过脚背。看看周围的红虫、小螃蟹，它们谁也不能比我自由自在。"

青蛙喋喋不休地夸耀自己的安乐："我独自享受这口井，真是快乐极了。"它邀请海龟到井里来游览观光一番。海龟经不住青蛙的怂恿，也走到井边去瞧瞧。谁知它的左足还没踏进井底，右足却被井栏绊住了。它进退不得，迟疑了一会儿，回到了原处。

海龟算是亲自领教了一番青蛙炫耀不已的井边环境。它忍不住向青蛙介绍东海的景象："我生活的大海以千里为单位都不足以形容海面的辽阔，用万尺深度都不足以穷尽海底。在大禹时代，10年中有9年遭水灾，海水也并不因此而上涨；商汤时代，8年中有7年遇旱灾，海水也并不因此而下降。你要知道，大海不受旱涝影响而涨落。这就是我栖息在广阔东海的乐趣！"

青蛙听了海龟对大海的描述，满脸涨得绯红，羞愧得一句话也说不出来……

2. 目的语复述

Learning how to drive is harder than it looks. Driving lessons are essential, of course. Teaching yourself will most assuredly end in disaster. Keep the following rules and suggestions in mind when you start driving.

Rule 1: Always be alert. Check the rear view and side mirrors; make sure you can see all traffic and pedestrians near your vehicle.

Rule 2: Watch out for trucks and buses that take up a lot of room on the road. These vehicles typically have visibility limitations that your car does not have. You'll need to compensate for any awkward situations that arise.

Rule 3: Don't do anything that is very quick, or sudden. Keep calm and assess each situation as it presents itself. Driving can be a nervous experience (especially at first). It's best to take your time and do the right thing at the right time.

Rule 4: Be safe. Following the rules of the road isn't enough. You need to anticipate any situation that could put you and your car in jeopardy. "Safety First" isn't just a meaningless platitude. It's the most important rule for all drivers.

2.4 公众演讲

2.4.1 技能讲解

掌握良好的公众演讲技巧是口译员必须掌握的一项重要技能。"口译是一种通过口头表达形式，将所听到的信息准确而快速地由一种语言转换成另一种语言，进而达到传递与交流信息之目的的交际行为。"因此，作为第二发言人（secondary speaker），口译员在用另外一种语言再现发言人的信息的同时，也承担着公众演讲的角色，需要利用自己的口头语言（语言手段）和体态语言（非语言手段），搭建好沟通的桥梁。

口译员需要通过语言手段来有效地将信息传达出去。一位优秀的口译员不仅要有良好的双语能力，还应该表达清晰，沉着自信，具有感染力。因此，掌握声音的艺术便显得尤为重要。这其中包括以下几个方面：

(1) 发音：一名合格的译员应在中英双语口头表达上符合规范，避免口音太重，影响听众理解说话内容。与此同时，还应该注意吐字清晰，避免过多的连读、弱读、吞音等。

(2) 音量：在进行公众演讲时，声音的平稳清晰很重要。在交替传译中，如果译员的音量太小，则显得底气不足，没有自信，观众听不清楚，便会对译员的能力产生质疑；如果译员的音量太大，一来耗费太多的体力，二来显得歇斯底里，也会在听众心中留下不良印象。因此，译员要时刻注意观察听众的反应，尤其是后排听众的表情，适时调整自己的音量。与此同时，口译员在工作中很多时候都需要用到麦克风，所以要注意麦克风礼仪，提前到会场检查并调整麦克风的距离和位置。

(3) 音调：著名的口译专家让·艾赫贝尔（Jean Herbert）说过，"口译员应避免语调呆板、平淡、毫无生气，用这种语调翻译，会使听众厌倦发困"。一般来说，口译中最好采用中音，因为中音显得沉稳可信，音调太低会让观众昏昏欲睡，而音调太高则会让观众听得很辛苦。此外，口译员还应该注意利用音调的变化表达不同的情感，避免过于沉闷。

(4) 语速：口译员在工作中应做到语速适当变换，因为一成不变的语速会造成沉闷。另外，口译切勿语速太快，不然观众会跟不上说话人的思维。在公众演讲中，尤其是在听众人数比较多的情况下，语速可以稍微放慢一些。口译员在工作中处于高度紧张的状态，有时候会越说越快，这个时候就要注意适时调整语速。

(5) 逻辑：口译员说话要注意逻辑，做到条理清晰，重点突出，主次分明。此外，当组织语言遇到障碍而进行思考时，应避免发出"嗯"、"呃"等声音。

除了以上提及的语言手段，口译员的身体语言也同样非常重要。身体语言能够更为强烈和丰富地让观众感受到口译员想要传达的信息。因此大方得体的仪态是成功的口译的必备条件，这其中包括以下几个方面：

(1) 着装：译员要根据工作场合调整自己的着装，总的来说要做到大方得体。在正式会议和商务谈判的场合，需要着正装，但要注意不要穿太鲜艳或明亮的颜色，以免喧宾夺主。男性译员应避免穿白色正装。女性译员应避免穿太短的裙子。如果不确定如何着装才合宜，可以提前主动和会议主办方进行沟通，了解他们对译员着装的要求。

(2) 眼神交流：在口译中，与听众进行适时的眼神交流会有助于提高口译效果。译员应注意避免只顾埋头念稿。眼神交流有四大作用：一是表示对听众的尊重，二是吸引听众的注意力，三是维持听众对讲话人或内容的信心，四是获取听众的反馈和反应。

(3) 站姿：为了防止身体晃动或倾斜，译员可以采取双脚八字形或丁字形站立。口译员还应避免双腿站得太直，这样会显得身体很僵硬，而且消耗大量的体力。口译时一手握笔记本，一手握笔，要保持端庄高雅的姿态。

(4) 手势：作为公众演讲者，口译员可以加入适当的手势。但是口译员毕竟不是发言人，过多的手势有抢风头之嫌，所以要特别注意保持端庄稳重，切勿手舞足蹈。

2.4.2 技能训练

1. 英汉口译

Bidding for Beijing 2008 Olympic Games
Yang Lan

Mr. President, Ladies and Gentlemen, good afternoon!

Before I introduce our cultural programs, I want to tell you one thing first about 2008. You're going to have a great time in Beijing.

China has its own sport legends. Back to Song Dynasty, about the 11th century, people started to play a game called Cuju, which is regarded as the origin of ancient football. The game was very popular and women were also participating. Now, you will understand why our women football team is so good today.

There are a lot more wonderful and exciting things waiting for you in New Beijing, a dynamic modern metropolis with 3,000 years of cultural treasures woven into the urban tapestry. Along with the iconic imagery of the Forbidden City, the Temple of Heaven and the Great Wall, the city offers an endless mixture of theatres, museums, discos, all kinds of restaurants and shopping malls that will amaze and delight you.

But beyond that, it is a place of millions of friendly people who love to meet people from around the world. People of Beijing believe that the 2008 Olympic Games in Beijing will help to enhance the harmony between our culture and the diverse cultures of the world.

Within our cultural programs, education and communication will receive the highest priority. We seek to create an intellectual and sporting legacy by broadening the understanding of the Olympic Ideals throughout the country.

Cultural events will unfold each year, from 2005 to 2008. We will stage multi-disciplined cultural programs, such as concerts, exhibitions, art competitions and camps which will involve young people from around the world. During the Olympics, they will be staged in the Olympic Village and the city for the benefit of the athletes.

Our Ceremonies will give China's greatest-and the world's greatest artists a stage for celebrating the common aspirations of humanity and the unique heritage of our culture and the Olympic Movement.

With a concept inspired by the famed Silk Road, our Torch Relay will break new ground, traveling from Olympia through some of the oldest civilizations known to man——Greek, Roman, Egyptian, Byzantine, Mesopotamian, Persian, Arabian, Indian and Chinese. Carrying the message "Share the Peace, Share the Olympics," the eternal flame will reach new heights as it crosses the Himalayas over the world's highest summit — Mount Qomolangma, which is known to many of you as Mt. Everest. In China, the flame will pass through Tibet, cross the Yangtze and Yellow River, travel the Great Wall and visit Hong Kong, Macau, Taiwan and the 56 ethnic communities who make up our society. On its journey, the flame will be seen by and inspire more human beings than any previous relay.

I am afraid I cannot present the whole picture of our cultural programs within such a short period of time. Before I end, let me share with you one story. Seven hundred years ago, amazed by his incredible descriptions of a faraway land of great beauty, people asked Marco Polo whether his stories about China were true. He answered: What I have told you was not even half of what I saw. Actually, what we have shown you here today is only a fraction of Beijing that awaits you.

2. 汉英口译

我的故事以及背后的中国梦
白岩松

过去的20年，中国一直在跟美国的三任总统打交道，今天到了耶鲁我才知道，其实他只跟一所学校打交道。但是透过这3位总统我也明白了，耶鲁大学的毕业生的水准也并不很平均。

接下来就进入我们这个主题，或许要起个题目的话应该叫《我的故事以及背后的中国梦》。我要讲5个年份，第一要讲的年份是1968年。那一年我出生了。那一年世界非常乱，在法国有它的这个，巨大的街头的骚乱，在美国也有，然后美国的总统肯尼迪遇刺了，但是的确这一切的原因都与我无关。而那一年我们更应该记住的是马丁·路德·金先生遇刺，虽然那一年他倒下了，但是"我有一个梦想"这句话却真正地站了起来，不仅在美国站起来，在全世界站起来。

当时很遗憾，不仅仅是我，几乎很多的中国人并不知道这个梦想，因为当时中国人，每一个个人很难说拥有自己的梦想。中国与美国的距离非常遥远，不亚于月亮与地球之间的距离。但是我并不关心这一切，我只关心我是否可以吃饱。很显然，我的出生非常不是时候，不仅对于当时的中国来说，对于世界来说，似乎都有些问题。

1978年，10年之后，我10岁，我依然生活在我出生的时候，那个只有20万人的非常非常小的城市里。它离北京的距离有2000公里，它要想了解北京出的报纸的话，要在3天之后才能看见，所以对于我们来说，是不存在新闻这个说法。那一年我的爷爷去世了，而在两年前的时候我的父亲去世了，所以只剩下我母亲一个人要抚养我们哥俩，她一个月的工资不到10美元。因此即使10岁了，梦想这个词对我来说，依然是一个非常陌生的词汇，我从来不会去想它。我看不到这个家庭的希望，只是会感觉，那个时候的每一个冬天都很寒冷，因为我所生活的那个城市离苏联更近。但是就在我看不到希望的1978年的时候，不管是中国这个国家，还有中国与美国这两个国家之间，都发生了非常巨大的变化，那是一个我们在座的所有人，今天都该记住的年份。

2.5 口译笔记

2.5.1 技能讲解

　　口译笔记法是口译员的一项重要技巧，这一点毋庸置疑。然而不了解口译的人以及一些口译初学者往往以为笔记法不但神乎其神而且是无所不能的，所以很多口译学生从一开始就希望老师传授给他们一套完整翔实的笔记法技巧，并将自己在口译练习中遇到的很多困难都归结为笔记没有做好。其实这是步入了一个误区。首先，职业译员的笔记法都具有鲜明的个人特色。口译笔记法的确遵循一些共同的规律和原则，但是总的来说并没有一套放之四海而皆准的方法。这是因为口译员的笔记是他们经过思考和分析，将接收到的信息进行个性化解码后有选择性地记录下的结果，因此每个人的笔记都不尽相同。其次，笔记在口译中的作用是为了减轻记忆的压力，帮助译员腾出更多的精力进行理解、分析和信息转化，所以笔记法相当于登山运动员的登山杖，如果用得好就能帮助译员走得更轻松，反之，如果使用不当或者过度依赖拐杖，就会本末倒置，使译员步履蹒跚。

　　总的来说，口译笔记有四大特点：第一，口译笔记具有"立即使用"这个特性，因此口译笔记应该简明清晰，易解读。第二，口译笔记牵涉到两种语言的转化。初学口译者往往会问一个问题："到底是该用译入语还是原语做笔记呢？"一般来说，笔记中译入语越多，越能反映译员经过思考并将原语信息解码。因此在初学阶段，应鼓励口译学习者尽量用译入语做笔记，以促使他们思考。第三，口译笔记法具有结构完整性。口译员的笔记必须层次分明，逻辑清晰，反映原文的信息结构。第四，口译笔记还具有"单次使用"的特性，不是为日后的翻阅而记录的。

　　虽然口译员的笔记法具有鲜明的个人特色，但是口译笔记还是有一些共性和原则的。

　　首先，笔记本的选择。口译员使用的笔记本最好是上下翻页的线圈本，约手掌宽，封底较硬，方便译员在没有任何支撑物的情况下做笔记。建议用圆珠笔或者铅笔而不是墨水笔或水写笔做笔记。避免用散页纸记录。

　　其次，口译笔记法的四大原则：纵写、内缩、分割和重叠。

　　（1）纵写。纵写的原因，首先是方便目光的游走，其次是为了体现信息的结构和逻辑关系。

　　（2）内缩。上下两行的信息靠内缩来体现层次关系，这样译员在读取笔记信息时一眼就能看出逻辑主次。

（3）**分割**。在记录某一层次的信息结束时，应该用横线来做区隔。区隔开的不一定是一个句子，也可能是一段话。初学者往往在使用分割线时掌握得不太好，有时分割线用得太多，有时会完全忘记使用分割线。分割线的重要性毋庸置疑，口译学习者要通过大量练习，理清信息之间的逻辑关系，用好分割线。

（4）**重叠**。具有排比意义的字词，应该使用自上而下的重叠法，并在排比的字词左边画一条竖线或括号，这样在阅读笔记的时候就能一眼看出信息之间的排比关系。

常用笔记符号：

箭头符号

↑　上升；提高；增强；上涨；增长；扩大；晋升（rise, go up, strengthen, skyrocket, increase, expand, promote）

↓　下降；降低；滑坡；恶化；降职；削减/裁减（drop, decrease, go down, deteriorate, reduce, demote, cut）

↗　上扬；渐渐好转（become better and better）

↘　下挫；不断亏损（become worse and worse）

→　出口；去；向前；前往；运往；导致；发展成为……（export to, go, go forward, send to, result in, cause, lead to）

←　回顾；进口；倒退；来自；源于（review, import, go back to, come from, result from）

数学符号

＋　增加；补充；除此之外；另外（furthermore, in addition to, with, and, besides, etc）

－　减少；删除；缺乏（minus, delete, lack）

×　不对的；错的；坏的；不好的；臭名昭著的（incorrect, wrong, bad, inappropriate, notorious）

＞　超过；大于；胜过；优于（more than, bigger than, surpass, better than）

＜　小于；不足；次于；逊色（fewer than, less than, worse than, inferior to）

＝　与……相同（equal to, the same as）

≠　不等于（not equal to）；或者"不是……对手"（no match for）

≈　大约，左右（approximately, around, about, or so）

∑　总和；总数（total, the total number/sum, totally）

∵　原因，理由（because, owing to, thanks to, due to）

∴　结果，结论（therefore, as a result, consequently, so）

标点符号
: 说；告诉；认为；宣称；声明；抗议；譬如（say, speak, tell, declare, announce, protest, such as）
? 问题；疑问；问（question, doubt, suspicious, skeptical, ask）
☆ 很重要（very important, vital, crucial, critical）
（ ） 包括；在……之中（including, within, among, inside）

其他符号
□ 国家（country, state, nation）
& 和；与；共同；与……在一起；陪同（and, together with, accompany）
√ 正确；对；好；肯定；著名；同意；支持（correct, right, good, affirmative/certain, well known/famous, agree, support）
° 人；人民（person, people）。如：中°（中国人），US°（美国人）
∈ 属于（belong to）
☆ 重要的（important）
⊕ 医院；红十字会（hospital, red cross）
TM 商标（trademark）
£ 英镑（pound）
$ 美元（dollar）
∈ 欧元（euro）
¥ 人民币（RMB）

笔记示范 1
我这次访问美国，是为增进互信、加强友谊、深化合作、推动 21 世纪积极合作全面的中美关系继续向前发展而来。中美建交 32 年来，两国关系已经成长为具有战略意义和全球影响的双边关系。奥巴马总统就职以来，在双方共同努力下，两国各领域合作成果丰硕，中美关系得到新的发展，为两国人民带来了实实在在的利益。

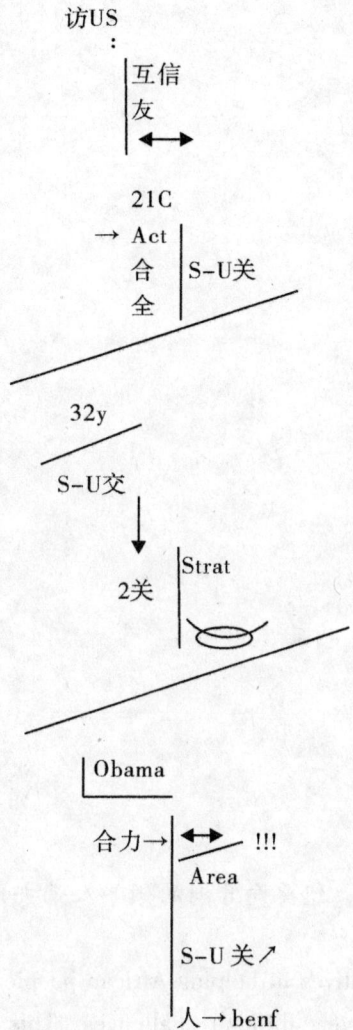

笔记示范 2

Twenty five years ago I came to Hong Kong as a student. The year was 1985. Deng Xiaoping and Margaret Thatcher had recently signed the historic Joint Declaration. The remarkable story of the successful handover of Hong Kong and the great progress Hong Kong has continued to make is an example to the world of what can be achieved when two countries cooperate in confidence and with mutual respect.

22   口译教程

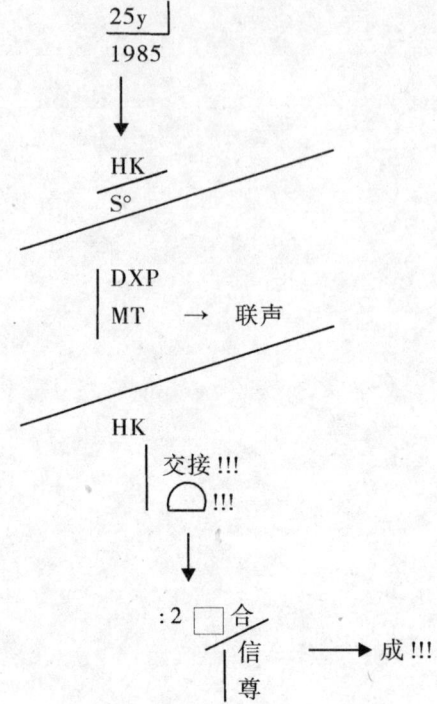

2.5.2 技能训练

1. 英汉互译

A：您这次来到北京是要出席中非合作论坛，您要向非洲的领导人带去什么样的信息呢？

B：China has been taking very important initiatives in helping African people and countries, to strengthen their capacities to address very difficult challenges. This is a great example of South-South cooperation. It's not only North-South Cooperation, but China is now a leading champion in promoting South-South Cooperation. As number two world economy, with a great economic strength and social and economic development, and political maturity, it is good that China shares whole experience, and technologies and know-how with the many African people. This is the core purpose. And as the Secretary-General of the United Nations, I will deliver my own message to not only African people but many developing countries, who are looking to such Chinese cooperation. I really count on China in continuing the support, working together with the United Nations.

A：我们知道在地球上最困难的工作就是做联合国的秘书长，一只耳朵要听发展中国家的诉求，另一只耳朵要听发达国家的抱怨。这个位置的工作有多难？为什么您还愿意做这份工作？

B: As a public servant, I have been working very hard. So whether it is difficult or not, that's not the big problem for me, because I'm committed to it. The most difficult thing is that, when I'm not able or the United Nations is not able to properly or be correctly understood by other people, when some terrorists or some radicals attack the United Nations, or killing the peace-keepers, or abducting humanitarian workers, this really saddens me. They simply do not understand what and why the United Nations is there.

2. 中译英

驻荷兰大使张军在"共品中国年味，同庆兔年新春"活动上的致辞

各位来宾、各位朋友：

再过一天就是中国农历新年。值此新春佳节来临之际，我谨代表中国驻荷兰使馆全体同事，向各位来宾和朋友致以节日的问候，衷心祝愿大家在新的一年里事业兴旺、家庭幸福、万事如意！

春节是中国最重要的传统节日，也最能集中地展示中国文化的深刻内涵。对中国人来说，春节最重要的内容就是家庭团圆。无论身在何方，人们都会设法赶回家中，共享亲人的关爱、家庭的和谐、团聚的欢乐。今天我们在这里举办这样一场国际大家庭的聚会，目的就是营造一个家的氛围，在这样的气氛中，"共品中国年味，同庆兔年新春"，一起享受节日的欢乐，共同期待充满希望的新的一年。

确实，随着全球化的快速发展，世界各国人民之间的联系越来越紧密，世界越来越像一个大家庭。在促进各国间关系发展的进程中，文化始终有着重要和不可替代的作用。沟通从文化开始。文化间的共性可以使我们克服肤色和语言的不同而相互认同，文化间的差异则为我们相互借鉴提供了可能。我衷心期待，通过文化这个桥梁，我们可以更多地相互了解，更多地相互借鉴，更多地相互信任，从而使我们的世界成为一个真正和平、和谐、繁荣的世界。

中华民族是一个多民族大家庭，56个民族的兄弟姐妹长期以来和睦相处，共同发展，也孕育了丰富多彩、充满魅力的多元中国文化。我们荣幸地邀请到中国青海省歌舞团为大家献上一台充满浓郁中国民族风情的演出。青海省位于中国西部，是多民族聚居区，有着丰厚的文化底蕴。相信通过他们精彩的表演，大家既能充分享受艺术之美，也更深切地感受中国各民族和谐共处的美好生活，增进大家对中国和中国文化的全面了解。

最后，祝兔年给所有的朋友带来好运、健康和幸福。我也祝愿中荷关系和各

领域合作，如同兔子奔跑一样，实现跨越式发展。

谢谢大家。

2.6 应对技巧

2.6.1 技能讲解

1. 数字难

数字表达的不同

数字口译经常会让译员感到头疼，在商务、科技等类型的口译中也是重点。能否迅速准确地翻译出数字，是对译员的一大挑战。

数字口译的难处在于中文和英文的数字表达方式不同。中文是"十、百、千、万、十万、百万、千万……"，以"十"的倍数表示；英语则是超过千位数以后用"千（thousand）"的倍数来表示，如"一万"是"ten thousand"，"十万"是"hundred thousand"，直到"百万"用"million"，之后就又用"百万"的倍数来表达，直到"十亿"的"billion"。

中英文数学表达如下表所示：

数字	1,	0	0	0,	0	0	0,	0	0	0,	0	0	0
中文	兆	千亿	百亿	十亿	亿	千万	百万	十万	万	千	百	十	个
英文	Tr	Hb	Tb	B	Hm	Tm	M	Hth	Tth	Th	H		

对于译员而言，很容易在"万"和"million"以及"亿"和"billion"的转换上出现问题，因此要特别加强这方面的训练。

数字的记录

关于记录数字的方法有很多种，下面笔者简单介绍两种常用的方法。

（1）填空法。上面的中英文数位表可以当成标尺使用，在听到数字之后把每个数字写到对应的位置上，这样无论是要中译英还是英译中都可以很顺利地译出。例如：

在听到"eighty-four billion forty-eight million three hundred and twelve thousand six hundred and eleven"时，可以在标尺下面填上：

兆	千亿	百亿	十亿	亿	千万	百万	十万	万	千	百	十	个
Tr	Hb	Tb	B	Hm	Tm	M	Hth	Tth	Th	H		
		8	4	0	4	8	3	1	2	6	1	1

之后便可以很轻松地读出"八百四十亿四千八百三十一万两千六百一十一"。

同样道理,如果是中文的话,听到"五十亿四千六百三十万七千零六十",同样可以在标尺下方写上:

兆	千亿	百亿	十亿	亿	千万	百万	十万	万	千	百	十	个
Tr	Hb	Tb	B	Hm	Tm	M	Hth	Tth	Th	H		
			5	0	4	6	3	0	7	0	6	0

之后就很轻松地读出"five billion forty-six million three-hundred-and-seven thousand and sixty"。

在口译任务开始前,可以另外准备纸张,或者在口译笔记本的空白位置先把标尺划好,遇到复杂数字时马上派上用场。

(2)分节法。英文数字的表达是三位一节,从千位开始每三位换一个单位,并且在书面上也用逗号隔开,每个逗号所处的位置分别是"thousand"、"million"、"billion"等,记住这些位置我们可以用逗号做标记。中文数字的表达是四位一节,从万位数开始每四位换一个单位,我们可以用"|"来隔开,"|"所处的位置应该是"兆"、"亿"、"万"等。具体操作请看下面的例子。

英译中时,借用上面同样的数字,在听到"eighty-four billion forty-eight million three hundred and twelve thousand six hundred and eleven"时,首先将其转换成罗马数字,并在听到"thousand"、"million"、"billion"时用逗号隔开,即"84,48,312,611",每个逗号后面应该有三位数,因此不足的要在最前面补零,变成"84,048,312,611",在产出前快速地用"|"分隔每四位数字,变成"84,0|48,31|2,611",然后就顺利读出"八百四十亿四千八百三十一万两千六百一十一"。

同样道理,中译英时,当听到"五十亿四千六百三十万七千零六十"时,可以快速地写下"50|4630|7060",在产出前用逗号分隔每三位数字,变成"5,0|46,30|7,060",之后就可以读出"five billion forty-six million three-hundred-and-seven thousand and sixty"。

数字的所指和单位

值得注意的是，仅仅掌握了数字的笔记方法并不足够。数字的出现是伴随着上下文的语境，一个包含数字的意群应该由三个部分组成，即事物、数字和单位。初学者在遇到数字时，很容易慌张，急急忙忙地把其他信息都撂一边，第一时间就将听到的数字写在了笔记本上，生怕错过。回过头看时却发现自己忘记了记录数字的所指以及数字的单位，面对干巴巴的一串数字，即使把数字翻译出来，也毫无意义。因此在记录数字的同时，译员还要留心数字的所指以及相应的单位。

初学者最常见的错误就是把单位漏掉，例如在提到公司某年的收入时，翻出了数字，却忘记了单位是美元还是人民币，这就会造成不小的麻烦，因此还必须建立一套常见的数字计量单位的符号或者缩略语。最常见的，如厘米（cm）、千克（kg）、立方米（m³）、人民币（RMB）等，这些都应该形成一套自己习惯使用且容易辨识的系统，方便在口译时进行记录。

数字特训

两人一组，其中一人用中文（英文）快速读出下面的数字，另外一人做笔记后用英文（中文）译出数字，之后交换练习。

14 19 30 68 89 110 456 589 1236 5720 9432 9854 30567
58932 62845 782356 982245 4567836 2375371 7129462 8133054
10328574 14832953 586739246 926395236 4267932952 4672893470
34671489761 346747197351 13375318571051 437890175011

2. 口音重

在译员做口译的时候，工作的对象并不总是说一口标准的牛津英语、华尔街美语或汉语普通话。实际上，职业译员在工作中大约有一半的外方客户是 native speaker，另外一半则可能来自天南海北。中方客户则来自祖国的各个角落，说着韵味独特的方言。译员在工作中，会时而遇到某些口音浓重，甚至很难听懂的发言人，这种情况要怎么处理呢？如何应对口音重的口译情景呢？

首先，译员需要在平时的学习和练习中熟悉不同的口音，不能只听标准英语。口音听力材料的来源可以是多种多样的，包括广播、电视以及大量的影视剧。比如美剧 *Big Bang Theory* 里面的四位主人公，就有一位操着印度口音、另一位是犹太口音。通过大量的口音听力练习，译员可以让自己更熟悉不同的英语口音。

其次，译员需要对各个地域的口音特点有基本的了解。一般来说，英音、美音、加音及澳音对译员而言不难应对，中欧和北欧的讲话者英语口音也足够标准，让译员"头疼"的客户主要来自南欧（法国、意大利、西班牙）、东亚（日本、韩国）、南亚（印度、东南亚岛国）和中东（阿拉伯国家）等地区。以下是几种常见口音特点的简要讲解：

法国

法语重音在单词的最后一个音节上，所以法国人说英语感觉比较拖拉，单词重音往往靠后。另外，法国人倾向把辅音发重，清辅音会变成浊辅音。法语里面字母 h 不发音，所以有些法国人会把 hospital 念成 ospital。

日本

日本人说英语的优点是速度比较慢，缺点是语法准确性一般。另外，日本人辅音发音往往不清楚干脆，会在辅音后加 o 或 a，例如 grid 会发成 grido。受日语影响，日本人说英语语调也比较平，会给听力造成一定困难。

印度

"咖喱"味的印度英语是最让译员头疼的一种口音之一。印度人不仅口音重，而且语速极快，好在语法还是相当准确的。印度英语同样会重发清辅音，r 音发成颤音，例如 three 会发成 dr～ee。

身处口译现场要如何应对口音难题呢？下面是几个有用的 tips：

（1）提前熟悉。译员需要提前到场，并不仅仅是防止堵车等意外造成迟到，到场后需要跟发言人提前交流，一般他们也会很愿意跟译员交谈。这段出于礼貌的谈话并不仅是合作双方的相识，更重要的是帮助译员了解和熟悉对方的口音，通过简单的对话总结对方的口音特点，并迅速熟悉发言人的特殊口音。

（2）教育讲者。译员需要帮助发言人了解与口译员合作的形式，即 educate the speaker。如果发现讲者口音浓重，会前可以礼貌地做出解释，并请他发言时语速放慢，尽量用清晰标准的英语发言，目的是帮助听众更好理解他的讲话。

（3）不懂就问。如果口译过程中实在无法理解讲话者的内容，不要尴尬地站在台上沉默不语，也切忌胡乱翻译。可以礼貌地提出疑问，或者寻求帮助。

（4）会后总结。每一次口译的过程都是锻炼自己、提高水平、总结经验的难得机遇。译员在口译中如遇到问题，在工作结束后要进行自我总结。如遇到口音浓重的发言人，不妨把他/她的讲话录下来，作为自己熟悉各国口音的练习材料。下次遇到有类似口音的发音人，自然有备无患。

3. 术语多

一般而言，口译学习者在培训课堂上做口译训练时多使用一般性的讲稿，但在实际工作中，译员所遇到的讲稿可能涉及很多相对具体且专业的内容，如航空航天热处理、智能电网、软件（仿真）、医疗器械、离岸金融、汽车发动机、电力、电子学等。这些行业的讲稿往往包含大量的高等数学、物理、化学等知识。

作为文科甚至语言专业的学生，需要如何翻译这些技术性高、专业术语多的口译内容呢？作为一名未来的口译员，要怎样让自己做好准备以应对如此复杂的口译环境呢？

首先，译员要做好心理准备，不要对术语和技术内容产生惧怕或抵触心理。如果不愿意做与技术有关的口译工作，那意味着一名译员的工作范畴很窄，未来发展也相应受到影响。

其次，要做好译前准备。提前与客户或会议主办方联系，索取相关资料并进行认真准备。对于不太熟悉的领域，还要了解相关背景。可以通过搜索引擎对该行业或主题进行搜索。

口译时，要调整好心态。不要因为一个生词或术语让自己惊慌失措，努力在讲话者和观众面前展现自己大方自信的形象。如果译员对自己的口译能力都不自信，自然会使客户丧失对其的信任。

遇到问题要及时与讲话者或观众沟通。在遇到难以理解的术语时，可以请讲话者解释一下该术语，譬如 sinusoid 这个词，如果讲话者解释为 a curve that goes like waves shape，译员便可理解为正弦曲线。另外，观众同样也是很好的助手。一些术语可以直接用英文表述，懂行的听众会告知译员正确的中文译法，这时译员可以马上将其记录下来，在后面的口译过程中便不会被相同的术语难住。

最后，工作结束后要做好总结。对不熟悉的生词和术语要进行分类总结，定时复习，确保下次翻译同类内容时可以更加熟悉有关背景和术语。

4. 段落长

在口译时，译员常戏称某些讲话者是"non-interpreter friendly"，这样的讲话者除了口音重之外，语速还很快，发言段落长，不照顾需要记笔记以及进行记忆的口译员。那么要怎样应对这些"非译员友好型讲话者"呢？

首先，口译员应具有熟练的口译技巧及扎实的口译功底，也就是口译笔译和短时记忆能够应对连续 3～5 分钟正常语速的讲话。在平常练习的时候如果可以人为地提高难度，训练自己的耐力，那么在口译现场就不会因为讲话者段落过长、语速过快而无法完成口译。

在讲者语速过快时，可以考虑放弃笔记，集中注意力听取演讲大意。因为在口译时，记录笔记占据了口译员大部分的精力，如果暂停笔记，全力听取和理解信息，就可以避免手忙脚乱、顾此失彼。这时可以仅翻译大意，细节部分可以适当丢失。

在讲者段落过长时，可以在笔记中着重关注中心句和关键细节，放弃部分不重要的细节。如果觉得自己的短时记忆无法延续过久，可以在讲者说到第三点的时候简单回顾一下前两点，这样在讲者结束时就不会辨认不出笔记或无法记得前面的内容。

其次，口译员要学会"educate the speaker"。译员一般需要提前半小时到一小时到场，这并不只是为了防止迟到。到场后，译员要在允许的情况下主动与讲者交流，适应对方的口音，并且熟悉合作流程，这就是所谓的"教育讲者"。

在"educating"的时候，一定要注意方式方法和礼貌尊重。一般先介绍自己，再询问讲话者背景，跟他/她说明口译的工作方式，然后申明为了观众更好地理解讲话内容，请讲话者放慢语速，尽量少用过难或过专业的词汇，并需要每1分钟（3～5句话）停顿一次（具体停顿间隔按照译员的习惯），方便译员口译。

此外，如果讲话者在演讲时出现过于紧张或兴奋的情况，不能控制段落长短或语速时，译员也可适时打断讲话者（在一个意群结束后为宜），开始进行口译。打断时最好道歉，可以有礼貌地询问"Can I do this part first?"或开玩笑地说"You forgot the interpreter is here."。

5. 笑话冷

在演讲中，口译员怕的是什么？是讲者讲冷笑话。更怕的是什么？是讲者讲跟双关语相关的冷笑话。最怕的是什么？是讲者讲完冷笑话，一半观众听得懂笑了，另一半观众目光灼灼地看着译员，等着听笑话。

下面是一位译员的亲身经历：

一次我在给培训班做交替传译时，老师是英国人，学员是一家外企的普通员工。一个学员做自我介绍的时候为了活跃气氛，说：老师我要给你讲个笑话！学员皆乐，老师很感兴趣，口译员只有硬着头皮开始翻译。

笑话开始："从前唐僧带着三个徒弟去西天……"我打断，说需要给英国老师解释一下什么是《西游记》，于是花了整整3分钟时间解释背景。笑话继续。

"唐僧问徒弟，你们说怎么上西天最快呢？悟空说'我翻筋斗云去，最快。'八戒说'猴哥，你out了，现在都坐飞机去，还头等舱呢。'沙僧说'上西天？师傅你找个高崖跳下去，不就上西天了吗？'"

费了很大力气，译完"Dying is the quickest way to go to paradise"，满堂大笑。老师却一脸严肃，很疑惑地问我"Why can Tang go to paradise? Isn't he a Buddhist?"我欲哭无泪。

由此可见，口译员实在不是件容易的工作，不仅要 know something about everything，还要会幽默，能用冷笑话把观众逗笑。在无法很快想到对应的笑料的时候，可以跟观众解释一下为什么这是个笑话。当然，如果有急智能转换为目的语的幽默，就更好了。

例如一个英文笑话：Two balloons were floating across the desert. One balloon said to the other："Look out for the cactusssssssssssss！"

对此，译员可以这样对听众解释：两只气球正飞越沙漠，其中一只对另一只说："小心仙人掌！"这是个笑话，因为英语"仙人掌"的最后一个音是s，这个气球万万没想到，自己的警告还没有说完，就"嘶"的一声先被扎破啦。

如果译员当时反应够快，还可以翻译成：两只气球正飞越沙漠，其中一只对另一只说:"小心仙人掌上的刺刺刺刺嗤嗤嗤嗤嗤……"

6. 文化浓

在口译中,译员同样不喜欢遇到文化气息浓郁的讲稿,这样的稿子对译员的语言水平、文化背景知识和遣词造句的能力有很大的挑战。所以,在遇到这样"拽文"的讲者时,译员要如何应对呢?

首先,译员本身要具备相关的双语文化、历史以及社会知识,这就要求译员平时要走到哪,学到哪。精通中文文化自不必说。除了掌握母语文化外,译员因有机会遇到世界各国的讲话者,因此平时应多注意积累方方面面的知识,口译时才能以不变应万变。

在近几年温家宝总理记者招待会上,译员张璐的出色表现博得了业内同行的一致肯定,其在口译现场对总理渊博的古文引用到位而传神的翻译更让人敬佩。以下是总理引用的部分古语以及张璐的临场口译译文:

(1) 行百里者半九十。

张璐译文: Half of the people who have embarked on a one hundred mile journey may fall by the way side.

(2) 华山再高,顶有过路。

张璐译文: No matter how high the mountain is, one can always ascend to its top.

(3) 亦余心之所向兮,虽九死其尤未悔。

张璐译文: For the ideal that I hold dear to my heart, I'd not regret a thousand times to die.

(4) 人或加讪,心无疵兮。

张璐译文: My conscience stays untainted in spite of rumors and slanders from the outside.

(5) 兄弟虽有小忿,不废懿亲。

张璐译文: Differences between brothers can not serve their blood ties.

严格来讲,张璐的译文并非完全正确无误,毫无瑕疵。但考虑到口译的及时性以及口译场合带给译员的无形压力,译员能有如此表现,已十分不易。

其次,除了平日里注重知识的积累外,口译时如遇到"古韵十足"、"文化浓重"的词句、篇章时,可采取以下三步骤:

(1) 将文言文或诗句理解为现代浅显汉语。

如,译员在为一位文化名人做口译时,讲话者引用《老子》里的名言"企者不立,跨者不行"。这句话在转化为现代汉语后可理解为:"踮起脚跟想要站得高,反而站立不住;迈起大步想要前进得快,反而不能远行。"

(2) 将浅显的汉语翻译成英文。

如能译得古典雅致固然好。做不到的话,也不必抓耳挠腮,支支吾吾,白费功夫。此种情况下，译员应立即将自己所理解的含义译成被听众所接受的英文即可。所以，"踮起脚跟想要站得高，反而站立不住；迈起大步想要前进得快，反而不能远行。"就可以译为："If you stand on your tiptop to be higher than others, you cannot stand stably. If you stride to go fast, you cannot go far."

（3）最后，讲话者提到的如果是名言警句、诗词歌赋，译员还可以加上它的出处。这样以来，既可以使译文更加完整，也可以增进听众对中国文化的了解。如不知出处，也可以灵活应对：An ancient saying in China goes like this … 或 There was a famous poem in China, which is …

那么最后，这句古语可以译为："Lao Tse, a famous philosopher in Chinese history once said: If you stand on your tiptop to be higher than others, you cannot stand stably. If you stride to go fast, you cannot go far."

2.6.2 技能训练

1. 英汉口译

The EU covers an area of 4,000,000 sq km, nearly half the size of China. Its total population is 454,400,000, the world's third largest after China and India, and accounts for some 7% of the total world population. The euro is the name of the single European currency that was put into circulation on 1 January 2002. The euro has replaced the old national currencies in 12 European Union countries so far. Having a single currency makes it easier to travel and to compare prices, and it provides a stable environment for European business, stimulating growth and competitiveness. Until recently, the GDP of the EU was more than USD 10 trillion, as a whole similar to that of its main competitor, the United States. The total volume of the economy and the total volume of trade account for 25% and 35% of the world total. The EU has a very good relationship with China. May this year will see the 30th anniversary of the establishment of EU China diplomatic relations. The total volume of imports and exports between the EU and China reached 200 billion euros last year. Germany is the largest trade partner with China, while the UK and the Netherlands rank 2nd and 3rd.

2. 汉英口译

"十一五"期间，我省服务业增加值年均增长11.7%，对经济增长的贡献率平均达到40.6%，年均拉动生产总值增长5个百分点。到2010年，全省服务业增加值达到20711.55亿元，占生产总值比重45%，其中现代服务业占服务业增加值比重达到54.8%。继广州之后，深圳成为我省第二个服务业比重超过50%的城市。同期，全省服务业新增就业人员457.1万人，占全部新增就业人员的62.7%。到2010年，全省服务业从业人员达到1954.02万人，占全部从业人员的34%，比2005年提高了4.2个百分点。服务业成为吸纳城乡居民就业的主要渠道。

3. 英汉口译

This week we celebrate the 80th birthday of one of the most respected people of our times, whose sense of duty and service has had a profound impact on our country, the Commonwealth and the world.

Years before the premature death of her father and her succession to the throne, the then Princess Elizabeth publicly dedicated her life to the service of her nation, but declared that she would need the support of the country to ensure that she could fulfill this promise. She has, as we know, carried out this pledge through all the changes, both in her life and in this country, with extraordinary grace and dedication, and her people, here and across the Commonwealth, who share in the celebration of her 80th birthday this year, have responded, as she hoped that they would, with their affection and their support.

In a world which has been transformed in her lifetime, she has been a truly remarkable source of constancy and strength. Our country has faced tremendous trials, witnessed the horrors of the World War II and celebrated some extraordinary triumphs in her 80 years. Throughout, as part of the royal family and as the Queen, she has been a reassuring and unifying presence for her people.

4. 汉英口译

中国电信有限公司（中国电信）是世界最大的固定电话和宽带服务提供商。中国电信有超过2.2亿固定电话用户和超过3500万的宽带网用户，覆盖中国城市、县镇和农村。深圳电信，中国电信在深圳的全资子公司，成功应用美国项目管理学会的项目管理指南对公司最大的项目之一进行了成功管理。这个项目被称为深圳电信2006年"1号项目"。

背景

2005年5月，深圳电信在竞标中获胜，取得了开发深圳南山区电讯网络的资格。这个项目将把政府部门、住宅区、学校、社区医疗中心（的通讯）连接起来。深圳电信负责在该地区铺设光纤电缆网络以提高沟通效率和政府服务当地民众的能力。在竞标成功后一年，即2006年7月6日，中国电信深圳子公司项目组进入南山区，并计划于2006年11月完成该项目。该项目的合同金额为300万美元。

挑战

南山区项目中，项目团队面临着各种挑战，保证进度是首当其冲的问题。项目正式启动的标志——合同签署晚于进度计划。合同签署时间延迟使项目团队在项目创立阶段只能按照用户提供的意图说明书来设计项目，但意图说明书中的内容和后来签署的正式合同中涉及的内容有差别，这使得项目组不得不在项目进行过程中进行修改，这影响了整个项目的周期。

南山区整体光纤网络由6张子网组成：政府网、教育网、医疗卫生网、社区网和警务法律网。全部6张网都和三级政府部门联通：南山区政府、管片办公室和社区办公室。连接对象的复杂性使项目小组必须确保每个单元中的所有活动都要进行良好的协作。

另外，项目规模也给团队管理带来挑战。由于项目庞大，深圳电信的10个部门都参与到这个项目中，在大量的统筹管理下，共同完成为数众多的设计、建设、监督等项目单元的工作。项目一共涉及搭建426条新光纤线路，覆盖整个南山区。项目执行中如此众多的人员给沟通带来了挑战。同时，项目必须履行一定的审批手续，这也威胁着项目的预定进度计划。

应对

为了在政府限定的条件下完成南山区项目，项目团队采用了美国项目管理学会的项目管理标准，以确保项目的成功和合作的愉快。

由于南山区网络项目涉及范围大，深圳电信的领导将其命名为"1号项目"以凸显其重要性。深圳电信组建了项目管理委员会，为各个小组提供步骤指导。委员会下，设立顾客协调小组、项目建设小组和后勤保障小组，这样的组织架构搭建了一个良好的项目管理平台。

为保证及时和有效的沟通，项目推出了"1号项目邮箱"，使团队有一个专属平台以分享最新信息、活动进展和进度安排。邮箱也使得每个项目参与者都变得"可视"了。另外，项目也高效率地利用了传统的项目管理沟通方式，如利用例会讨论项目问题、利用周报追踪项目进展。"整合沟通界面"也加强了项目的沟通效果。"整合沟通界面"指各个项目单元与客户都有一个预先指定的联络人。通过给予每个联络人个性化的关注，用户的变更请求以及其他事项都能快速地反映到项目团队中。

项目文件处理程序便利了团队对每个活动的回顾，使进度和预算等方面的问题在恶化到无法控制前得到识别和调整，从而帮助项目进行平滑管理。作为文件处理流程的一部分，一个项目成员被指定负责管理、比较、更新文件，保证团队的信息更新，以对不断变化的项目进行控制。

为进一步确保项目按期顺利完成，项目团队对阻碍按时完工的因素进行评估，然后制订计划克服这些潜在问题。例如，利用项目管理学会的原则和标准，每个项目单元的工作表现都视觉化地反映在一个程序中，特别是那些可能延误的工作。这使得团队能随时保持对情况的更新，并且激励成员努力工作以取得个人和项目的成功。另外，在项目的最后阶段，项目团队设立了"1号项目决策中心",负责每日发布倒计时公报,以制造一种紧张而有成就的气氛,从而帮助项目按期完成。

结果

南山区电讯网络项目于2006年11月8日成功完成,比预计工期提前。通过系统应用项目管理方法,深圳电信项目团队不仅保证了工期,而且各项活动的实施也富有成效。南山区政府对深圳电信该项目的执行过程和执行成果深表满意,赠送锦旗以示表彰。这个项目不仅为南山区政府带来了许多成果,而且也为深圳电信带来了可观的经济和社会效益。南山电讯网络项目的成功加强了深圳电信作为顶级电信服务提供商的信誉,因此也成为深圳电信2006—2007年度当之无愧的"1号项目"。

第 3 章 口译实战

3.1 礼仪致辞

3.1.1 背景阅读

An epideictic or ceremonial speech is a speech of praise or blame, celebration or thanksgiving, condemnation or mourning. Ceremonial speaking stresses sharing of identities and values that unites people into communities. Eulogies, Fourth of July orations, speeches of condemnation or commendation, farewell addresses, etc. are instances of epideictic discourse. Ceremonial speeches often serve to establish standards for action or provide the ethical and moral basis for future arguments.

You should use language that is clear, vivid, inspiring and arousing. Your style will be critical in the delivery of the epideictic speech; style is your word preference and syntax (i.e., the structure of your sentences). Two major techniques of ceremonial speaking are identification and magnification.

Identification creates the feeling of closeness, familiarity, universality.

Magnification expounds overcoming obstacles, exceeding the boundaries, shifting paradigms, achieving the unparalleled, benefiting humankind.

The language you choose will influence how your audience will envision the subject. Words express an attitude toward the object, the idea, the event, or the person. Your words will convey a perspective or a reality.

Five basic guidelines for the epideictic speech:

Use concrete rather than abstract terms.

Use personal rather than impersonal references.

Use simple rather than complex sentences.

Use active rather than passive verbs.

Use more repetition of ideas to enhance comprehension and memory.

Speeches of Introduction

The speech of introduction welcomes the speaker, establishes his or her ethos, and tunes the audience for the message to follow. The introduction should place the speaker within the context of the topic to be presented, the occasion, or the context that has special meaning for the audience. Make certain you:

Know how to pronounce the speaker's name.

Ask the speaker what he would like you to emphasize.

Make the speaker feel welcome.

Focus on the relevant areas of the speaker's background.

Spotlight the topic or title of the speech; introduce the speaker, do not present the speech.

Be brief, warm, and gracious.

Presenting Awards or Honors

There are four basic guidelines you should follow when presenting an award or honor:

Announce the person's name (unless the award or honor is to be a surprise!).

Outline the criteria for the award or honor; explain how the person was selected, and by whom (e. g., letter of recommendation or ballot).

Highlight achievements or qualities of the individual; use brief anecdotes; capture the unique qualities of the person.

If presenting a plaque, certificate, key to the city, group, building, etc., explain what the item symbolizes or means to the group recognizing the individual.

Accepting an Award or Tribute

After receiving an award or honor, you may be expected to respond with a speech of acceptance. Your speech should express gratitude, an acknowledgement of the group presenting you with the award, and recognition of the underlying principles and values the award or tribute represents. We suggest you follow these guidelines when accepting an award or tribute:

Accept the honor with grace and confidence. The stylistic techniques of magnification are most useful in speeches of acceptance.

Acknowledge and give credit to those who deserve recognition (i. e., those who assisted or played some part in your effort, those who have influenced your life or the choices you have made).

Give a gift back to the audience—i. e. express your awareness of its deeper meaning and leave the audience with an insight or tribute to their work and/or the work that inspired you.

Conclude with a future-oriented statement—i. e., what this means to you, to society, to the group, and how you will continue this work.

(http://www.pitt.edu/~present/cermony.htm)

3.1.2 口译精讲

1. 英汉口译

（1）词语必备。

the Chinese delegation	中国代表团
extraordinary hospitality	盛情款待
strategic priority	战略重点
intellectual property rights	知识产权
unconscionable	昧着良心的，不合理的
regime	政治制度，政权，政体

（2）口译课文。

Well, thank you all for being here. And it's an honor to welcome Vice President Xi, along with the entire Chinese delegation.

Madam Secretary, this lunch is a great start. I hope we can match the extraordinary hospitality that the Vice President showed me in my four-day visit to China last August.

The highlight of that trip for me, Mr. Vice President, was the time we spent in conversation together in Beijing, in Chengdu, and I look forward to continuing the conversations we started this morning over the next four days you're here.

The Vice President has already participated in three meetings prior to this lunch and they've covered a broad range of constructive discussions, and we have a very ambitious agenda in the coming days as well.

As the Vice President and I have discussed at some length, the United States and China have much to do together, quite frankly, because our relationship is literally going to help shape the 21st century. We're not only the two — the world's two largest economies, we're both Pacific powers. And every day the affairs of our nations and the livelihoods of our citizens grow more connected.

The President and I came to office determined to rebalance America's strategic priorities toward those regions that are most critical to our nation's future, and that meant refocusing on Asia, the most dynamic region of the global economy. And to state the obvious, the US-China relationship is a critical component of our broader Asian strategy. Our people, both American and Chinese, are indeed people — quite frankly, people all around the world will benefit from this mutual effort to build a more cooperative partnership between our countries.

I first visited China in 1979, and the prosperity achieved since then, which I saw as recently as this past August is — as all of you know who visit it — stunning, absolutely stunning. Few other nations in history have come so far, so fast, and it's a great credit to the talent and industriousness of the Chinese people. But I respectfully suggest that this remarkable growth did not occur in a vacuum.

Mr. Vice President, even as our cooperation grows, as we've discussed, the United States and China will continue to compete. And, as Americans, we welcome competition. It's part of our DNA and it propels our citizens to rise to the challenge.

But cooperation, as you and I have spoken about, can only be mutually beneficial if the game is fair. That's why in the meetings we've had this morning were essentially a continuation of the multiple meetings we had in your country in August, and we spent a great deal of time discussing the areas of our greatest concern, including the need to rebalance the global economy, to protect intellectual property rights and trade secrets, to address China's undervalued exchange rate, to level the competitive playing field and to prevent the forced transfer of technology, and to continue a constructive dialogue on policies that would benefit our citizens and the world.

While the United States and China — as you have pointed out, Mr. Vice President — will not always see eye to eye, it is a sign of the strength and maturity of our relationship that we can be candid about our differences as we have been. We saw this in the recent U.N. Security Council debate about Syria, where we strongly disagreed with China and Russia's veto of a resolution against the unconscionable violence being perpetrated by the Assad regime.

Despite our differences, China and the United States are working more closely together on a broader range of issues than ever before. These include pressing security challenges in North Korea and Iran, maritime security, cyber security and the important work of developing cooperation between our militaries.

As you and the President briefly discussed in the Oval Office, it also includes our efforts in Sudan and in South Asia, and on global issues such as climate change and nuclear security. We appreciate your candid responses as we discuss these issues, Mr. Vice President, and I believe you appreciate ours as well.

So, Mr. Vice President, once again welcome to the United States. I've always believed that the best way — sometimes, the only way — to truly understand a country is to see it with your own eyes. As you know, there's an old Chinese saying, better to travel 10,000 miles than read 10,000 books. Although I read Dr. Kissinger's book on China, I felt that my trip to your country was at least as important last summer.

Actually, Mr. Vice President, I can't thank you enough for the hospitality you extended to me in my trip. And I would like to, with your permission, propose a toast — a toast to a successful visit for the Vice President and the increasing cooperation and understanding that will help both our nations continue to increase this relationship and may it benefit not only us, but the whole world.

(*Excerpted from the speech by Vice President Biden at the State Department Luncheon Honoring Vice President Xi Jinping of China on February 14, 2012*)

(3) 参考译文。

感谢各位的光临。我十分荣幸地欢迎习副主席以及全体中国代表团成员的来访。

国务卿女士，这个午宴是一个非常好的开端。去年8月我在中国进行了为期4天的访问，期间受到了副主席的盛情款待，希望今天我们也能让他感受到同样的盛情。

副主席先生，我认为我那次访问的重要内容就是我们在北京和成都所进行的交谈，我期待着您在接下来4天的访问期间继续进行我们今天上午已经开始的讨论。

副主席在出席这个午宴前已经参加了3个会议，这些会议涵盖了广泛的建设性议题，而且我们在接下来的几天还有非常紧密的议程。

我和副主席已经深入地讨论过，美国和中国在许多事务上可以携手合作，坦率地说，这是因为两国关系将势必影响21世纪的发展进程。我们不仅是全世界最大的两个经济体——我们也是太平洋地区的两个大国。中美两国的国情和民生日益紧密相连。

总统和我在就职之时便决心重新平衡美国的战略重点，主要针对那些对于美国的未来至关重要的地区，这意味着我们的战略重心将重回亚洲，这个全球经济最活跃的区域。显而易见，美中关系是我们更广泛的亚洲战略的一个关键部分。我们的人民，美国人民和中国人民，还有——坦率地说，全世界人民都将从两国为加强合作伙伴关系所做出的努力中获益。

1979年我第一次访问中国，自那之后中国不断繁荣发展，正如我在去年8月访华时所看到的——所有去过中国的人都知道的——是令人赞叹的，着实令人赞叹。历史上没有几个国家有过这么大、这么快的发展，这要归功于中国人民的聪明才智与辛勤劳动。不过，我谨指出，如此令人瞩目的成就并不是凭空产生的。

副主席先生，虽然我们的合作不断加深，但正如我们已讨论过的，美国与中国之间的竞争仍将继续。作为美国人，我们欢迎竞争。这是我们基因的一部分，它能激励美国人民奋起迎接挑战。

但正如您和我所谈到的，只有在公平的环境中，合作才会带来双赢。这就是为什么我们今天早上的会议基本上是去年8月我们在贵国进行的多次会谈的延续。我们花了大量时间讨论我们最关注的问题，包括重新平衡全球经济、保护知识产权和商贸机密、解决中国汇率低估问题、创造公平竞争的环境、防止强迫转让技术、继续就有利于两国公民及全球的政策问题进行建设性对话。

副主席先生，正如您所指出的那样，美国与中国的观点不总是一致的，但这也是我们两国关系愈加牢固与成熟的标志，它表明我们可以坦诚地面对我们之间的分歧。这一点，我们在联合国安理会最近关于叙利亚的辩论中可以看到，我们坚决反对中国和俄罗斯否决了制止阿萨德政权实施暴政的决议的做法。

尽管中美两国之间存在着一些分歧，但我们却在更广泛的议题上进行着比以往任何时候都要紧密的合作，其中包括来自朝鲜与伊朗的安全挑战、海事安全、网络安全和发展两国军队之间合作的重要工作。

正如您和奥巴马总统在白宫椭圆形办公室内简短地谈到的那样，双方的合作还包括我们在苏丹和南亚以及在气候变化和核安全等全球问题上所作的努力。副主席先生，我们赞赏您在讨论这些问题时所作出的坦率应答，我相信您也同样赞赏我们的坦诚。

因此，副主席先生，再一次欢迎您来访美国。我一向认为，真正了解一个国家的最好的方式——有时，也是唯一的方式——就是亲眼观察这个国家。如您所知，中国有句古话，读万卷书不如行万里路。虽然我读过基辛格博士撰写的关于中国的书，但是我觉得去年夏天我对贵国访问的经历至少与读书同样重要。

副主席先生，承蒙您对我上次访问时的款待，感谢之情难以言尽。如果您同意的话，我想举杯祝酒——祝您此次访问成功，祝中美两国之间愈加紧密的合作与理解有助于增进两国的合作关系，并希望这种关系不仅使我们受益，也使全世界人民受益。

（4）口译点津。

1) I hope we can match the extraordinary hospitality that the Vice President showed me in my four-day visit to China last August.

英语重形合，事件的先后顺序可以用语法手段表示。译为汉语时，则按时间先后顺序。

译文：去年8月我在中国进行了4天访问，期间受到了副主席的盛情款待，希望今天我们也能让他感受到同样的盛情。

2) The Vice President has already participated in three meetings prior to this lunch

and they've covered a broad range of constructive discussions, and we have a very ambitious agenda in the coming days as well.

断句和顺句驱动是口译的两个重要技巧。按语法结构和意群断句，顺势处理，是比较有效的口译策略。断句，即通过判断句子的语法结构，将长句切短。一般情况下，将长句（sentence）切分为小句（clause）后即可进入第二步，顺句驱动，即快速判断每个小句的主干和枝叶，理解并通顺地译出。本句包含了3个简单句：The Vice President has already participated in three meetings prior to this lunch, they've covered a broad range of constructive discussions 与 we have a very ambitious agenda in the coming days as well，其中第一个小句还可以根据意群继续切短为主干部分 The Vice President has already participated in three meetings 和枝叶部分 prior to this lunch，即状语；第二步，顺句驱动，抓主干，理枝叶，用符合汉语习惯的表达译出即可。

译文：副主席在出席这个午宴前已经参加了3个会议，这些会议涵盖了广泛的建设性议题，而且我们在接下来的几天还有非常紧密的议程。

3) ... to level the competitive playing field.

playing field 指的是体育场，运动场；词组 a level playing field 指的是公平竞争的环境、场所。此处，level 作为动词，与 playing field 单配，意思是"创造一个公平竞争的环境"。

4) We spent a great deal of time discussing the areas of our greatest concern, including the need to rebalance the global economy, to protect intellectual property rights and trade secrets, to address China's undervalued exchange rate, to level the competitive playing field and to prevent the forced transfer of technology, and to continue a constructive dialogue on policies that would benefit our citizens and the world.

本句语法结构简单，由主句 We spent a great deal of time discussing the areas of our greatest concern 和一个动名词结构，即伴随状语 including the need to ...组成；动名词结构较长，可根据意群继续切短为6个不定式结构，再进行翻译。需要注意的是，最后一个不定式结构较长，包含一个修饰先行词 policies 的定语从句 to continue a constructive dialogue on policies that would benefit our citizens and the world。对包含定语从句的成分进行翻译时，处理方法有两种：内容较长的定语从句可单独译成一个成分；内容较短时，一般译成其先行词的定语。此处定语从句内容较短，所以将其译为先行词的定语，即"有利于两国公民和全球的政策"。

译文：我们花了大量时间讨论我们最关注的问题，包括重新平衡全球经济、保护知识产权和商贸机密、解决中国汇率低估问题、创造公平竞争的环境、防止强迫转让技术、继续就有利于两国公民和全球的政策问题进行建设性的对话。

5) I can't thank you enough for the hospitality you extended to me in my trip.

口译中不能死板地拘泥于原文的形式，有时需要根据译入语的表达习惯做结构调整。此处就涉及口译中正话反译、反话正译的处理方法。另外，正式场合的现代汉语使用中若能恰当自如地插入文言套词，也会为译文增色。

译文：承蒙您对我上次访问时的款待，感谢之情难以言尽。

2. 汉英口译

（1）词汇必备。

中国国际广播电台	China Radio International
中国人民广播电台	China National Radio
中央电视台	China Central Television
香港特别行政区同胞	compatriots in Hong Kong
海外侨胞	overseas Chinese
"十一五"规划	the 11th Five-Year Plan
"三个代表"重要思想	the important thought of Three Represents
中国特色社会主义伟大旗帜	the great banner of socialism with Chinese characteristics
一国两制	the principles of "one country, two systems"
港人治港	Hong Kong people governing Hong Kong

（2）口译课文。

女士们，先生们，同志们，朋友们，

新年钟声即将敲响，人类就要进入2011年。在这辞旧迎新的美好时刻，我很高兴向全国各族人民，向香港特别行政区同胞、澳门特别行政区同胞、台湾同胞和海外侨胞，向世界各国的朋友们，致以新年的祝福！

2010年，对中国人民来说是很不平凡的一年。面对国际国内环境的复杂变化，中国人民团结一心、开拓前进，成功举办上海世博会、广州亚运会，保持经济平稳较快发展，着力提高人民生活水平和质量，经济实力和综合国力进一步增强。中国加强同各国的友好合作，积极参与应对国际金融危机、气候变化、核安全等问题的国际合作，发挥建设性作用，为促进世界和平与发展作出了新的贡献。

在这里，我谨代表中国政府和人民，向今年以来在各方面给予我们大力支持的各国政府和人民，表示衷心的感谢！

此时此刻，世界上还有不少民众经受着战火、贫困、疾病、自然灾害等带来的苦难。中国人民对他们的不幸遭遇抱着深深的同情，衷心希望他们早日摆脱困境。中国人民将一如既往地向他们提供力所能及的帮助。我相信，只要各国人民携手努力，世界发展前景一定会更加美好，各国人民福祉一定会不断增进。

最后，我从北京祝大家在新的一年里幸福安康！

(2010年12月31日中国国家主席胡锦涛发表的新年贺词，节选)

(3) 参考译文。

Ladies and Gentlemen, Comrades and Friends,

The New Year's bell is about to ring, and 2011 is arriving. At this beautiful moment of bidding farewell to the old and ushering in the new, I am delighted to extend New Year greetings to Chinese of all ethnic groups, to compatriots in Hong Kong and Macao Special Administrative Regions and Taiwan, to overseas Chinese and to friends all over the world!

For the Chinese people, the year of 2010 has been quite unusual. Confronting the complicated changes of domestic and international situations, Chinese people of all ethnic groups worked together, with pioneering spirit. We successfully held Shanghai World Expo and Guangzhou Asian Games. We maintained a stable and relatively fast economic growth. The living standard of the Chinese people has been improved and the economic strength and the overall national strength have been strengthened. China enhanced the friendly exchanges and cooperation with the rest of the world and played a constructive role in dealing with the issues like the global financial crisis, climate change, and nuclear safety through international cooperation, which all together made further contributions to world peace and development.

Here on behalf of the Chinese government and people, I would like to express the most sincere thanks to the governments and people of all the countries that have supported us in the past year!

At this moment, there are still numerous people who are suffering the misery caused by war, poverty, disease and natural disasters in the world. The Chinese people have great sympathy for their pain, hoping they can overcome the difficulties. Also, we will continue to provide assistance for those in need. I believe, with concerted efforts of people of all countries, the world is sure to witness a bright future and the well-being of people worldwide is certain to improve.

Finally, from here in Beijing, I would like to wish you all happiness, peace and good health in the New Year!

(4) 口译点津。

1) 在这辞旧迎新的美好时刻……

一般来讲，汉语是动态的语言，较多地使用动词；英语是静态的语言，较多地使用名词，相应地，也较多地使用介词，用以搭配动词。此处，"辞旧""迎新"两个动宾结构译为英语时可处理成两个名词性词组。译为 at this beautiful moment of bidding farewell to the old and ushering in the new。

2)我很高兴向全国各族人民,向香港特别行政区同胞、澳门特别行政区同胞、台湾同胞和海外侨胞,向世界各国的朋友们,致以新年的祝福!

汉语的结构往往较松散,而英语的结构和逻辑则更加严谨。口译过程中,迅速找出原文的主干"我很高兴向……致以新年的祝福",进而确定译入语的主干结构,即 I am delighted to extend New Year greetings to…,其余的成分则根据其意思处理为定语、状语或补语等。此句中,"向全国各族人民,向香港特别行政区同胞、澳门特别行政区同胞、台湾同胞和海外侨胞,向世界各国的朋友们"处理为后置补语。

译文:I am delighted to extend New Year greetings to Chinese of all ethnic groups, to compatriots in Hong Kong and Macao Special Administrative Regions and Taiwan, to overseas Chinese and to friends all over the world!

3)中国人民团结一心、开拓前进,成功举办上海世博会、广州亚运会,保持经济平稳较快发展……

汉语的结构松散还体现在主语缺失。在口译过程中,可适当添加主语,将长句断句为简单句后再译。本句中几个并列成分"成功举办……"、"保持……"的逻辑主语均为"中国人民",在译为英语时,可将几个并列成分处理为几个并列小句,并添加主语。

译文:Chinese people of all ethnic groups worked together, with pioneering spirit. We successfully held Shanghai World Expo and Guangzhou Asian Games. We maintained a stable and relatively fast economic growth.

4)我相信,只要各国人民携手努力,世界发展前景一定会更加美好,各国人民福祉一定会不断增进。

口译中应注意语言的多样性,如此句中"携手努力"的翻译,既可使用动词或动词词组 cooperate, work together, join hands, 也可以使用介词词组 with concerted efforts, with joint efforts。

5)我从北京祝大家在新的一年里幸福安康!

汉语重意合,因而表达形式较为灵活。翻译时,可考虑将一些成分,如状语、补语等单独划分出来,以便于更好地把握原句的主要意思,确定译入语的主干结构。本句中,可将状语"从北京"单独置于句首或句末,剩下的成分便不难处理。

译文:From here in Beijing, I would like to wish you all happiness, peace and good health in the New Year!

3.1.3 实战演练

1. 口译听解与表达

(1) 口译听辨。

Thank you all very much. Please be _____. And it's an honor to welcome all of you to the State Department this afternoon. It's always good to have Vice President Biden here, and we are particularly pleased to have our very special guest of _____. I'd also like to recognize Ming Tsai, the talented chef who has prepared this delicious lunch for us, fusing the flavors of Chinese and American cuisine.

This year marks the 40th _____ of President Nixon's historic trip to China. And we are very pleased that Dr. Kissinger is here with us, who, along with Zhou Enlai, was _____ in transforming the relationship between our two countries. Today, cooperation between the United States and China is _____ to address the many vexing challenges we face, from countering proliferation, to addressing climate change, to promoting global economic _____. Now, developing the habits of cooperation is not easy. We have a lot of work to do. But we are both _____ to building a lasting framework of trust that will support a cooperative partnership for the next 40 years and beyond.

Vice President Xi first came to the United States on an _____ program over 25 years ago to Iowa. He will travel there tomorrow to see some old friends. That visit illustrates how important the _____ between our people are. That's why we support programs like 100,000 Strong to send more American students to study in China, and many more people-to-people exchanges.

So it is a great _____ to welcome Vice President Xi and to celebrate the bonds of friendship between our nations' governments and peoples. And it is now my great honor to introduce Vice President Biden.

(2) 复述练习。

There are so many people who are proud of you — your parents, family, faculty, friends — all who share in this achievement. So please give them a big round of applause. To all the moms who are here today, you could not ask for a better Mother's Day gift than to see all of these folks graduate. I have to say, though, whenever I come to these things, I start thinking about Malia and Sasha graduating, and I start tearing up and — it's terrible. I don't know how you guys are holding it together.

I will begin by telling a hard truth: I'm a Columbia college graduate. I know there can be a little bit of a sibling rivalry here. But I'm honored nevertheless to be your commencement speaker today — although I've got to say, you set a pretty high bar given the past three years. Hillary Clinton, Meryl Streep, Sheryl Sandberg, these are not easy acts to follow.

But I will point out Hillary is doing an extraordinary job as one of the finest Secretaries of State America has ever had. We gave Meryl the Presidential Medal of Arts and Humanities. Sheryl is not just a good friend; she's also one of our economic advisers. So it's like the old saying goes — keep your friends close, and your Barnard commencement speakers even closer. There's wisdom in that.

（3）公众演讲。

假设你是某所高校的校长，对新入学的大一新生做欢迎致辞，分别以英语及汉语作3～5分钟的演讲。

2. 单句口译

（1）英汉口译。

1) I would like to begin by expressing, on behalf of the World Tourism Organization, our congratulations to the grand inauguration of the festival and promotion conference.

2) It is with great pleasure that I welcome you to the city of Shenzhen, China, home of the 26th edition of the Summer Universiade for the next 11 days.

3) I would like to compliment especially the authorities of the City of Shenzhen and of the Guangdong Province for preparing such quality venues.

4) On behalf of the entire FISU Family worldwide, I would like to extend our best wishes to all of the competitors who came from the far reaches of the globe to take part in this Universiade.

5) I would like to propose a toast to the enduring friendship between our two countries. Cheers!

（2）汉英口译。

1) 新年肇始，气象更新，在这辞旧迎新的美好夜晚，很高兴和新老朋友们欢聚畅谈，共迎新年。

2) 我代表中华人民共和国外交部，并以我个人名义，向各位来宾致以最美好的节日祝福。

3) 我谨代表中国政府和人民，向出席中国国家馆日活动的各位来宾表示热烈的欢迎和诚挚的感谢！

4) 借此机会我谨代表广东省人民政府对长期以来关心支持广东旅游业、经贸事业以及各项建设事业发展的朋友们表示深深的谢意。

5) 祝中国与世界各国的互利友好合作关系不断发展，祝各位来宾、朋友新年快乐，干杯！

3. 段落口译

（1）英汉口译。

Paragraph 1

Those are the folks who inspire me. People ask me sometimes, who inspires you, Mr. President? Those quiet heroes all across this country — some of your parents and grandparents who are sitting here — no fanfare, no articles written about them, they just persevere. They just do their jobs. They meet their responsibilities. They don't quit. I'm only here because of them. They may not have set out to change the world, but in small, important ways, they did. They certainly changed mine. But whenever you feel that creeping cynicism, whenever you hear those voices say you can't make a difference, whenever somebody tells you to set your sights lower — the trajectory of this country should give you hope. Previous generations should give you hope. What young generations have done before should give you hope. So whether it's starting a business, or running for office, or raising an amazing family, remember that making your mark on the world is hard. It takes patience. It takes commitment. It comes with plenty of setbacks and it comes with plenty of failures.

Paragraph 2

For a long time, China has dreamed of opening its doors and inviting the world's athletes to Beijing for the Olympic Games. Tonight that dream comes true. Congratulations, Beijing! You have chosen as the theme of these Games One World, One Dream. That is what we are tonight. As one world, we grieved with you over the tragic earthquake in Sichuan Province. We were moved by the great courage and solidarity of the Chinese people. As one dream, may these Olympic Games bring you joy, hope and pride. Athletes, the Games were created for you by our founder, Pierre de Coubertin. These Games belong to you. Let them be the athletes' Games. Have Fun! Remember that they are about much more than performance alone. They are about the peaceful gathering of 204 National Olympic Committees — regardless of ethnic origin, gender, religions or political system. Please compete in the sprit of Olympic values: excellence, friendship and respect. Dear athletes, remember that you are role models for the youth of the World. Reject doping and cheating. Make us proud of your achievements and your conduct. As we bring the Olympic dream to life, our warm thanks go to the Beijing Organising Committee for their tireless work. Our special thanks also go to the thousands of gracious volunteers, without whom none of this would be possible.

(2) 汉英口译。

段落1

在这辞旧迎新之际，很高兴与各位新老朋友再次聚集一堂，共迎新的一年。首先，我要特别欢迎和感谢有关部门负责人拨冗出席今天的招待会，与各位使节和朋友们见面交流。一年来，各位驻华使节、代表以及驻华外交官们为促进中国同各国及国际组织的友好合作关系付出了辛勤的努力，作出了积极的贡献。我谨代表外交部，向你们及各位来宾致以最美好的新年祝福，向所有关心和支持中国外交的朋友们表示衷心的感谢！

段落2

在这里我还想特别提及，明年我们将迎来上海世博会的召开。在各方大力支持和积极配合下，各项筹备工作正在紧锣密鼓地顺利开展。我们期待着各国在世博会的精彩展示，也热情欢迎各国领导人和人民利用这个难得的机会，到上海及中国各地多走走，多看看。为此，今晚上海交响乐团还将献给朋友们一台精彩纷呈的演出。岁月不居，天道酬勤。在新的一年里，我们期待着继续与各位使节和朋友保持良好合作，为世界和平、稳定和发展而共同努力！

4. 对话口译

A: Thank you so much for your hospitality. This is my first visit to Shanghai, and we've been so impressed with the incredible growth in the city and the great warmth of the people who have received us.

B: 上海是一座见证了过去30年间中国与美国外交关系发展的城市。1972年，《上海公报》在上海这座城市宣布，这已经为两国之间外交关系的正常化奠定了坚实基础。

A: Well, obviously both countries have benefited greatly from the progress that we've made over the last three decades. I know that many U.S. businesses are now located here in Shanghai and they consider it really the center for the region, commercially and financially. And it is very impressive to travel through the city and to see what extraordinary progress has been made.

B: 上海市民非常高兴，因为上海是您中国之行的第一站。

A: Well, thank you.

B: 在众多驻上海的美国公司当中，最有名的制造企业之一是通用汽车。通用汽车在上海的业务很好。截至今年10月底，他们的销售额比去年同期增长了40%以上。我认为他们在上海的出色业绩肯定会推动他们在美国的业务。

A: Absolutely. I think they can learn from their operations here in terms of increasing sales back in the United States.

(2009年11月16日美国总统奥巴马和上海市委书记俞正声在双边会议前的

讲话，节选）

5. 篇章口译

（1）英汉口译。

Each year that passes seems to have its own character. Some leave us with a feeling of satisfaction, others are best forgotten. 2009 was a difficult year for many, in particular those facing the continuing effects of the economic downturn.

I am sure that we have all been affected by events in Afghanistan and saddened by the casualties suffered by our forces serving there. Our thoughts go out to their relations and friends who have shown immense dignity in the face of great personal loss.

But, we can be proud of the positive contribution that our servicemen and women are making, in conjunction with our allies.

Well over 13,000 soldiers from the United Kingdom, and across the Commonwealth — Canada, Australia, New Zealand and Singapore — are currently serving in Afghanistan.

The debt of gratitude owed to these young men and women, and to their predecessors, is indeed profound.

It is 60 years since the Commonwealth was created and today, with more than a billion of its members under the age of 25, the organization remains a strong and practical force for good.

Recently I attended the Commonwealth Heads of Government Meeting in Trinidad and Tobago and heard how important the Commonwealth is to young people.

New communication technologies allow them to reach out to the wider world and share their experiences and viewpoints. For many, the practical assistance and networks of the Commonwealth can give skills, lend advice and encourage enterprise.

It is inspiring to learn of some of the work being done by these young people, who bring creativity and innovation to the challenges they face.

It is important to keep discussing issues that concern us all — there can be no more valuable role for our family of nations. I have been closely associated with the Commonwealth through most of its existence.

The personal and living bond I have enjoyed with leaders, and with people the world over, has always been more important in promoting our unity than symbolism alone.

The Commonwealth is not an organization with a mission. It is rather an opportunity for its people to work together to achieve practical solutions to problems.

In many aspects of our lives, whether in sport, the environment, business or culture, the Commonwealth connection remains vivid and enriching.

It is, in lots of ways, the face of the future. And with continuing support and dedication, I am confident that this diverse Commonwealth of nations can strengthen the common bond that transcends politics, religion, race and economic circumstances.

We know that Christmas is a time for celebration and family reunions; but it is also a time to reflect on what confronts those less fortunate than ourselves, at home and throughout the world.

Christians are taught to love their neighbours, having compassion and concern, and being ready to undertake charity and voluntary work to ease the burden of deprivation and disadvantage.

We may ourselves be confronted by a bewildering array of difficulties and challenges, but we must never cease to work for a better future for ourselves and for others.

I wish you all, wherever you may be, a very happy Christmas.

(*Christmas Message by Queen Elizabeth II on December 25, 2009*)

(2) 汉英口译。

尊敬的胡锦涛主席和夫人,
各位嘉宾、各位朋友,
女士们、先生们:

我们十分荣幸,在中华人民共和国澳门特别行政区成立10周年前夕,国家领导人胡锦涛主席再次亲临澳门,并出席今晚的盛会。

首先,请让我代表澳门特别行政区政府和全体澳门市民,向胡锦涛主席和夫人,以及中央政府代表团各位领导,致以热烈的欢迎和崇高的敬意。同时,亦请让我向在座各位嘉宾和朋友的光临表示热烈的欢迎和衷心的感谢。

10年以来,在中央的正确领导和大力支持下,并在广大市民的紧密配合下,澳门特区政府严格按照《澳门基本法》积极施政,全面落实"一国两制"的伟大方针。今天,澳门社会民心稳定、综合实力有所提升、市民生活持续改善、制度建设逐步完善、爱国传统薪火相传,"一国两制"、"澳人治澳"、高度自治的实践初见成效,并充分展现出其科学正确和强大生命力。

各位嘉宾、各位朋友,在澳门特区成立10年之际,我们深深体会到邓小平先生提出"一国两制"伟大构想的雄才伟略;我们再次回忆起江泽民主席在澳门回归1周年时对我们的鼓励嘱托;我们更加始终紧记,胡锦涛主席在特区成立5周年时,亲临澳门并发表重要讲话,对我们提出了具有重大指导意义的"四点希望"。特区10年的发展历程充分显示,"一国两制"能在澳门顺利实施,实在有赖于中央政府和全国人民一直以来所给予的深厚关怀和大力支持。在这里,让我们向胡锦涛主席、向中央政府、向全国人民表示衷心的感谢。借此机会,衷心感谢胡锦涛主席和中央政府对本人一直以来的信任和支持。同时,我亦衷心感谢广大市民和公务员一直以来的理解和支持。

明天,澳门特区将迈进新的历史阶段。我们深信,在中央的正确领导和全力支持下,第三任行政长官崔世安先生必将带领新一届的特区政府和广大澳门居民,全面贯彻基本法,坚持团结奋进,努力开创澳门繁荣和谐新局面,确保"一国两制"伟大实践不断取得新的成功。

女士们、先生们,现在,请大家举杯——

为胡锦涛主席和夫人的健康,

为各位嘉宾和朋友们的健康,

为伟大祖国的繁荣富强和澳门的美好明天,

干杯!

(2009年12月19日澳门特别行政区行政长官何厚铧在庆祝中华人民共和国澳门特别行政区成立10周年晚宴上的欢迎辞)

3.1.4 词语拓展

本着……精神	in the spirit of
闭幕式	closing ceremony
陛下	His (Her, Your) Majesty
殿下	His (Her, Your) Royal Highness
阁下	His (Her, Your) Honor/ Excellency
总统先生阁下和夫人	His Excellency Mr. President and Mme…
常设机构	standing body
答谢宴会	reciprocal banquet
大会	assembly, congress, conference
代表团主席	head of the delegation, leader of the delegation
悼词	memorial speech
东道国	host country
发展友好合作关系	develop the relations of friendship and cooperation
繁荣富强	prosperity and strength
以掌声表示对……热烈欢迎	give the warmest applause to welcome…
共同关心的问题	questions of common interest; questions of common concern
顾问委员会,咨询委员会	advisory committee, consultative committee
贵宾	distinguished guest
国宴	state banquet

贺电	message of greeting, message of congratulation
欢迎宴会	welcoming banquet
检阅仪仗队	review the guard of honour
健康长寿	good health and a long life
结婚宴会	wedding dinner, a wedding reception
借此机会	take this opportunity to
酒宴	banquet
祝酒词	toast
举杯，敬酒	propose a toast to…
开幕/闭幕式	opening/closing ceremony
开幕词	opening speech/address
全会	plenary meeting
盛情接待	cordial hospitality
午宴	luncheon
惜别会	farewell party
新年会	New Year's banquet
宣布……开幕	declare …open
由衷的谢意	heartfelt thanks
友好访问	friendly visit, goodwill visit
圆满成功	a complete success
征求……的同意	request the consent of…
正式邀请	official invitation
执行委员会	executive council, executive board
起草委员会	drafting committee
致以衷心的祝贺和最好的愿望	express one's sincere congratulations and best wishes
主管团体	governing body
祝国家繁荣人民幸福	wish prosperity to the country and well-being to the people

3.1.5 厚积薄发

在各种社交场合出现的礼仪致辞，其表达是较为仪式化的。口译学习者不妨积累一些场合惯用的句型和表达，从而更轻松地完成口译任务。

1. 出席活动

It is my great pleasure to join …

It is a great honor to be…

I am very pleased to be invited to…

I am delighted today to have the opportunity to meet you here at …

I am delighted to be given this opportunity to address …

2. 开幕/闭幕

It is a privilege to open…

I now have the honor of asking …to open …

Now I declare the opening/commencement of…

I declare the closing/conclusion of…

It is my great pleasure to address these closing remarks to you at …

3. 欢迎

It is an honor/a great honor to welcome you to…

It is a pleasure to have …with us tonight.

On behalf of …, I would like to extend a very warm welcome to …

On the occasion of …, please allow me to extend my warmest welcome to…

4. 问候、致谢、祝福

On behalf of …, I would like to extend New Year's greetings to…

We send our warmest wishes to …

We bring you good wishes from …

I would like to convey my sincere thanks to…

On behalf of …, I would like to extend my heartfelt thanks to…

Thank you for your warm/extraordinary hospitality.

I wish…a great/complete success.

I wish…good health and a long life.

5. 祝酒

Now I would like to propose a toast to…

Now I would like to invite you to join me in a toast to the cooperation and friendship between our two countries. Cheers!

3.2 旅游观光

3.2.1 背景阅读

The Importance of Tourism to Britain

Tourism is an often underestimated but tremendously important sector of the UK's economy. It's already one of our six biggest industries and our third-largest export earner. It accounts for almost £ 90bn direct spend each year, contains over 200,000 businesses and provides 4.4% of our nation's jobs. Equally importantly, it creates wealth and employment in all parts of the country, not just the south-east, and it's a cost-effective way to regenerate run-down communities. A thriving tourism industry creates beautiful places to visit all round the country, which also improves the quality of life for everyone who lives near them as well.

Our Goals

Whilst there is no doubting the importance of the UK's visitor economy, there are still opportunities to grow the sector, making it more productive, competitive and profitable than it is today. The next few years also offer an unprecedented series of opportunities which our tourism industry must grasp. Starting with the Royal Wedding in 2011 we will stage a slew of major international events, including the Queen's Diamond Jubilee and the London 2012 Olympic and Paralympic Games. The Government will work to ensure that we harness the full potential of this industry, building on the strengths we have while also addressing the weaknesses in the sector.

Increasing Domestic Tourism

Britain runs a large tourism trade deficit, partly because we are far more likely to travel abroad for our holidays than most other countries. Currently less than 40% of our total holiday spending goes on domestic tourism and we are worse than our neighbours too: just 20% of us spending holiday at home, compared to 28% on average for other European countries. This means that domestic tourism offers significant scope for economic growth. The Government should look at what it can do to help the tourism sector to fulfill its potential.

* We will consult on whether to move the first bank holiday in May. Possible alternatives include either a new St George's Day bank holiday in England (St David's

Day in Wales); or a new 'UK Day' or 'Trafalgar Day' bank holiday during the October half term instead. This would lengthen the summer tourism season and create new national holidays for our domestic tourism industry to celebrate.

　　* Brown signs have been criticised as not meeting the needs of the Tourism Industry. We will therefore work with the Highways Agency to ensure that Brown Signs can be as informative as possible to road users, whilst helping tourist destinations.

　　The Government's role is to create the right environment in which the domestic tourism sector can flourish. Our plans address the failures which previous Governments have ignored. Where possible the Government wants to do all that is possible to facilitate the growth of Britain's tourism industry.

Improving Productivity

　　Our tourism industry has many well-run, professional and productive organizations which offer great value for money at every price point. But, inevitably, there are some which are less successful. An unproductive industry would mean our visitor economy will progressively be relegated to being a high-end, high cost niche player. Given that much of the global growth in visitor numbers over the next 20 years will come from newly-emerging middle classes in countries such as Brazil, Russia, India and China, pricing ourselves out of the mass or middle markets would be a huge mistake. We want to encourage the industry to raise its game and prepare to embrace and an ever changing market:

　　We will give the industry and consumers responsibility for hotel 'star rating' quality schemes. Maintaining official government-sponsored schemes is expensive, and stops the industry from taking responsibility for its own standards. Consumer led websites offer significant potential to drive up standards, and we will allow the industry to work with them to ensure ratings are transparent and fair.

　　We will help to improve staff and management skills across the entire industry by increasing the number of apprenticeships and other courses teaching these skills. We have more well-qualified and experienced staff than ever before, but we still suffer from skills shortages. For example, hospitality and service is still sometimes seen as a poor-quality job for students or low-skilled workers, rather than a structured and professional career in its own right. We will put this right.

　　We will help the industry prepare for changes in technology, so tourism information can be provided through iphone and android apps, as well as through traditional leaflets and websites. This will make every destination far easier and more accessible for visitors to navigate, in more languages, no matter where they are.

We will create an industry task force, led by senior industry figures from across the UK, to cut red tape. They will be asked to identify sector specific rules, regulations, inspections and forms which are holding the industry back so we can cut, modify or abolish as many of them as possible.

We will make tourist visas far simpler, faster and more convenient to get, by increasing the number of visa biometric ID centres around the world, putting applications online and publishing application guidance in more local languages too.

Our plans will give the tourism sector much greater control over its destiny and ensure that they are ready to face the demands of the future. The Government's role will be to deregulate where necessary and ensure that tourism policy is coordinated across Government. Improving staff and management skills will raise standards and ensure we have the capabilities needed to expand the industry.

(*Excerpted from the UK's The Government Tourism Policy, 2011*)

3.2.2 口译精讲

1. 英汉口译

(1) 词语必备。

archipelago	群岛，列岛；多岛屿的海
accolade	嘉奖，表扬
a popular tourist destination	旅游胜地
scuba diving	戴水肺潜水
snorkeling	浮潜
bungalow	平房
diesel fuel	柴油

(2) 口译课文。

It is my privilege as President to introduce you to the Republic of Vanuatu. My country is an archipelago of 83 islands, situated in the South West Pacific Ocean, about 2.5 flying hours from the east coast of Australia, North of New Zealand, not far from the Fiji Islands, and a little over 7,000 km south east of Shanghai.

The people of Vanuatu are very special. Having travelled the vast Pacific Ocean to land on these islands over 2,000 years ago, the Ni Vanuatu, as we are called, from the Melanesian race, have lived for centuries in close harmony with the environment.

In this 21st century, Vanuatu won an international accolade as the happiest country in the world, based upon an independent assessment of the low environmental footprint caused by its people, the long life expectancy, and high quality of life and sense of community experienced by its people. It is indeed the natural welcoming smile of the Ni Vanuatu, their openness and friendliness to outsiders that makes Vanuatu a special place to visit.

After living in splendid isolation for centuries, Europeans visited then settled in the country. Vanuatu was one of the few places that was colonised jointly by two countries. In our case we were a colony of France and Britain for 75 years until independence in 1980. Since Vanuatu's independence, the nation has rapidly matured in terms of its institutions of state, the development of a mature economy, and its engagement with the outside world as an independent nation of about 200,000 people.

Because of its beauty and culture, the country has become a popular tourist destination in the South West Pacific. Tourists like Vanuatu for its diversity, the potential for soft adventure in its islands, whether visiting beauty spots, scuba diving or snorkeling the ever present coral reefs, sailing, fishing, hiking through magnificent scenery, observing traditional culture up close, or just sitting under a massive banyan tree on the beach admiring the unspoilt world. There is accommodation ranging from large luxury resorts in the major centres of Port Vila or Luganville through to small local family-owned bungalows on the outer islands.

Agriculture is the second largest sector, providing both the local food supply, and some exports, mostly, copra, sandalwood, and kava, the latter a specialised root crop that produces the social drink of choice around the Pacific and now in places around the world, and on sample at World Expo 2010 Shanghai. Vanuatu kava is renowned around the Pacific as the most noble variety.

Vanuatu is a world leader in the adoption of coconut oil as a replacement for diesel fuel. Manufacturing in Vanuatu is small, but specialised, and largely derived from natural products. Specialised medicines produced from the Beche-La-Mar or Sea Cucumber are produced in Vanuatu and sold around the world, with major research now being undertaken by the US Food and Drug Administration, to establish the effectiveness of some of these medicines for treating cancer. Vanuatu is a high quality coffee exporter, and produces many health care products.

Vanuatu strongly promotes private-sector-led growth. Many of the major international accounting firms and a number of major international financial institutions have representation in the capital of Port Vila, and the second city, Luganville.

The Ni Vanuatu are happy people and this happiness is infectious. We invite you to share this happiness, by coming to our exhibit at World Expo 2010 Shanghai, and participating in our events during Expo. We hope that from the sharing of our lifestyle experience, we can help inspire city dwellers to reinvigorate their sense of being an important member and contributor to the well-being of their community environment.

(*Speech by Vanuatu's President Iolu Johnson Abbil at 2010 Shanghai Expo*, 2010)

(3) 参考译文。

我很荣幸以总统的身份向您介绍瓦努阿图共和国。瓦努阿图共和国由83个岛屿组成，位于太平洋的西南部。距澳大利亚东海岸和新西兰北部约2.5小时飞行距离，离斐济群岛不远，距上海的东南部约7000多公里。

瓦努阿图人民非常特别。我们所称的尼－瓦努阿图人是美拉尼西亚族人。2000多年前，他们驶过浩瀚的太平洋，来到这片群岛。从此他们与当地环境和谐相容，在岛上居住长达数世纪之久。

21世纪的今天，瓦努阿图赢得国际美誉，被称为世界上最快乐的国家。据独立评估结果显示，瓦努阿图人民尽可能地降低对自然环境的影响，人民的平均寿命长，生活质量高，社会团结。尼瓦努阿图人民真挚的笑容，开放友好的态度，使得瓦努阿图成为一处独特的旅游之地。

经过数百年的与世隔绝，这片土地迎来了第一批欧洲人，他们随后在此定居。瓦努阿图是少数几个由两个国家共同殖民的国家之一。瓦努阿图作为法国和英国的殖民地长达75年，直到1980年获得独立。自从瓦努阿图独立以来，国家迅速发展，国家机构逐步完善，经济日益发展，并与世界其他各国建立往来，人口已达到20万。

由于风景迷人，文化独特，瓦努阿图已成为太平洋西南部的旅游胜地。游客们喜欢瓦努阿图，因为这里有丰富的休闲活动，可以到众多岛屿去探险，可以参观名胜，潜水或浮潜观赏珊瑚礁，乘帆船航行，钓鱼，登山观看壮丽风景，近距离了解传统文化，或者坐在海滩边的大榕树下欣赏世界的自然之美。这里有位于维拉港和卢甘维尔湾中心地区的大型豪华度假村，也有建在外岛上的小型家庭式平房。

农业是瓦努阿图的第二大产业，即为本国人民提供食物，也出口销往国外，出口以椰干、檀香和卡瓦为主。卡瓦是一种块根作物，在太平洋地区专门用于制作饮料，现已在全世界推广，并将在这次上海世博会上展出。瓦努阿图的卡瓦在太平洋地区享有最珍贵品种的美誉。

瓦努阿图在使用椰子油代替柴油燃料方面领先于其他国家。瓦努阿图的生产规模小但专业化程度高，主要加工天然产品。当地人将海参制作成药品并销往世界各地。美国食品药物监督管理局正在对这些药品进行研究以确认其对治疗癌症的功效。此外，瓦努阿图还出口高品质咖啡，生产大量保健产品。

瓦努阿图大力推动私营经济的增长。许多大型国际会计事务所和主要金融机构已经在首都维拉港以及第二大城市卢甘维尔设立了代表处。

尼瓦努阿图人是快乐的民族，而快乐是可以传染的。我们邀请大家参观瓦努阿图上海世博会的展馆并参与我们的活动，分享我们的快乐。我们希望，通过分享我们的生活方式可以让城市居民增强社会归属感，为社会福祉作出贡献。

（瓦努阿图总统 尤路·约翰逊·阿比尔在2010年上海世博会上的讲话）

(4) 口译点津。

1) Vanuatu won an international accolade as the happiest country in the world, based upon an independent assessment of the low environmental footprint caused by its people, the long life expectancy, and high quality of life and sense of community experienced by its people.

口译过程中，译者理解语言和组织语言的时间很紧，所以顺句驱动是口译中常用的策略。原句词汇密度较大，多用静态词，动词名词化和名词词组较多。鉴于汉语多用动态词，译时可将名词词组译为几个小句，即断句和拆译的方法相结合。

译文：瓦努阿图赢得国际美誉，被称为世界上最快乐的国家。据独立评估结果显示，瓦努阿图人民尽可能地降低对自然环境的影响，人民的平均寿命长，生活质量高，社会团结。

2) Since Vanuatu's independence, the nation has rapidly matured in terms of its institutions of state, the development of a mature economy, and its engagement with the outside world as an independent nation of about 200,000 people.

英语中，一个简单句只能有一个谓语动词，其余的动词则只能用非谓语动词形式，名词性、形容词性和副词性派生词，或者介词词组等形式。汉语中的动词形式则不受此约束。在顺句驱动的策略下，原文中包含的 independence, in terms of, development, engagement, of 等名词、介词词组和介词等成分可在汉语中转换为动词形式，译成几个小句单位。

译文：自从瓦努阿图独立以来，国家迅速发展，国家机构逐步完善，经济日益发展，并与世界其他各国建立往来，人口已达到20万。

3) Tourists like Vanuatu for its diversity, the potential for soft adventure in its islands…

英语较多用抽象词，汉语则较多用具体词，所以 diversity 可处理成具体的汉语表达。

译文：游客们喜欢瓦努阿图，因为这里有丰富的休闲活动，可以到众多岛屿去探险……

4) Vanuatu is a world leader in the adoption of coconut oil as a replacement for diesel fuel.

口译和笔译的策略一样，有时需要在翻译的过程中对词性进行转换。本句中的"leader"处理成汉语中的动词形式"领先",既简练又符合汉语的表达习惯。

译文:瓦努阿图在使用椰子油代替柴油燃料方面领先其于他国家。

5) Manufacturing in Vanuatu is small, but specialised, and largely derived from natural products.

口译应尽可能准确地传递原文的意义,"manufacturing"有"制造"的意思,但根据本句的上下文,译为"生产"则较为恰当,并可以根据意思的需要,添加"规模"、"程度"等表示抽象范畴的词语,以便更符合汉语表达习惯。

译文:瓦努阿图的生产规模小但专业化程度高,主要加工天然产品。

2. 汉英口译

(1) 词汇必备。

中共海南省委	CPC Hainan Provincial Committee
科学发展观	the scientific outlook of development
岛屿型经济	island economy
海岛型旅游	sea island tourism
支柱产业	the pillar industry
制高点	the commanding height
突破口	the breaking point

(2) 口译课文。

女士们、先生们、朋友们,

首先,请允许我代表中共海南省委、海南省人民政府向大家表示感谢,衷心感谢各位一直以来对海南的热情关注和大力支持!

日前,国务院颁布了《关于推进海南国际旅游岛建设发展的若干意见》(以下简称《意见》),这是国务院着眼我国改革开放和现代化建设全局,作出的一项重大战略决策,体现了党中央对海南经济特区的高度关注和支持。这个《意见》的出台,标志着海南国际旅游岛建设正式上升为国家战略,是继1988年建立省办经济特区之后,海南发展史上又一件具有里程碑意义的大事。

建设国际旅游岛,是海南省委、省政府贯彻落实科学发展观,转变经济发展方式,结合海南省情提出的发展思路。其主要内涵,是发挥海南省生态环境和热带岛屿资源优势,借鉴国际上岛屿型经济的成功经验,加快推进旅游要素国际化进程,不断提升旅游设施建设及管理服务水平,实现旅游业转型升级,进而推动经济社会全面发展,逐步把海南建设成为旅游国际化程度高、生态环境优美、文化魅力独特、社会文明祥和的世界一流的海岛型旅游和休闲度假目的地,建设成中国人民的四季花园。

把海南建成国际旅游岛的发展思路提出后,得到了中央领导同志的充分肯定,社会各界和全省上下的一致认同。2008年4月,胡锦涛总书记视察海南时明确指出，海南要积极发展服务型经济，提高旅游业国际化程度，努力使旅游业成为海南的支柱产业。2009年4月，温总理视察海南时提出，"建设国际旅游岛要成为海南深化改革开放、促进经济增长的制高点和突破口"，并要求国家发改委牵头，会同有关部门制定海南国际旅游岛建设的系统性指导意见。2009年6月，国家发展改革委会同财政部、交通部、国土资源部等22个国家部委单位，组成联合调研组赴海南进行了实地调研，在充分吸收各方意见的基础上形成了国务院《关于推进海南国际旅游岛建设发展的若干意见》，以国务院文件形式颁布。

各位记者、朋友们，建设国际旅游岛，为海南的发展描绘了令人振奋的美景蓝图，但我们也清醒地认识到，这是一项长期而艰巨的历史任务。我们将认真按照科学发展、和谐发展的要求，带领全省各族人民扎实抓好《意见》的贯彻落实。第一是抓规划，引入先进的发展理念，按照国际化程度高，地方特色鲜明，"高品位、有特色"的要求，认真编制国际旅游岛建设规划，确保各项建设在科学规划指导下有序进行。第二是抓政策落实，对国务院《意见》中提出的各项政策，完善配套措施，使其具体化、可操作，确保国际旅游岛建设有强劲而又持续的吸引力和支撑力。第三是抓项目，高标准、高水平建设好各个重点项目，确保每个项目都成为国际旅游岛的坚强基石和亮丽风景。

（2010年1月6日，中共海南省委书记卫留成在国务院海南国际旅游新闻发布会上的讲话，节选）

（3）参考译文。

Ladies and Gentlemen, Dear Friends,

First of all, on behalf of CPC Hainan Provincial Committee and People's Government of Hainan Province, please allow me to extend my heart-felt appreciation and gratitude to you for your constant concerns and full support to Hainan.

The newly released *Opinions on Promoting Construction of Hainan as an International Tourism Destination* is a significant strategic decision made by the State Council, focusing on the overall situation of reform and opening up and modernization in China and reflecting the concerns and support from the Central Committee of the CPC to Hainan. The release of the document symbolizes that the project of building Hainan into an international tourism destination has been upgraded to a state strategy, which is another milestone in Hainan's development history since Hainan was established as a province and a special economic zone in 1988.

The idea of "building an international tourism destination" is a development path proposed by Hainan Provincial Party Committee and Hainan Provincial Government. It is based on the implementation of the scientific outlook of development and the policy of changing economic development mode as well as Hainan's local conditions. The plan is to build Hainan into a world-class sea island tourism and resort destination and an all-year-round garden, displaying highly internationalized tourism, excellent eco-environment, distinctive and attractive culture, and harmonious civilization. To achieve this, we will give full play to the advantages of the ecological environment and tropical island resource in Hainan, learn from successful international island economies, accelerate the internationalization course of tourism sectors, and upgrade the construction of tourism facilities as well as management and services. We will achieve the transformation and upgrading of tourism industry, and promote the overall economic development and social progress.

The proposal gains full recognition from both the state leaders and people of all sectors. When President Hu Jintao was on his inspection trip to Hainan in April 2008, he demanded that Hainan actively develop service sectors and promote tourism internationalization to build tourism into the pillar industry of the province. When Premier Wen Jiabao inspected Hainan in April 2009, he pointed out that, "to build Hainan into an international tourism destination should be taken as the commanding height and breaking point for Hainan's further reform and opening up and economic growth". And he urged the State Development and Reform Commission to draft systematic instructions for this campaign in company with other state ministries concerned. In June 2009, the State Development and Reform Commission headed an investigation group to Hainan, joint by 21 other state ministries including the Ministry of Finance, the Ministry of Communications, and the Ministry of Land and Resources. After full consultation with all parties, *Opinions on Promoting Construction of Hainan as an International Tourism Destination* was released as a State Council document on Dec. 31, 2009.

Dear friends, to build an international tourism destination is an attractive blueprint for Hainan's development. However, we are fully aware that it is a long and tenuous historic task. We will follow the scientific and harmonious development approach and mobilize people of all ethnic groups in the province to implement the document. Firstly, to address the planning. We will introduce advanced development notions and make the construction planning in compliance with the requirement of high internationalization and "refined taste, distinctive local features" to ensure all the work to be proceeded in order. Secondly, the implementation of the policies. All the policies stipulated in the document must be implemented with explicit practical supporting measures to maintain strong and sustained attraction and support for the construction. Thirdly, the projects.

We must build projects of high quality and high level and ensure every project to be the cornerstone and new attraction of Hainan.

(4) 口译点津。

1) 国务院颁布了《关于推进海南国际旅游岛建设发展的若干意见》，这是国务院着眼我国 改革开放和现代化建设全局，作出的一项重大战略决策……

口译的过程是理解、断句、翻译的过程，译者可尽量使用顺句驱动的方法，当顺句驱动行不通时，就通过"抓主干、理枝叶"的方法重组信息，将主干处理为译入语的基本框架，其余信息则处理为定状补等成分，然后用恰当的词汇和符合译入语表达习惯的方式译出。本句有两种处理方式：第一种，将主干理解为："国务院颁布《意见》。《意见》是决策"，其余成分处理为定语、状语或补语等。

译文：The State Council has released *Opinions on Promoting Construction of Hainan as an International Tourism Destination*, which is a significant strategic decision focusing on the overall situation of reform and opening up and modernization in China.

第二种，将主干理解为"《意见》是重大战略决策"，其余的信息处理成定语、状语或补语等。

译文：The newly released *Opinions on Promoting Construction of Hainan as an International Tourism Destination* is a significant strategic decision made by the State Council, focusing on the overall situation of reform and opening up and modernization in China.

2) 这个《意见》的出台，标志着海南国际旅游岛建设正式上升为国家战略；是继1988年建省办经济特区之后，海南发展史上又一件具有里程碑意义的大事。

汉语形散，逻辑结构不如英语严谨；原句主干可理解为"《意见》的出台标志着……，是大事"，可考虑顺句驱动，将其处理为小句＋非限定性定语从句的英语结构，翻译"继1988年建省办经济特区之后"时，可考虑将其置于句末，作时间状语成分。

译文：The release of that document symbolizes that the project of building Hainan into an international tourism destination has been upgraded to a state strategy, which is another milestone in Hainan's development history since Hainan was established as a province and a special economic zone in 1988.

3) 其主要内涵，是发挥海南省生态环境和热带岛屿资源优势，借鉴国际上岛屿型经济的成功经验，加快推进旅游要素国际化进程，不断提升旅游设施建设及管理服务水平，实现旅游业转型升级，进而推动经济社会全面发展，逐步把海南建设成为旅游国际化程度高、生态环境优美、文化魅力独特、社会文明祥和的世界一流的海岛型旅游和休闲度假目的地,建设成中国人民的四季花园。

　　口译过程中,需要在理解原文的基础上对原文的逻辑层次进行归纳,重组信息,翻译信息。原文较长,主干可理解为"内涵是通过(途径)把海南建设成……",从而确定译文的基本结构为"The plan is to build Hainan into a world-class sea island tourism and resort destination and an all-year-round garden, displaying highly internationalized tourism, excellent eco-environment, distinctive and attractive culture, and harmonious civilization, by way of …",同时,考虑到实现途径的内容较长,"是发挥海南省生态环境和热带岛屿资源优势,借鉴国际上岛屿型经济的成功经验,加快推进旅游要素国际化进程,不断提升旅游设施建设及管理服务水平,实现旅游业转型升级,进而推动经济社会全面发展",也可将这一部分从原句拆开来译,并添加包含指示代词、增强上下文衔接的成分"to achieve this"。

　　译文：To achieve this, we will give full play to the advantages of the ecological environment and tropical island resource in Hainan, learn from successful international island economies, accelerate the internationalization course of tourism sectors, and upgrade the construction of tourism facilities as well as management and services. We will achieve the transformation and upgrading of tourism industry, and promote the overall economic development and social progress.

　　4)国家发展改革委会同财政部、交通部、国土资源部等22个国家部委单位,组成联合调研组赴海南进行了实地调研……

　　政府机构的名称,如"国家发展改革委会"、"财政部"、"交通部",可以通过平时积累和译前准备解决。理解原文,抓主干,可理解为"国家部委单位组成联合调研组。调研组进行调研"。

　　译文：22 state ministries, including the State Development and Reform Commission, the Ministry of Finance, the Ministry of Communications, and the Ministry of Land and Resources, formed an investigation group. The group headed to Hainan to conduct an investigation.

　　也可将"财政部、交通部、国土资源部等22个国家部委单位"拆分出来处理为补语,将主干理解为"国家发展改革委会组成联合调研组赴海南进行了实地调研",从而简化原文结构,降低处理难度。

　　译文：The State Development and Reform Commission headed an investigation group to Hainan, joined by 21 other state ministries including the Ministry of Finance, the Ministry of Communications, and the Ministry of Land and Resources.

　　5)首先是抓规划,引入先进的发展理念,按照国际化程度高,地方特色鲜明,"高品位、有特色"的要求,认真编制国际旅游岛建设规划,确保各项建设在科学规划指导下有序进行。

口译中，会经常用到词性转移的方法，如原句"抓规划"不一定非得译出"抓"，将其处理成名词性意义译出也未尝不可；汉语常使用排比句式，有时会因此而出现语义重复的现象。原句中"国际化程度高，地方特色鲜明，'高品位、有特色'"中的"地方特色鲜明"与"有特色"就是这种情况，口译过程中可以略去重复的意义；原句中有几处主语缺失，翻译时可以考虑添加相应的逻辑主语。

译文：Firstly, to address the planning. We will introduce advanced development notions and make the construction planning in compliance with the requirement of high internationalization and "refined taste, distinctive local features" to ensure all the work to be proceeded in order.

3.2.3 实战演练

1. 口译听解与表达

（1）口译听辨。

I'm pleased to congratulate China on the opening of the Shanghai _____, a major event of the world this year and one that will allow Americans and Chinese to continue to get to know each other on the deeper and broader bases.

America has _____ and participated in many World Expos since 19th century and we're excited to see this tradition carry on at the Shanghai Expo. Our participation demonstrates America's _____ to a forward-looking, positive relationship with China.

I invite you to visit American pavilion to learn about America's _____ to creating "a better city and a better life". We have prepared a special theatre _____ that we hope will entertain visitors of all ages and inspire them to be part of efforts to improve their own _____.

The USA _____ will also feature an array of American cultural performers — from Blue Grass to Hiphop, to Jazz to classical music. One of the Grammy Award winning artists _____ to perform is American Jazz legend Herbie Hancock.

I'm also particularly proud of our "Student Ambassador" program. Visitors to American pavilion will be _____ by American college students from schools across America. They have many different life experiences they will share with you. And all 160 student ambassadors speak Chinese, which demonstrates the importance American younger generation is placing on learning about China.

While the Expo is an opportunity to present some of the best of America to visitors, it is also an opportunity to learn from China and many of countries will be _____ about how they are working to improve their communities. I personally look forward to visiting other national pavilions to see the many exciting things they will have to offer.

I congratulate China on what I'm sure will be a spectacular world's fair. Come and see at the US pavilion.

(2) 复述练习。

The theme of this year's World Tourism Day, "Tourism — linking cultures", highlights the powerful role of tourism in building international understanding and mutual respect.

There is no better way to learn about a new culture than to experience it first-hand. Tourism offers a wonderful connecting thread between visitor and host community. It promotes dialogue and interaction. Such contact between people of different backgrounds is the very foundation for tolerance. In a world struggling for peaceful coexistence, tourism can build bridges and contribute to peace.

Tourism's contributions to development also advance the cause of global solidarity. At a time of profound global economic uncertainty, tourism's ability to generate socio-economic opportunities and help reduce the gap between rich and poor, is more important than ever.

I encourage all involved in tourism to embrace the ten principles of the Global Code of Ethics for Tourism. These guidelines for sustainable and responsible tourism development, approved by the UN General Assembly in 2001, are based on the proven interaction between tourism and peace, human rights and understanding.

World Tourism Day is an opportunity to reflect on the importance of tourism to global well-being. As we travel, let us engage with other cultures and celebrate human diversity. On this observance, let us recognize tourism as a force for a more tolerant, open and united world.

(3) 公众演讲。

就你出生或生活的城市，以"魅力城市"为题，宣传值得游览的地方。分别以英语和汉语做 3～5 分钟的演讲。

2. 单句口译

(1) 英汉口译。

1) The income generated by sustainable tourism can provide important support for nature conservation, as well as for economic development.

2) International tourist arrivals grew in 2004 by an exceptional 10.7% to almost 763 million.

3) By the end of 2004, the province had 1120 star hotels, including 40 five-star hotels and 136 four-star hotels, the highest number of star hotels among all cities of

China.

4) World tourism has become more resilient and prepared to absorb external shocks and the new destinations are becoming more and more competitive.

5) Through the collaboration with the UN family, national tourism authorities and the private sector, the World Tourism Organization is helping to highlight the links between tourism, poverty alleviation and biodiversity.

(2) 汉英口译。

1) 新北京,一个充满活力的现代化大都市,呈现出崭新的城市面貌。

2) 广东的旅游业得到了蓬勃的发展,去年广东旅游收入达到208亿美元,占全国的1/4;旅游外汇收入53亿美元,占全国的1/5。

3) 未来旅游业的发展将以政府投入为主,发挥市场配置资源的基础性作用,全力推进旅游基础设施和配套设施建设。

4) 目前,西藏已有国家4A级旅游景区8个,3A级旅游景区2个,2A级景区3个,1A级旅游景区2个;有国家级自然保护区6个,国家地质公园2个;中国优秀旅游城市一座,可供旅游者游览的景点297处,形成了以拉萨为中心、辐射西藏的旅游资源开发利用格局。

5) 不到6平方公里的世博园,千姿百态的万国建筑毗邻而居,独具匠心的创意布展争奇斗艳,丰富多彩的文艺演出竞相绽放,各领风骚的最佳实践区熠熠生辉,启迪智慧的论坛对话精彩纷呈,生动体现了世界的多样性,构成一幅多元文化、多种文明和谐共融的美好画卷。

3. 段落口译

(1) 英汉口译。

Paragraph 1

According to the latest data of the WTO World Tourism Barometer, international tourist arrivals grew this year up to July by almost 6%, which represents an increase of 25 million new tourist arrivals worldwide. Such growth trend was particularly strong in Asia, where after 28% increase in 2004; arrivals still went up by 9%. Again Asia's tourism is growing above the world average, and above the long term forecast growth of around 6%. 2005 is estimated to yield to end with 5% to 6% growth, while in Asia the growth estimates to the end of the year are projected at 10%. This growth is much driven by China's exceptional performance where tourist arrivals grew by 14% until October this year. Looking at the development of international tourism in the past 5 years, we see that the world gained during this period, and this was a trouble period, 19% more arrivals. And more important, international tourist arrivals reached an increment of almost 50% in Asian destinations, making thus Asia as the second most visited region in the world, after Europe, and ahead of the Americas.

Paragraph 2

Due to its excellent performance in 2004, China is already the 4th most visited destination in the world, with a volume of almost 42 million international tourist arrivals, after having surpassed Italy for the first time in 2004. China is also the 7th most important country in terms of tourism earnings. It represents a volume of 26 billion US dollars. According to the World Tourism Organization's long-term forecast — Tourism 2020 Vision, China is set to become by the year 2020 the most important tourism destination in the world. With the volume of 130 million tourist arrivals or 8% of world total, an expected 8% year average growth was estimated by the time the projections were made. However, up to the moment, the country has been performing much better than expected as tourist arrivals grew by 30% between 1990 and 1995, and by 30% a year between 1995 and 2000. As we can see the projected volume of 39 million arrivals for 2004 was already surpassed. China's tourism is growing in a very favourable world and regional environment.

（2）汉英口译。

段落 1

基于丝绸之路带来的灵感，我们的火炬接力将有新的突破，从奥林匹亚开始，穿越一些最古老的文明古国——希腊、罗马、埃及、拜占庭、美索不达米亚、波斯、阿拉伯、印度和中国。携带着信息"分享和平，分享奥运"，永恒的火焰将达到新的高峰，因为它将穿越喜马拉雅山在世界的最高峰——珠穆朗玛峰。在中国，圣火还将穿过西藏，穿越长江与黄河，游历长城，并拜访香港、澳门、台湾和56个民族的人们，在这一历程之中，圣火的观看人数将超越所有之前的传递，而它也将激励更多的人参与到奥林匹克的大家庭中。

段落 2

屹立于上海世博园的中国馆"东方之冠"，光彩夺目，气势磅礴，它以"城市发展中的中华智慧"为主线，让人从中感受中国人民创造美好生活的生动实践，领略中华文化世代传承的和谐理念，畅想中国科学发展的美好未来。中华民族有着悠久的历史和灿烂的文化，在5000多年的漫长岁月中，各族中华儿女在这片广袤的大地上薪火相传、生生不息，孕育了勤劳勇敢、自强不息的优秀品格，铸就了海纳百川、兼容并蓄的博大胸怀，形成了鼎故革新、勇于探索的进取精神，为人类社会的文明进步作出了不可磨灭的重大贡献。

4. 对话口译

A：为什么您会被邀请搬移"小美人鱼"？

B：There is a very small market for this kind of business and, though it might sound pretentious, I am the most experienced in this field. It is impossible for me to keep track on how many statues and works of art I have moved but it must be several thousands.

A：您以前有参与过涉及"小美人鱼"的工作吗？

B: Not really, because she is made out of bronze and I work with stone. But I did remove some graffiti from her once in the early 80's after she had been targeted by vandals (the statue has repeatedly been subjected to vandalism, as for example on 11 September 2003 when unknown perpetrators toppled her from her stone).

A：您将怎样搬移"小美人鱼"？

B: First I will measure up exactly how she sits on her rock at Langelinie so that she is placed in the same way in the Danish Pavilion. I will separate her from the rock underneath her, and later she will be lifted away by a crane to be taken by plane to Shanghai. When she arrives, I will place her in the Harbour Pool inside the pavilion. I will bring my own tools to Shanghai to make sure that everything goes according to plan.

A："小美人鱼"雕像于1913年完成，这样算来她是一位老太太了。如此让她长途跋涉合适吗？

B: She is very fit. She is almost new compared to some of the older statues you can find in Copenhagen. You can also say that bronze sculptures like her, generally speaking, stay fit for a long time.

A：你认为"小美人鱼"前往上海途中及在上海期间是否安全？

B: I think she will be very safe. I don't think that anyone will try to steal the Little Mermaid because she is too famous. I mean, what would they do with her? No one would buy her knowing that it was the real Little Mermaid.

A：您长期从事石头雕刻。您是否认为此次任务将是您的主要挑战之一？

B: I would not say that this is one of my most difficult assignments. The modern or postmodern sculptures are much more complicated to work on. But she is by far the most famous. I cannot recall any other statue that has such a great history as the Little Mermaid. She is an essential part of Denmark and when I meet Chinese people, they often don't know Denmark but they have all heard about the Mermaid, Hans Christian Andersen and Copenhagen.

A：您将前往中国，以确保"小美人鱼"安全抵达上海。您自身和中国渊源颇深，可以和我们讲讲吗？

B: I started doing business in China eight years ago and now the basic work on many of my sculptures is done in China in Fujian Province. I give the Chinese workers a step-by-step manual on how to make the sculptures and then I come to China around five times a year to supervise the work.

(*Excerpted from the interview with Flemming Brian Nielsen about moving Little Mermaid to Shanghai Expo, 2010*)

5. 篇章口译

(1) 英汉口译。

This is a very special occasion. We are here to recognize the top five tour operators in the Shanghai region who arrange group travel to the US. Travel and tourism between our countries is crucial to building stronger cultural and economic ties. This generates greater understanding and friendship between our people. And it also generates greater prosperity.

As you all know, the US—China Memorandum of Understanding on Cooperation in Travel and Tourism was signed in 2007. It opened the door for packaged leisure travel to our country by Chinese groups. Since then, the number of Chinese people traveling to the US has grown significantly. So far this year, travelers from China have increased 40 percent over the same period in 2011! We are very happy to welcome these visitors, and we look forward to welcoming many more.

And under the leadership of the Department of Commerce, the United States government is taking a number of steps to ensure continued growth in travel and tourism from China to America. As you no doubt know, at the direction of President Obama, our State Department has increased our capacity to process visa applications here in China. Also, we are working with America's travel and tourism leaders to make sure that our travel hubs — such as airports — are easier to navigate. In addition, we are working to educate our hotel owners and service providers about the needs and wants of Chinese travelers. And we are doing more to share information about all of the diverse cultural, recreational and entertainment opportunities that America offers.

These are important steps, because over the next five years, the number of international visitors traveling to the US from all over the world is expected to grow significantly. We expect over 65 million visitors in 2012 alone. This reflects the fact that travel and tourism is America's number-one services export — and it continues to get stronger each day. We project that China will — by far — have the largest percentage growth in tourism to the US over the next five years, at nearly 200 percent. Our message to China and people across the globe is clear: "the United States welcomes you."

Before I go any further, let me recognize two groups. First, thank you to the National Tour Association for developing the program that qualifies the US—inbound tour operators. Without this program we could not have entered into the agreement that allows selling packaged travel to the United States. Second, thank you to the China National Tourism Administration, which has been a good partner in developing travel and tourism for both countries. We look forward to working with all of you to strengthen US—China ties and reap all the economic and cultural benefits that flow from our relationship.

And finally, thank you to the Shanghai Commercial Service and Shanghai Tourism Bureau for all their work to support this event and to continue promoting US—China travel and tourism.

Now let me turn the microphone back over before we officially present today's awards.

(*Speech by US Commerce Secretary John Bryson at Tourism Award Ceremony on May 7, 2012*)

(2) 汉英口译。

世界旅游组织秘书长弗朗加利先生，
联合国常务副秘书长弗莱切特女士，
各位代表，女士们，先生们：

十月的北京，天高气爽，秋色宜人。世界旅游组织第15届全体大会今天在这里隆重开幕。我代表中国政府，向各位来宾表示诚挚的欢迎！向大会表示热烈的祝贺！

旅游是一项集观光、娱乐、健身为一体的愉快而美好的活动。旅游业随着时代进步而不断发展。20世纪中叶以来，现代旅游在世界范围迅速兴起，旅游人数不断增加，旅游产业规模持续扩大，旅游经济地位显著提升，旅游活动愈益成为各国人民交流文化、增进友谊、扩大交往的重要渠道，对人类生活和社会进步产生越来越广泛的影响。

古往今来，旅游一直是人们增长知识、丰富阅历、强健体魄的美好追求。在古代，中国先哲们就提出了"观国之光"的思想，倡导"读万卷书，行万里路"，游历名山大川，承天地之灵气，接山水之精华。新中国成立后，特别是改革开放以来，中国政府高度重视旅游工作，旅游业持续快速发展，已经成为一个富有蓬勃活力和巨大潜力的新兴产业。目前，中国入境旅游人数和旅游外汇收入跃居世界前列，出境旅游人数迅速增加，中国已经成为旅游大国。今年上半年，尽管我国遭遇了一场突如其来的"非典"疫情冲击，但我们一手抓防治"非典"，一手抓经济建设，及时采取有力扶持政策，使一度受到重创的旅游业得以迅速恢复和发展。

中国是一个历史悠久的文明古国，也是一个充满时代生机的东方大国，拥有许多得天独厚的旅游资源。自然风光旖旎秀美,历史文化博大精深,56个民族风情浓郁,目前已被列入世界文化遗产地和世界自然遗产地达29处。在改革开放政策的推动下,现代化建设突飞猛进,城乡面貌日新月异。古代中国的风采神韵与现代中国的蓬勃英姿交相辉映。这些都为发展国内外旅游创造了优越的条件。

21世纪头20年,是中国全面建设小康社会、加快推进社会主义现代化的重要战略机遇期,也是中国旅游业发展的有利时期。我们要把旅游业培育成为中国国民经济的重要产业,合理保护和利用旅游资源,努力实现旅游业的可持续发展。中国政府欢迎各国朋友到中国旅游观光,我们将全力保障广大旅游者的健康和安全;同时鼓励更多的中国人走向世界。我们愿同各国广泛开展合作,推动世界旅游业的发展。

多年来,世界旅游组织为促进全球旅游业的繁荣与发展,做出了积极而富有成效的努力。最近,世界旅游组织成为联合国专门机构,我们谨表示衷心祝贺。我们相信,这次大会必将对实现全球旅游业的更大繁荣和发展,起到重要的推动作用。

祝世界旅游组织第15届全体大会圆满成功!

谢谢大家!

(2003年10月19日温家宝在世界旅游组织第15届全体大会开幕式上的讲话)

3.2.4 词语拓展

出境旅游	outbound travel
出境游客	outbound tourist
度假胜地	holiday resort
动植物	flora and fauna
大教堂	cathedral
佛教名山	famous Buddhist mountain
国画	traditional Chinese painting
国家4A景区	national AAAA (4A) tourist scenic area
国家公园	national park
国内旅游	domestic tourism
观光	sightseeing
湖光山色	landscape of lakes and hills
纪念品	souvenir
景观设计	landscape design
莲花池	lotus pond

联合国教科文组织	United Nations Educational, Scientific and Cultural Organization (UNESCO)
旅行日程	itinerary
旅行社	travel agency
旅游管理局	tourism administration bureau
旅游景点	tourist spot, scenic spot
旅游业	tourism industry/sector
名山大川	famous mountains and great rivers
名胜古迹	scenic spots and historical sites
木/竹/贝雕	wood/bamboo/shell carving
鸟瞰	overlook
青山绿水	green hills and clear waters
人文景观	places of historic figures and cultural heritage
山水/水墨画	landscape/ink painting
石刻碑文	stone inscription
手工艺品	artifact; handicrafts
世界文化遗产	World Heritage
世界旅游组织	World Tourism Organization
世界文化遗产地	World Cultural Heritage site
世界自然遗产地	World Natural Heritage site
耸立的	towering
五岳	five great mountains
由导游带领的旅游	conducted/guided tour
延绵起伏的山脉	rolling mountains
中国古典园林	classical Chinese garden
中国国际旅行社	China International Travel Service
中国国家旅游局	China National Tourism Administration
自然保护区	nature reserve
自然景观	natural scenery/attraction
壮丽景色	spectacular scene

3.2.5 厚积薄发

中式英语（Chinglish），简单地说，是指生成的英语在语音、词汇、语法、表达方式和思维习惯等方面有受汉语母语影响的痕迹，是不地道、甚至错误的英语表达方式，可能会在交流中引起误解或达不到沟通效果。下面仅举一些常见标语中的中式英语为例,表达有误的原因可能是英语词汇语法知识的欠缺,对汉语原文理解有误,或者对英语国家文化知识的了解不够。

(1) No standing.

此标示语的正确意思是"不许停车",但由于国人望文生义,将其误用为"此处请勿站人"或"请勿在此停留",常见于楼梯口处。正确的译文为 Standing clear 或是 To avoid congestion please do not stand near the stairs。

(2) Please notice the distance between the train and the platform.

(3) Don't stop the door from closing.

上面两个中式标识语常见于国内的地铁站内。想要表达"小心列车与站台之间的空隙",可以参考伦敦地铁站里反复播放的"Mind the gap"。"请勿阻止车门关闭"不妨译为"Mind the door"。

(4) Slide carefully.

标识语"小心地滑"译为英文可以使用"Caution! Slippery when wet"或者"Caution! Wet floor"。如果只是简单地字字对译,译为"Slide carefully"的话,意思则是"要小心翼翼地摔倒",这样的英文标识语不仅不能起到提示、警告的作用,反而成了一个笑话。

(5) Workpeople passage.

此标识语本想要表达"员工通道",但与中文"工作人员"或"员工"相对应的英文词为"crew"、"employee"或"staff"。而英文中的 workpeople 指的是工人或体力劳动者。因此,机场的标识语可用 Crew and employees enter here,其他场合也以用 Staff only。

由上面的例子可见,杜绝中式英语,正确、地道地使用英语,不仅要求译者有过硬的语言功底,还要求译者了解语言的文化内涵以及中英文两种语言的差异所在。

3.3 文化教育

3.3.1 背景阅读

The Overall Situation of Studying Abroad

It has been more than 100 years since China began to send its students and scholars to study abroad. Though with different scales and various forms during different stages of history, the underlining principle remains:

Before the foundation of the People's Republic of China, there were already a lot of Chinese going abroad for further studies in order to bring home knowledge that could help build a stronger country. After the establishment of new China, bearing in mind the ideas of fighting against the capitalist Western Bloc and speeding up the development of a socialist country, the Communist Party of China (CPC) and the central government decided to send students and scholars to the former Soviet Union and other socialist countries to study the advanced S&T and management skills. Beginning from the 1960s, with the change of international political climate, the central government accordingly made adjustments in policies related to sending students and scholars abroad. In 1978, with strategic insight, late Chinese leader Deng Xiaoping made the important decision of expanding the scales of sending students and scholars abroad. Based on the past experience, in 1992, the CPC Central Committee and central government promulgated the guideline for students and scholars studying abroad, that is — to support students and scholars studying abroad, to encourage them to return to China after their completion of studies and guarantee them the freedom of coming and going.

Ⅰ. General information of students and scholars studying abroad since the reform and opening up in 1978:

Since the reform and opening up in 1978, the work related to students and scholars studying abroad has seen rapid developments and now it serves as a window for China's reform and opening up as well as for the cultural exchanges between China and other countries. In harmony with the socio-economic development, a managing and implementing system for the work related to students and scholars studying abroad has been set up in higher education institutes (HEIs) as well as in S&T research institutes, from the national level to local levels. This system mainly consists of three complementary channels for students and scholars, namely, state-funded, employer-funded and self-funded.

In 2003, the total number of students and scholars studying abroad is 117,300, among which 3,002 people are state-funded, 5,144 employer-funded and 109,200 self-funded. In the same year, a total number of 20,100 students and scholars returned from overseas studying, among which 2,638 are state funded, 4,292 employer-funded and 13,200 self-funded.

From 1978 to 2003, a total number of 700,200 Chinese students and scholars studied in 108 countries and regions all over the world, covering almost all disciplines.

Both the quantity and scale was unprecedented in the history of China. During the same period, a total of 172,800 returned. As for 527,400 who haven't returned yet, 356,600 are still studying, doing researches or visiting as scholars in foreign HEIs.

As for the geographic distribution of the overseas Chinese students and scholars, the statistics for destination in 2003 is as follows: 10.5% to Asia, 1.8% to Africa, 49.8% to Europe, 15.4% to North America and Latin America, and 22.5% to Oceania. Among those who have returned in 2003, 25.1% are from Asia, 0.2% from Africa, 42.7% from Europe, 22.7% from North America and Latin America, and 9.3% from Oceania. As for those who are still studying abroad, 22% are in Asia, 0.6% in Africa, 28.1% in Europe, 36.4% in North America and Latin America, and 12.9% in Oceania.

II. General information of the efforts of the Ministry of Education (MOE) to attract outstanding students and scholars abroad to return to China or make contributions for China through various ways:

The CPC Central Committee and the central government have always been attaching great importance to the work related to students and scholars studying abroad. And the Ministry of Education has been strictly implementing the guideline of "supporting students and scholars studying abroad, encouraging them to return to China after their completion of studies and guaranteeing them the freedom of coming and going". Meanwhile, the MOE has taken effective measures to attract outstanding students and scholars to return to China or to make contributions through various ways.

The returned students and scholars play an leading role in areas like education, S&T, high-tech industries, finance, insurance, trade and management etc, and serve as a driving force for the country's economic and social development. At same time, many students and scholars staying abroad take initiatives to make contributions to China through various ways, such as giving lectures during short-term visit to China, having academic exchanges, conducting joint researches, bringing in projects and investments and providing information and technical consultancy etc. Accordingly, governments at all levels as well as enterprises and institutions have all come up with supportive policies in this regard. Relevant institutions, special funds and talent-reserves have been established to facilitate the returnees in their careers. As for the MOE, it has been conducting some exemplary programs to attract students and scholars to return as well as to facilitate their careers.

With China's further reform and opening up, the work related to students and scholars studying abroad will surely play a greater role in the economic and social development of China.

(http://www.moe.gov.cn/publicfiles/business/htmlfiles/moe/s3917/201007/91574.html)

3.3.2 口译精讲

1. 英汉口译

（1）词语必备。

sclerosis	硬化症
instill	灌输
integrity	正直
languishing	日渐衰弱
fortitude	坚定

（2）口译课文。

I'm honored to meet you, the future leaders of Great Britain and this world. And although the circumstances of our lives may seem very distant, with me standing here as the First Lady of the United States of America, and you, just getting through school, I want you to know that we have very much in common, for nothing in my life's path would have predicted that I'd be standing here as the first African-American First Lady of the United States of America. There is nothing in my story that would land me here.

I wasn't raised with wealth or resources or any social standing to speak of. I was raised on the South Side of Chicago. That's the real part of Chicago. And I was the product of a working-class community. My father was a city worker all of his life, and my mother was a stay-at-home mom. And she stayed at home to take care of me and my older brother. Neither of them attended university. My dad was diagnosed with multiple sclerosis in the prime of his life. But even as it got harder for him to walk and get dressed in the morning — I saw him struggle more and more — my father never complained about his struggle. He was grateful for what he had. He just woke up a little earlier and worked a little harder. And my brother and I were raised with all that you really need: love, strong values and a belief that with a good education and a whole lot of hard work, that there was nothing that we could not do.

I am an example of what's possible when girls from the very beginning of their lives are loved and nurtured by the people around them. I was surrounded by extraordinary women in my life: grandmothers, teachers, aunts, cousins, neighbors, who taught me about quiet strength and dignity. And my mother, the most important role model in my life, who lives with us at the White House and helps to care for our two little daughters, Malia and Sasha. She's an active presence in their lives, as well as mine, and is instilling in them the same values that she taught me and my brother: things like compassion, and integrity, and confidence, and perseverance — all of that wrapped up in an unconditional love that only a grandmother can give.

I was also fortunate enough to be cherished and encouraged by some strong male role models as well, including my father, my brother, uncles and grandfathers. The men in my life taught me some important things, as well. They taught me about what a respectful relationship should look like between men and women. They taught me about what a strong marriage feels like: that it's built on faith and commitment and an admiration for each other's unique gifts. They taught me about what it means to be a father and to raise a family, and not only to invest in your own home but to reach out and help raise kids in the broader community.

You are the women who will build the world as it should be. You're going to write the next chapter in history. Not just for yourselves, but for your generation and generations to come. And that's why getting a good education is so important. That's why all of this that you're going through — the ups and the downs, the teachers that you love and the teachers that you don't — why it's so important, because communities and countries and ultimately the world are only as strong as the health of their women. And that's important to keep in mind.

Part of that health includes an outstanding education. The difference between a struggling family and a healthy one is often the presence of an empowered woman or women at the center of that family. The difference between a broken community and a thriving one is often the healthy respect between men and women who appreciate the contributions each other makes to society. The difference between a languishing nation and one that will flourish is the recognition that we need equal access to education for both boys and girls.

If you want to know the reason why I'm standing here, it's because of education. I never cut class. Sorry, I don't know if anybody is cutting class. I never did it. I loved getting As. I liked being smart. I liked being on time. I liked getting my work done. I thought being smart was cooler than anything in the world. And you too, with these same values, can control your own destiny. You too can pave the way. You too can realize your dreams, and then your job is to reach back and to help someone just like you do the same thing.

History proves that it doesn't matter whether you come from a council estate or a country estate. Your success will be determined by your own fortitude, your own confidence, your own individual hard work. That is true. That is the reality of the world that we live in. You now have control over your own destiny. And it won't be easy — that's for sure. But you have everything you need. Everything you need to succeed, you already have, right here.

(*Excerpted from the speech by America's First Lady, Michelle Obama at the Elizabeth Garrett Anderson School on April 3, 2009*)

(3) 参考译文。

我很荣幸见到你们，你们是英国和世界未来的领导者。尽管目前我们的生活境况差距很大，我作为美国的第一夫人站在这里，而你们还正在上学，但是我想让你们知道我们有很多共同之处，因为我的生命中从没有什么东西曾预示过我能作为美国的第一位非洲裔的第一夫人站在这里。我的生活经历中也没有什么能让我站在这个位置上。

我并不是由财富和资源培养长大的，我的家庭也没什么社会地位可言。我生长在芝加哥的南部，那是芝加哥最真实的地方。我出生于工人阶级，我的父亲一生都是市政工人，我母亲是位家庭妇女。她呆在家里照顾哥哥和我。我的父母亲都不曾上过大学。我父亲在壮年的时候被诊断出患有多种硬化症。这使得他行走和早上穿衣都越来越困难——我看着他挣扎得越来越厉害——尽管如此，父亲从不曾对此有抱怨。他对于所拥有的一切怀有感恩之心。他只是起得更早一点，工作更努力一点。我哥哥和我在成长中拥有我们所需的一切：爱、坚定的价值观和信念，我们坚信只要获得良好的教育和努力工作，就没有什么是我们做不到的。

我的例子证明了女孩子只要从生命之初就被周围的人呵护和教育，是可以取得非凡成就的。在我的生命中，身边围绕着许多杰出的女性，我的祖母、老师、姨妈、表姐妹、邻居，她们教会我沉默的力量和尊严。还有我的母亲，我一生中最重要的榜样，她和我们一起住在白宫，帮助照顾我的两个小女儿，玛利亚和萨莎。她在我们的生活中积极而活跃，她将曾经教给我哥哥和我的价值观灌输给我的女儿们，如同情心、正直、自信和坚持不懈，这一切都包含在了只有祖母才能给予的无条件的爱当中。

我也很幸运地从一些坚强的男性榜样那里得到珍爱和鼓励，他们包括我的父亲、哥哥、叔伯和祖父。他们也教会了我一些重要的东西，如相互尊重的男女关系应是什么样子的，牢固的婚姻应如何维系——婚姻应建立在信任和承诺的基础上，夫妻双方应对彼此独特的才能互相欣赏，以及如何成为一名称职的父亲，承担起家庭的责任。他们还教会我不应只是为自己的家庭付出，也要伸出援手，帮助养育更加广大的社区里的孩子。

你们是将在未来建立理想世界的女性。你们将会谱写历史的崭新篇章。不只是为了你们自己,还为了你们这一代人以及你们的子子孙孙。这就是为什么获得良好的教育至关重要。这就是为什么现在你们要经历这一切——起起伏伏,你喜欢的老师和不喜欢的老师。为什么这些是如此的重要,因为只有女性保持健康,她们所在的社区、国家以及最终这个世界才会变得强大。你们要牢牢记住一点。

这份健康中的一部分就包括了出色的教育。一个困难的家庭与一个健康的家庭的区别往往在于是否有一个或几个能干的女性处于家庭核心地位,当家做主。一个破败的社区与一个欣欣向荣的社区的区别往往在于男女之间是否能够彼此尊重,相互欣赏对方为社会作出的贡献。一个日渐衰弱的国家与一个日益强盛的国家的区别在于是否认同男孩和女孩都应该享有平等的教育机会。

如果你想知道我为什么站在这里,其原因就是教育。我从不逃课。抱歉,我不知道你们当中是否有人逃课,我从没有那样做。我喜欢得"优",喜欢做聪明人,喜欢准时。我喜欢把我的功课做完。我认为做聪明人是世界上最酷的事情。如果你们与我拥有相同的价值观,你们同样可以掌控自己的命运,为自己的未来铺路。你们也可以实现梦想,然后你们要做的就是伸出手去帮助像你们一样的人实现梦想。

历史证明,出身贫寒或富裕并不重要。你的成功取决于你的坚毅、你的信心和你自己的辛勤工作。这是真的。这就是我们所生活的世界的实际情况。你现在可以掌控自己的命运。但可以肯定的是,这并不是容易的事情。不过你已经拥有了你所需要的一切。你已经拥有了可以使你获得成功的一切,它们就在这里。

(4) 口译点津。

1) I wasn't raised with wealth or resources or any social standing to speak of.

be raised with sth 是指"用……把……养大",此句可翻译为"我并不是由财富和资源培养长大的,我的家庭也没有什么社会地位可言",也可基于演讲者想要强调自己出身平民的用意,翻译为"我并不是生长在一个资源丰富、地位显赫的富裕家庭"。

2) My dad was diagnosed with multiple sclerosis in the prime of his life.

此句中,in the prime of one's life 指的是某人正值壮年或正处于年富力强时期。

3) I am an example of what's possible when girls from the very beginning of their lives are loved and nurtured by the people around them.

I am an example of what's possible 中的 example 在翻译时可使用转译法,将名词转换为动词"证明了",将 possible 转译成"取得非凡成就",两次转译法的使用既能表达原文的意思,又使句子更符合汉语的表达习惯。

4) They taught me about what a respectful relationship should look like between men and women. They taught me about what a strong marriage feels like: that it's built

on faith and commitment and an admiration for each other's unique gifts. They taught me about what it means to be a father and to raise a family.

这3句话结构相同，内容相近，且主语相同，又接近汉语中的排比修辞手法，在翻译时可将其合并成一个句子，使行文更简洁明了。

5) The difference between a struggling family and a healthy one is often the presence of an empowered woman or women at the center of that family. The difference between a broken community and a thriving one is often the healthy respect between men and women who appreciate the contributions each other makes to society. The difference between a languishing nation and one that will flourish is the recognition that we need equal access to education for both boys and girls.

此处3句话的结构相同，在翻译时应采用相同的方法和结构。原文句子的结构是 the difference between…is…，是肯定的陈述句，在翻译时，应增加"是否"二字，译成"……与……的区别在于是否……，"以体现出对指定话题的立场选择，到底是肯定还是否定便能看出根本的区别，此增词法的使用使语义更加清晰，句子的编排更加符合汉语的思维习惯。

2．汉英口译

(1) 词语必备。

隔阂	estrangement
培生（传媒集团）	Pearson
麦克米伦	Macmillan
新兴文化产业	emerging cultural industry

(2) 口译课文。

事实告诉我们，中英关系的潜力和前景，有赖于人文交流所奠定的坚实民意基础。站在中英关系新的起点上，我们应以建立中英高级别人文交流机制为契机，为文明的对话和人民的相知构建更加宽广的桥梁。我认为可在四个方面共同努力：

第一，尊重和维护文明多样性。文明多样性是人类历史发展的宝贵财富，是当代世界的基本特征。全球有200多个国家和地区，2500多个民族，6000多种语言。各民族历经千百年的磨练，创造了独具魅力的灿烂文化。世界之美在于文明多元多样多彩。在多样中求大同，在差异中求和谐，在交流中求发展，是人类社会应有的文明观。我们应当充分理解各国不同国情、发展阶段和历史文化特点，尊重各国自主选择社会制度和发展道路，这样的世界才能异彩纷呈。

第二，深化和扩大文化互信共识。文化渗透在经济、社会和制度的各个层面，具有超越时空、跨越国界的影响力。当今世界，人类同住"地球村"，这是一个不同文化相互走近的时代，也是一个最需要包容和理解的时代，交流对话是文化和谐共生的根本途径，是人们理解互信的重要基础。我们应以宽广的胸怀对待其他文化,相互学习,博采众长。我们应最大限度地寻求共识、减少纷争,避免将分歧转化为对抗。这不但是各国人民的愿望,也是人类社会繁荣和谐的强劲动力。

第三,重视和推进人与人的交流。人文交流沟通的是人们的心灵和情感。坦率地说,目前中英民众交流还不够深入,误解与隔阂有时仍困扰双方的情感和认同。我们要构建官民并举、多方参与的交流格局,面向人人,植根社会,为各层次、各领域、各年龄段的人们相互了解创造条件。

第四,挖掘和拓展出版传媒合作新领域。中英出版传媒合作开启较早、潜力巨大。英国是世界出版创意强国,中国是图书出版大国。新中国成立以来,中国从英国引进图书3.4万多种,英国已成为中国对外版权贸易第二大国。近年来,中英出版传媒合作多样化多渠道开展,牛津、剑桥、培生、企鹅、麦克米伦等知名传媒集团与中国建立了良好合作关系。中国有底蕴深厚的历史人文资源,英国有表现力强大的现代技术手段;中国有广阔的文化消费市场,英国有成熟的商业运营模式,我们完全可以形成优势互补、合作共赢的格局。随着信息网络技术的快速发展,出版传媒业正面临巨大转型。双方应把握好数字时代文化传播的新特征,开拓新媒体、新技术和新兴文化产业的合作领域,联合打造具有战略性标志性的项目,把最优秀的文化产品带给对方,让双方民众享受多元文化的滋养。

(2012年4月15日刘延东在伦敦中英出版传媒产业投资论坛上的演讲,节选)

(3) 参考译文。

Facts have shown that the potential and prospects of Sino-UK relationship rely on the solid public support forged through cultural and people-to-people exchanges from both countries. Standing on a new starting point of our bilateral relationship, we should make the best of the High-Level People-to-People Exchange mechanism, to build wider bridges for dialogue between civilizations and greater understanding between the peoples. I suggest that we should work together from the following four aspects.

First, respect and safeguard the diversity of civilizations. This diversity is a valuable treasure of the development of human history and the basic feature of the modern world. There are more than 200 countries and regions in the world, with over 2,500 ethnic groups and over 6,000 languages. These ethnic groups, through hundreds of years of development, have created splendid cultures of unique charm. The beauty of the world lies in the diversity and richness of different civilizations. To pursue common ground among diversity, to seek harmony in differences, and to achieve development through exchanges are the right approach to human civilizations. We should fully understand the different conditions, development stages and history and culture of different countries, therefore respect their independent choices of social systems and development paths. Only in this way, the world will be colorful.

Second, deepen and enlarge the mutual trust and consensus in cultures. Cultures can be found in different aspects of economy, society and institutions and its influence is beyond time and borders. Nowadays, human beings are living in a global village. It is a time when different cultures are closer to each other and tolerance and understanding are more needed than ever before. Dialogue and exchanges are the fundamental way for harmonious coexistence of cultures and an important basis for mutual trust. We should approach other cultures with a broad mind, and learn from their strengths. We should seek consensus and reduce disputes whenever possible, and prevent differences from degenerating into confrontation. This is not only the wish of people of all nations, but also the driving force for a harmonious and prosperous human society.

Third, value and promote people-to-people exchanges. People-to-people exchanges are communication of their hearts and feelings. To be honest, exchanges between Chinese and British peoples are not sufficient enough, and misunderstanding and estrangement still undermine our feelings and recognition for each other sometimes. Therefore, we need to institute an exchange pattern, with multiple participants from both government and non-government sectors, and oriented towards all members of society, to enable deeper understanding between people from all ages and walks of life.

Fourth, explore and expand new areas of cooperation in media and publishing. The cooperation between two countries in media and publishing has an early history and huge potential. The UK is a great power of publishing and creative industry while China is a big publisher of books. Ever since the founding of PR China, our country has introduced from the UK more than 34,000 published books, which renders the UK the second largest copyright trading partner of China. In recent years, this cooperation has developed and diversified in many channels. Well-known publishers such as Oxford, Cambridge, Pearson, Penguin and Macmillan have established friendly cooperative relationships with China. China enjoys rich historical and cultural resources and a large market for cultural consumption, while the UK has expressive modern technologies and mature business model. Therefore, we can complement each other to achieve a win-win progress. With the fast development of information and network technologies, the publishing industry is facing great transformation. Both of us should make good use of the new features of cultural communication in the digital era to explore cooperative areas for new media, new technologies and emerging cultural industries, and to jointly foster key strategic projects, so as to offer the best of our cultural products to each other and let our people benefit from the diversity of cultures.

(4) 口译点津。

1) 站在中英关系新的起点上，我们应以建立中英高级别人文交流机制为契机，为文明的对话和人民的相知构建更加宽广的桥梁。

"以……为契机"是常见的中文句式，暗含了比喻，如果直译容易造成译文受众的误解，或者产生中式英语，此处译为 we should make the best of, make the best of ...意思与"以……为契机"对等，舍弃了源语的比喻修辞，用平实的词组把原文的意思翻译出来反而使译文更显地道。"为……构建更宽广的桥梁"也是常见的句式，"桥梁"在此处也是比喻，指沟通的渠道，但是，由于此喻体形象清晰，直译后不会造成译文读者的误解，固采用了直译的手法，译为 build wider bridges for。

2) 在多样中求大同，在差异中求和谐，在交流中求发展，是人类社会应有的文明观。

"在多样中求大同，在差异中求和谐，在交流中求发展"是典型的中文并列排比结构，译文也以并列的介词短语（among, in 和 through）体现排比的修辞：To pursue common ground amid diversity, to seek harmony in differences, and to achieve development through exchanges，同时，动词 pursue，seek，achieve 三者并列也对应了3个"求"字，以及3个 to 的不省略译出，以使结构对等，译文在内容和形式上都做到了忠于原文。

3) 我们应最大限度地寻求共识、减少纷争，避免分歧转化为对抗。

"最大限度"译为"whenever possible"，相比"to the greatest extent"更加具体。由"分歧"到"对抗"，是指对立程度、事态愈加严重，因此"转化"一词译为 degenerate，与文中想要表达的含义更加契合。

4) 我们要构建官民并举、多方参与的交流格局，面向人人，植根社会，为各层次、各领域、各年龄段的人们相互了解创造条件。

四字词的成语式修饰语是中文的一大特色，比如，"官民并举，多方参与，面向人人，植根社会"，这些词语朗朗上口，信息内涵多，却不易翻译，其内容与形式往往不能同时兼顾。译文采用了意译的方法，把"官民并举，多方参与"整合到一起，译为"with multiple participants from both the government and non-government sectors"，在意思上忠于原文，舍弃了成语的形式反而使译文更为简洁。同理，"面向人人，植根社会"译为"oriented towards all members of society"，也是在忠于原文的基础上做了信息整合，使译文的表达更为简洁与地道。

5) 中国有底蕴深厚的历史人文资源，英国有表现力强大的现代技术手段；中国有广阔的文化消费市场，英国有成熟的商业运营模式，我们完全可以形成优势互补、合作共赢的格局。

这是一句典型的汉语长句，翻译时可进行信息整合，将"中国有底蕴深厚的历史人文资源"与"中国有广阔的文化消费市场"合并为一句，将"英国有表现力强大的现代技术手段"与"英国有成熟的商业运营模式"并为一句，译为：China enjoys rich historical and cultural resources and a large market for cultural consumption, while the UK has expressive modern technologies and mature business model.

3.3.3 实战演练

1. 口译听解与表达

（1）口译听辨。

The chief goal is to see that all students are ready to _____ the product that you, as colleges and universities are providing. That is a major _____. We want to serve you, the colleges, at the same time, serve the students. That is our _____ and our _____ to see that your customers have the tools they need to succeed when they come into your business. And it's our goal to see that the students have the tools they need to succeed and take advantage of _____. It is no longer just a matter of getting to high school and try to get into the college, _____. We've seen more and more of American system of _____ rather than just American systems of _____, where people are allowed to dip in and out of the education system through their process of learning throughout their careers and recognizing especially during all this fair trade, the _____ place on them for more _____, more _____, more _____ that they are able to get back into the systems and learn more. And two things happen in order for the world _____. And that is, the _____ and adults and _____ have to have the basics through the systems that they needed to begin with. And secondly, you have to be able to deliver in the system those opportunity for them to come back in. The workforce for American comes of every single state. You and I have to get on. All of the _____, all of the states have the responsibility of providing the America workforce. And that workforce is going to determine how much _____ there is in the United States of America. And that in turn will determine how strong we are, whether we continue to _____ or whether we slip to a _____.

（2）复述练习。

Through education, you can better yourselves in other ways. You learn how to learn — how to think critically and find solutions to unexpected challenges. I remember we used to ask our teachers, "Why am I going to need algebra?" Well, you may not have to solve for X to get a good job or to be a good parent. But you will need to think through tough problems. You'll need to think on your feet. You'll need to know how to gather facts and evaluate information. So, math teachers, you can tell your students that the president says they need algebra. Education also teaches you the value of discipline — that the greatest rewards come not from instant gratification but from sustained effort and from hard work. This is a lesson that's especially true today, in a culture that prizes flash over substance, that tells us that the goal in life is to be entertained, that says you can be famous just for being famous. You get on a reality show — don't know what you've done — suddenly you're famous. But that's not going to lead to lasting, sustained achievement. And finally, with the right education, both at home and at school, you can learn how to be a better human being. For when you read a great story or you learn about an important moment in history, it helps you imagine what it would be like to walk in somebody else's shoes, to know their struggles. The success of our economy will depend on your skills, but the success of our community will depend on your ability to follow the Golden Rule — to treat others as you would like to be treated.

(3) 公众演讲。

以"中国的留学热"为题,分别用英语和汉语作 3～5 分钟的演讲。

2. 单句口译

(1) 英汉口译。

1) In Britain, the Open University, founded in 1969, encourages home-based students to study for Bachelor of Arts and Bachelor of Science degrees using a combination of television and radio programs and correspondence work, where students send in assignments to their tutors and have them returned after assessment.

2) Despite almost universal acknowledgement of the vital importance of women's literacy, education remains an elusive dream for far too many women in far too many countries of the world.

3) To further indicate its support for this idea, the World Bank announced in late 1995 that it was earmarking up to $900 million each year for loans to promote the education of girls.

4) Over the past two years, 620,000 Chinese have gone abroad to study, which is more than a quarter of the total number who have studied overseas since the start of China's reform policies in 1978.

5) China's overseas student body has traditionally been dominated by only the very best, who have chosen to study as undergraduates at China's top universities before doing postgraduate studies abroad.

(2) 汉英口译。

1) 进入21世纪，经济全球化、信息网络化，已经把世界连成一体，文化的发展将不再是各自封闭的，而是在相互影响中多元共存。

2) 中国将永远坚持开放兼容的方针，既珍视传统，又博采众长，用文明的方式、和谐的方式实现经济繁荣和社会进步。

3) 我们将以教师、教材、教法为重点，积极推进人才培养模式和教育体制改革，更好地激发学校和教师的创造活力。

4) 中国有2.6亿学生，我们要努力提供公平的受教育机会和高质量的教育，为每个孩子的成功和幸福创造条件。

5) 特别是近年来哈佛与我的母校清华大学联合举办公共管理高级培训项目，中国有68名省部级干部和近400名厅局级干部来此研修，成为中美人文交流的典范。

3. 段落口译

(1) 英汉口译。

Paragraph 1

The United Nations Educational, Scientific and Cultural Organization (UNESCO) has long supported the work of poets, publishers and teachers worldwide. This year, once again, on the occasion of World Poetry Day, UNESCO wishes to highlight the artistic importance and the power of poetry in encouraging people to read and in creating one of humanity's most authentic and dynamic art forms. Poets convey a timeless message. They are often key witness to history's great political and social changes. Their writings inspire us to build lasting peace in our minds, to rethink relations between man and nature and to establish humanism founded on the uniqueness and diversity of peoples.

Paragraph 2

While many governments are making efforts to protect education budgets, teachers' jobs, salaries and decent teaching conditions, we are deeply concerned by the probable impact of the global economic slowdown on the teaching profession. As a catalyst for human growth and development, education is key to the achievement of all the Millennium Development Goals and Education for All targets. But without sufficient numbers of well-trained and professionally motivated teachers, we risk falling short of the promise made ten years ago at the World Education Forum to the world's children and youth, because teachers are at the heart of the education system.

(2) 汉英口译。

段落 1

中国未来的发展，根本靠人才，基础在教育。去年中国颁布了未来10年的教育规划纲要。其核心有三点：一是把育人为本作为根本要求。教育的核心和全部任务就是培养人才，促进学生的全面发展。二是把促进公平和提高质量作为两大重点。教育公平是社会公平的基础，收入不公影响人一时，教育不公影响人一生。三是把优先发展和改革创新作为两大保障。优先发展教育是中国政府的长期方针，近10年来，教育的财政投入年均增长20%，2012年将比2010年增加50%以上。

段落2

中华文化千古传承。众所周知，世界古代五大文明，其中四大文明都因外族侵略而中断，唯有中国，尽管历史上曾屡遭外族入侵，面临亡国灭种灾难，但侵略者或可征服我们的国土，却始终未能切断中华文化命脉，甚至被我们的文化同化。由此可见中国文化的博大精深。以儒家思想为代表的中华文化倡导以文化人，以和为贵，主张己所不欲，勿施于人。中国自古以来每一次崛起都是以先进的文化和思想立足于世界民族之林，从未侵略其他国家。今天中国必将坚持和平发展之路，创造大国和平崛起的先例，为构建和谐世界作出重要贡献。

4．对话口译

A：我知道您作为联合国秘书长，工作非常繁忙。那么您每天大概要工作多少个小时呢？

B: Sometimes I sleep very little. Sometimes I have to sleep two hours or three hours, but normally I try to sleep four or five hours a day. For me, there is no such thing as weekends.

A：这样的话，想必您也没有时间做一些工作以外的事情，比如一些业余爱好。

B: Almost no time for hobbies. But whenever I'm free, even with a few hours, I try to practice calligraphy.

A：那么您为什么喜欢书法呢？练习书法对您有什么帮助呢？

B: That really helps for your mind and your body. That really makes you concentrate and focus. That makes your mind peaceful. You don't think about other things but to concentrate. I often think that calligraphy and diplomacy have something in common.

A：书法与外交会有相同的地方？您为什么会这样认为呢？

B: When you see a beautiful calligraphy art, you don't appreciate how much time and effort have been spent there. You just appreciate the beauty without knowing how much time and energy have been spent. When you hammer out these difficult and complicated issues, a lot of things have to be done behind the scenes. It's not visible, as what I have been doing for the past five and a half years behind the scenes, and speaking to the world leaders, then you will see peace and harmony. But people should appreciate more how much time and energy you have spent behind this.

5. 篇章口译
(1) 英汉口译。

I know that some of you are still adjusting to being back at school. But I'm here today because I have something important to discuss with you. I'm here because I want to talk with you about your education and what's expected of all of you in this new school year.

I've given a lot of speeches about education. And I've talked about responsibility a lot. I've talked about teachers' responsibility for inspiring students and pushing you to learn. I've talked about your parents' responsibility for making sure you stay on track, and you get your homework done, and don't spend every waking hour in front of the TV or with the Xbox. I've talked a lot about your government's responsibility for setting high standards, and supporting teachers and principals, and turning around schools that aren't working, where students aren't getting the opportunities that they deserve.

But at the end of the day, we can have the most dedicated teachers, the most supportive parents, the best schools in the world — and none of it will make a difference, none of it will matter unless all of you fulfill your responsibilities, unless you show up to those schools, unless you pay attention to those teachers, unless you listen to your parents and grandparents and other adults and put in the hard work it takes to succeed. That's what I want to focus on today: the responsibility each of you has for your education.

I want to start with the responsibility you have to yourself. Every single one of you has something that you're good at. Every single one of you has something to offer. And you have a responsibility to yourself to discover what that is. That's the opportunity an education can provide. Maybe you could be a great writer — maybe even good enough to write a book or articles in a newspaper — but you might not know it until you write that English paper — that English class paper that's assigned to you. Maybe you could be an innovator or an inventor — maybe even good enough to come up with the next iPhone or the new medicine or vaccine — but you might not know it until you do your project for your science class. Maybe you could be a mayor or a senator or a Supreme Court justice — but you might not know that until you join student government or the debate team.

And no matter what you want to do with your life, I guarantee that you'll need an education to do it. You want to be a doctor, or a teacher, or a police officer? You want to be a nurse or an architect, a lawyer or a member of our military? You're going to need a good education for every single one of those careers. You cannot drop out of school and just drop into a good job. You've got to train for it and work for it and learn for it. And this isn't just important for your own life and your own future. What you make of your education will decide nothing less than the future of this country. The future of America depends on you. What you're learning in school today will determine whether we as a nation can meet our greatest challenges in the future.

You'll need the knowledge and problem-solving skills you learn in science and math to cure diseases like cancer and AIDS, and to develop new energy technologies and protect our environment. You'll need the insights and critical-thinking skills you gain in history and social studies to fight poverty and homelessness, crime and discrimination, and make our nation more fair and more free. You'll need the creativity and ingenuity you develop in all your classes to build new companies that will create new jobs and boost our economy.

(*Excerpted from the speech by American President Obama in a National Address to America's Schoolchildren on September 8, 2009*)

(2) 汉英口译。

从在座的同学们一张张稚气、可爱的笑脸上，我仿佛看到了你们对汉语这门新课的新鲜和好奇。你们也许会问，汉语是什么样的语言呢？它难学吗？学它有用吗？我想告诉你们，汉语是一门日益普及的语言，是一门充满趣味的语言，学汉语必将助你成才。

第一，汉语应用广泛，日益普及。汉语是世界上最重要的语言之一，也是全球使用人数最多的语言，目前全世界会讲汉语的人口已达16亿。随着中国国力和国际影响力的提升，汉语备受推崇，世界各国纷纷掀起学习汉语和中华文化的热潮。现在，全世界已建起435所孔子学院，开设644个汉语课堂，分布在117个国家。各国在中小学开设汉语课的热情也越来越高，仅在美国就有1000多所中小学教授汉语，学习汉语的中学生人数已突破10万。英国、德国、俄罗斯等欧洲国家也有数万中小学生学习汉语，你们的邻国塞尔维亚也在中小学开设了汉语课。

第二，汉语简单易学，趣味无穷。汉语由汉字构成，汉字具有集形象、声音和辞义三者于一体的特性，易学易记，且学习过程犹如游戏，充满趣味。例如，汉字"人"，由一撇一捺两部分组成，看起来就像一个直立的人，字义一目了然。汉语的构词方式也颇具形象性。例如，汉语中"电脑"一词由"电"和"脑"搭配组成，有电子脑之义。学汉语可以望文生义，易于理解掌握，学习过程毫不枯燥，兴味盎然。我特别想要告诉大家的是，在阿国有一批你们爷爷奶奶辈的人曾到中国学习汉语，汉语讲得非常地道。

第三，学习汉语大有必要。一方面，汉语正在成为国际化的语言，你们要想成为国际化人才就要学习汉语。另一方面，随着中国经济发展壮大和中阿两国关系日益密切，越来越多的中国企业和中国游客来到阿尔巴尼亚，阿国主要企业均与中方建立了合作关系，懂汉语、了解中华文化的人才愈发紧俏。你们今天在汉语学习上的少量投入将为明天的就业增添一枚重要砝码。

我相信，你们一定能够在学习汉语和中华文化的道路上取得成就，将来成为中阿友好交往的桥梁和阿尔巴尼亚民族复兴的栋梁之材。

（2013年驻阿尔巴尼亚大使叶皓在阿中小学汉语课开课仪式上的讲话，节选）

3.3.4 词语拓展

出版传媒	publishing and media
成人教育	adult education
初等教育	primary education
当代艺术	contemporary art
高等教育	tertiary education
歌德学院	Goethe Institute
汉语热	the rise of Chinese language learning
函授教育	correspondence education
卷轴	scroll
科举制度	imperial examination system
孔子学院	Confucius Institute
历史人文资源	historical and cultural resources
美国大学理事会	US college board
民为邦本	people being the fundamental of the state
民办大学	non-government-run colleges and universities
普通话	mandarin
培养人才	nurture talents
区域差异	regional discrepancies
人文交流	cultural and people-to-people exchanges
人才培养模式和教育体制	the model of cultivating talents and the education system
软实力	soft power
儒家思想	Confucianism
数字时代	the digital era

素质教育	quality-oriented education
省部级干部	minister-level officials
世界遗产	world heritage
水墨艺术	ink art
天人合一	harmony between man and nature
文明多样性	the diversity of civilizations
文化和谐共生	harmonious coexistence of different cultures
文化消费市场	market for cultural consumption
新兴文化产业	emerging cultural industry
小学	elementary school
学术课程	academic curricula
学龄儿童	school-age children
学科	discipline
义利兼顾	taking into account both interests and obligations
义务教育	compulsory education
印欧语系	Indo-European languages
研究生阶段的学习	postgraduate studies
远程教育	distance learning
在职培训	on-the-job training
职业教育	vocational education
终身教育体制	a system of lifelong education
中等教育	secondary education

3.3.5 厚积薄发

古语云"民以食为天",可见饮食是中国文化的重要组成部分。中国的菜式命名方式独特,形式多样,有些还包含典故,比如"过桥米线"和"宋嫂鱼羹"。如何才能正确又地道地把中国的菜式翻译出来,同时又不失菜肴的文化特色,是值得译者深入研究的话题。就口译而言,对菜名的翻译首先要注重其交际功能。下面列举中国菜名英译的若干方式,供译者参考。

1. 烹调法+原料

烹调法包括了煮(boil)、煎(fry)、炸(deep-fry)、炒(stir-fry)、炖(stew)、蒸(steam)等。翻译时把烹调方法译出,再以主要的原料为中心词即可。比如:

清蒸桂鱼	steamed mandarin fish
西红柿炒鸡蛋	stir-fried eggs with tomatoes

炖牛肉	stewed beef

2. 原料 + with + 佐料

鱼香肉丝	shredded pork with garlic sauce
椒盐排骨	spare ribs with pepper and salt

3. 佐料 + 原料

咖喱鸡	curry chicken
糖醋排骨	sweet & sour ribs

4. 原料 + 地名 + style

麻婆豆腐	spicy tofu in Sichuan style
湖南肉	pork in Hunan style

5. 音译 + 释义法

馒头	mantou steamed bread
锅贴	guotie pot stickers

6. 直译 + 释义

狮子头	lion's head — pork meat balls
叫花鸡	beggar's chicken — roast whole chicken wrapped in mud

对于包含有比喻或夸张等修辞，以及文化典故的菜名，在口译时应首先注重把意思直白地译出，即吃的到底是什么菜。对于其文化附加意，如果能在有限的篇幅和时间内兼顾，那是最好的，如果不能，可适当地舍弃。

3.4 能源环境

3.4.1 背景阅读

The Copenhagen Accord

1. We underline that climate change is one of the greatest challenges of our time. We emphasize our strong political will to urgently combat climate change in accordance with the principle of common but differentiated responsibilities and respective capabilities. To achieve the ultimate objective of the Convention to stabilize greenhouse gas concentration in the atmosphere at a level that would prevent dangerous anthropogenic interference with the climate system, we shall, recognizing the scientific

view that the increase in global temperature should be below 2 degrees Celsius, on the basis of equity and in the context of sustainable development, enhance our long-term cooperative action to combat climate change. We recognize the critical impacts of climate change and the potential impacts of response measures on countries particularly vulnerable to its adverse effects and stress the need to establish a comprehensive adaptation programme including international support.

2. We agree that deep cuts in global emissions are required according to science, and as documented by the IPCC Fourth Assessment Report with a view to reduce global emissions so as to hold the increase in global temperature below 2 degrees Celsius, and take action to meet this objective consistent with science and on the basis of equity. We should cooperate in achieving the peaking of global and national emissions as soon as possible, recognizing that the time frame for peaking will be longer in developing countries and bearing in mind that social and economic development and poverty eradication are the first and overriding priorities of developing countries and that a low-emission development strategy is indispensable to sustainable development.

3. Adaptation to the adverse effects of climate change and the potential impacts of response measures is a challenge faced by all countries. Enhanced action and international cooperation on adaptation is urgently required to ensure the implementation of the Convention by enabling and supporting the implementation of adaptation actions aimed at reducing vulnerability and building resilience in developing countries, especially in those that are particularly vulnerable, especially least developed countries, small island developing States and Africa. We agree that developed countries shall provide adequate, predictable and sustainable financial resources, technology and capacity-building to support the implementation of adaptation action in developing countries.

4. Annex I Parties commit to implement individually or jointly the quantified economywide emissions targets for 2020, to be submitted in the format given in Appendix I by Annex I Parties to the secretariat by 31 January 2010 for compilation in an INF document. Annex I Parties that are Party to the Kyoto Protocol will thereby further strengthen the emissions reductions initiated by the Kyoto Protocol. Delivery of reductions and financing by developed countries will be measured, reported and verified in accordance with existing and any further guidelines adopted by the Conference of the Parties, and will ensure that accounting of such targets and finance is rigorous, robust and transparent.

5. Non-Annex I Parties to the Convention will implement mitigation actions,

including those to be submitted to the secretariat by non-Annex I Parties in the format given in Appendix II by 31 January 2010, for compilation in an INF document, consistent with Article 4.1 and Article 4.7 and in the context of sustainable development. Least developed countries and small island developing States may undertake actions voluntarily and on the basis of support. Mitigation actions subsequently taken and envisaged by Non-Annex I Parties, including national inventory reports, shall be communicated through national communications consistent with Article 12.1 (b) every two years on the basis of guidelines to be adopted by the Conference of the Parties. Those mitigation actions in national communications or otherwise communicated to the Secretariat will be added to the list in appendix II. Mitigation actions taken by Non-Annex I Parties will be subject to their domestic measurement, reporting and verification the result of which will be reported through their national communications every two years. Non-Annex I Parties will communicate information on the implementation of their actions through National Communications, with provisions for international consultations and analysis under clearly defined guidelines that will ensure that national sovereignty is respected. Nationally appropriate mitigation actions seeking international support will be recorded in a registry along with relevant technology, finance and capacity building support. Those actions supported will be added to the list in appendix II. These supported nationally appropriate mitigation actions will be subject to international measurement, reporting and verification in accordance with guidelines adopted by the Conference of the Parties.

6. We recognize the crucial role of reducing emission from deforestation and forest degradation and the need to enhance removals of greenhouse gas emission by forests and agree on the need to provide positive incentives to such actions through the immediate establishment of a mechanism including REDD-plus, to enable the mobilization of financial resources from developed countries.

7. We decide to pursue various approaches, including opportunities to use markets, to enhance the cost-effectiveness of, and to promote mitigation actions. Developing countries, especially those with low emitting economies should be provided incentives to continue to develop on a low emission pathway.

8. Scaled up, new and additional, predictable and adequate funding as well as improved access shall be provided to developing countries, in accordance with the relevant provisions of the Convention, to enable and support enhanced action on mitigation, including substantial finance to reduce emissions from deforestation and forest degradation (REDD-plus), adaptation, technology development and transfer and

capacity-building, for enhanced implementation of the Convention. The collective commitment by developed countries is to provide new and additional resources, including forestry and investments through international institutions, approaching USD 30 billion for the period 2010. 2012 with balanced allocation between adaptation and mitigation. Funding for adaptation will be prioritized for the most vulnerable developing countries, such as the least developed countries, small island developing States and Africa. In the context of meaningful mitigation actions and transparency on implementation, developed countries commit to a goal of mobilizing jointly USD 100 billion dollars a year by 2020 to address the needs of developing countries. This funding will come from a wide variety of sources, public and private, bilateral and multilateral, including alternative sources of finance. New multilateral funding for adaptation will be delivered through effective and efficient fund arrangements, with a governance structure providing for equal representation of developed and developing countries. A significant portion of such funding should flow through the Copenhagen Green Climate Fund.

9. To this end, a High Level Panel will be established under the guidance of and accountable to the Conference of the Parties to study the contribution of the potential sources of revenue, including alternative sources of finance, towards meeting this goal.

10. We decide that the Copenhagen Green Climate Fund shall be established as an operating entity of the financial mechanism of the Convention to support projects, programme, policies and other activities in developing countries related to mitigation including REDD-plus, adaptation, capacitybuilding, technology development and transfer.

11. In order to enhance action on development and transfer of technology we decide to establish a Technology Mechanism to accelerate technology development and transfer in support of action on adaptation and mitigation that will be guided by a country-driven approach and be based on national circumstances and priorities.

12. We call for an assessment of the implementation of this Accord to be completed by 2015, including in light of the Convention's ultimate objective. This would include consideration of strengthening the long-term goal referencing various matters presented by the science, including in relation to temperature rises of 1.5 degrees Celsius.

(http://unfccc.int/2860.php)

3.4.2 口译精讲

1. 英汉口译
(1) 词语必备。
foul   肮脏的

carbon capture and storage (CCS) technology	碳捕获和储存技术
Recovery Act	复兴法案
carbon-free electricity	无碳发电
proliferation	扩散
natural gas reserves	天然气储量
Special Climate Envoy	气候特使
UN Framework Convention on Climate Change	联合国气候变化框架公约会议
Copenhagen conference	哥本哈根会议
low-carbon growth	低碳经济增长

(2) 口译课文。

Just like China, the United States has abundant supplies of coal. But if we burn coal in the 21st century using 20th century technologies, our air will be foul and disruptions to our climate will threaten us all. Secretary Chu has made carbon capture and storage (CCS) technology a priority and mobilized the Department of Energy's expertise and resources around this critical issue.

While coal accounts for nearly half of electricity generated in the United States, nuclear energy accounts for 70 percent of the United States' carbon-free electricity. President Obama has stated that nuclear must be "part of the energy mix". To this end, Secretary Chu is exploring ways to help re-start the US nuclear industry and will establish a panel of experts to explore ways to safely store nuclear waste while preventing proliferation. The Department of Energy recently awarded $44 million to more than 70 nuclear research projects at universities across the country.

These policies will go a long way toward reducing carbon emissions and ending our dependence on oil. However, in the short – and medium-term, conventional fossil fuels will still play a significant role in our energy supply. Recently, our ability to locate and extract fossil fuels has improved considerably — for instance, US natural gas reserves have more than doubled in the past five years, thanks in large part to new technologies. President Obama has stated that he supports expanded domestic oil drilling as part of a comprehensive energy plan.

Internationally, the United States is committed to helping lead the world in promoting clean energy and fighting climate change. As Special Climate Envoy Todd Stern said in a recent speech at a meeting of the UN Framework Convention on Climate Change, "the US is back". Our policy is guided by a combination of science and pragmatism — doing what the science requires while delivering concrete results. We are working hard with partners from around the world to achieve a successful outcome at the Copenhagen conference this December and protect the planet for our children and grandchildren. This will of course require the work of both our great countries.

In recent years, China has taken significant steps to improve its energy efficiency and reduce its emissions. As you all know, the 11th Five-Year Plan includes the goal of reducing the energy intensity of the economy 20% by 2010, and the aim of increasing the share of renewable energy in the primary energy supply to 15% by 2020. China has implemented stringent auto emissions standards, stronger than our own, and its domestic stimulus package contained substantial clean energy investments. And there are many other initiatives underway, with respect to electric vehicles, renewable energy and more.

China deserves significant credit for these actions, which are both strengthening its economy and contributing to the solution to a global problem. Yet China can and will need to do much more if the world is going to have any hope of containing climate change.

China is such a large and important force in the global economy that, according to one recent analysis, even if every other country in the world cut its emissions 80% by 2050, China's business-as-usual emissions alone would cause global average temperatures to increase by 2.7 degrees Centigrade — far above dangerous levels, according to scientists.

China does not need to take the same actions that developed countries are taking, but it does need to take significant action. When it comes to climate change, China must be part of the solution.

This is in fact the road to prosperity and success. China has abundant opportunities to cut emissions by improving energy efficiency and promoting low-carbon economic growth. In the years ahead, the economic race will be won by those who have responded best to the imperative of low-carbon growth.

In sum, clean energy and climate change are top priorities for the Obama administration. And just as my colleagues and I hope to learn more this week about China's goals, concerns and capabilities in energy and climate, I hope that you now have a deeper understanding of the United States' new approach.

(*Excerpted from the speech by Assistant Secretary for Policy & International Affairs David Sandalow on June 9, 2009*)

(3) 参考译文。

美国与中国一样，有丰富的煤炭供应。但是，如果我们在21世纪仍使用20世纪的技术烧煤，我们的空气将被污染，人们将受到气候变化的威胁。朱部长把碳捕获和储存（CCS）技术作为优先事项，并利用能源部的专业知识和资源处理这个关键问题。

美国近一半的发电量来自煤炭，而其无碳发电的70%依靠的则是核能。奥巴马总统曾表示，核能必须成为"能源组合的一部分"。为此，朱部长正在探索如何帮助重启美国的核工业，并将设立一个专家小组，探讨如何在安全储存核废料的同时防止核扩散。能源部最近向全美各地大学的70多个核研究项目提供了4400万美元的经费作为奖励。

这些政策将大大有利于减少碳排放量和结束我们对石油的依赖。然而，从中短期来看，传统化石燃料仍将在我们的能源供应中发挥重要作用。最近，我们在定位与提取化石燃料方面的能力已得到显著提高——例如，在过去5年中，美国天然气储量增加了一倍多，这在很大程度上归功于新技术。奥巴马总统曾表示，作为一个全面能源计划的一部分，他支持扩大国内石油开采。

在国际方面，美国致力于带头促进推广清洁能源和应对气候变化。如气候特使托德·斯特恩最近一次在联合国气候变化框架公约会议上的发言中所说，"美国回来了"。我们的指导方针是将科学与务实相结合——既符合科学要求，同时取得切实成果。我们正在与来自世界各地的伙伴们努力合作，以期在今年12月的哥本哈根会议上获得成果以及为我们的子孙后代保护地球。这当然需要我们两个伟大国家做更多的努力。

近年来，中国已采取有效措施来提高能源效率和减少排放量。众所周知，中国第11个五年计划包括到2010年经济能源强度减少20%的目标，和到2020年，可再生能源达到主要能源供应量的15%。中国实施的汽车尾气排放标准比我们的还要严格。其国内刺激计划包含了大量清洁能源方面的投资。还有许多针对电动汽车，可再生能源等的方案仍在进行之中。

这些举措既能够促进其经济增长，又有助于解决全球性问题，为此中国应该得到赞扬。然而，如果世界想要在遏制气候变化方面有任何希望的话，中国能够而且必须做更多的工作。

最近的一项分析表明，即使世界上所有其他国家到2050年将减排80%，仅中国的日常排放量就会导致全球平均气温上升2.7摄氏度，而科学家认为这远远超过了危险水平，可见，中国对于全球经济而言是一股巨大而且重要的力量。

中国并不需要采取与发达国家相同的措施，但它必须付诸有效行动。当涉及解决气候变化问题时，中国的参与是不可或缺的。

这实际上是通往繁荣和成功的道路。中国有充足的机会通过提高能效和促进低碳经济的增长来减少排放量。今后，谁能最好地应对低碳增长这一当务之急，谁就将赢得经济竞赛。

总之，推广清洁能源和应对气候变化是奥巴马政府工作的重中之重。正如我和我的同事希望在这个星期进一步了解中国有关能源和气候的目标、忧虑和能力，我希望现在你们对美国的新的处理方式有了更深理解。

（4）口译点津。

1）在翻译这类发言稿时，总会出现长串的术语，并且在会议过程中可能被反复提及。但是并非每次都要将其全称译出。例如，carbon capture and storage (CCS) technology 在第一次出现时可以全部译出，再次出现时，则只需说"该技术"，在减轻口译员负担的同时，也让听众听得更舒服。

2）对于许多专题口译而言，总会有一些知识因与会议的主题紧密相关，在会议中被讲话者提及的几率非常高，这些知识应该纳入译员的译前准备中。如谈到"能源环境"，就不能不提联合国的千年发展目标、哥本哈根会议以及《京都议定书》等关键词，谈到"经济发展"，就不能不去了解经济危机和复苏。

3）He supports expanded domestic oil drilling as part of a comprehensive energy plan.

口译时要注重理解，不能字对字地翻译，因此有时进行词性转换更能帮助听众理解。在英译中时最常见的就是过去分词和名词等转变成动词。此句中的 expanded 是过去分词作定语，没有必要翻译成"扩大的"，直接处理为动词"扩大"，让表达更简洁易懂。

4）China is such a large and important force in the global economy that, according to one recent analysis, even if every other country in the world cut its emissions 80% by 2050 — which is very unlikely, to say the least — China's business-as-usual emissions alone would cause global average temperatures to increase by 2.7 degrees Centigrade — far above dangerous levels, according to scientists.

英文中会频繁使用插入语，不论插入语作何成分，若不调整位置，定会显得生硬。上面这段文字中便出现几处插入语，口译时对插入语的语序进行调整是十分必要的。

5）When it comes to climate change, China must be part of the solution.

某些语句在英文中完全可以理解，若直接翻译为中文，却会让人摸不着头脑，这时候有必要进行解释，采用意译的手法。例如"China must be part of the solution"，如果翻译成"……中国必须作为解决办法的一部分"，所指并不明确。结合上下文，其实说的就是"中国必须参与到气候变化的解决之中"或"对于解决气候变化问题，中国的参与是不可或缺的。"

2. 汉英口译

(1) 词汇必备。

薪柴时代	the era of burning wood
煤炭时代	the era of burning coal
油气时代	the era of burning oil and gas
化石能源	fossil fuel
节能减排	energy conservation and emission reduction
装机容量	installed capacity
火力发电	coal-fired power generation
循环经济	circular economy
低碳经济	low-carbon economy

(2) 口译课文。

能源是支撑人类文明进步的物质基础，也是现代社会发展须臾不可或缺的基本条件。人类对能源的利用，从薪柴时代到煤炭时代，再到油气时代，每一次变迁都伴随着生产力的巨大飞跃。当然，传统化石能源的开发利用，也给人类的可持续发展带来了严峻挑战。近年来，绿色发展在全球蓬勃兴起。其核心是，减少对能源资源的过度消耗，追求经济、社会、生态全面协调可持续发展。为此，世界各国进行了积极探索，中国也做出了不懈努力。

——积极调整经济结构，加大节能减排力度。我们推进了工业、交通、建筑、居民生活等领域的节能减排。在电力、钢铁、水泥、电解铝等高耗能行业中，淘汰大批落后生产能力，新上一批先进生产能力。5年来，电力行业共关闭了落后小火电机组8000万千瓦，相当于欧洲一个中等国家的装机容量。政府对这些企业给予必要补偿，并相应安排了60多万职工再就业。这是我们在应对国际金融危机非常困难的情况下完成的。仅此一项，一年就少烧原煤9200万吨，减排二氧化碳1.84亿吨。据统计，2005年至2010年，中国单位国内生产总值能耗下降近20%，相当于减排二氧化碳14.6亿吨，为减缓全球气候变化作出了贡献。

——加大政策扶持，加快清洁能源发展。截至2011年，中国水电装机突破2亿千瓦，居世界第一；风电装机达4700万千瓦，太阳能装机达300万千瓦，成为全球发展最快的地区；核电装机容量1000多万千瓦，有27台机组正在建设，在建规模居世界首位。中国发展清洁能源，投入之大、建设之快、成效之显著，为世界所公认。

——加快传统产业改造，提高能源利用效率。我们以信息化带动工业化，积极采用先进适用技术改造传统产业，大幅度提高企业的能效水平。近5年来，在全国实施了锅炉改造、电机节能、建筑节能、绿色照明等一系列节能改造工程，成效显著。其中，每千瓦时火力发电煤耗降低了37克，降幅达10%；吨钢综合能耗降低了13%；新建设的有色、建材、石化等重化工项目，其能源利用效率达到或接近世界先进水平。

——倡导低碳生活方式，推行绿色消费。虽然中国人均能耗水平比OECD国家少很多，但我们仍在全社会倡导节俭、文明、适度、合理的消费理念。我们在大中城市、工业园区和企业广泛开展循环经济试点和低碳经济试点，大力推行清洁生产和资源综合利用。我们在国家机关及公共建筑实行严格的节能措施，夏季室内不低于26摄氏度，冬季不高于20摄氏度。由于政府带头，崇尚节约，绿色消费越来越成为公民的自觉行动。

(2012年1月16日国务院总理温家宝在世界未来能源峰会上的讲话，节选)

(3) 参考译文。

Energy is the material foundation that supports human progress, also an indispensable element that contributes to the development of modern society. From burning wood to burning coal and to the era of oil and gas, every change in how people use energy is accompanied by the great leap of productivity. Of course, the exploitation and utilization of traditional fossil fuel has brought grim challenges to the sustainable development of human race, thus giving impetus to the worldwide trend of green development, which focuses on reducing excessive consumption of energy and resources so as to pursue comprehensive, balanced and sustainable economic, social and ecological development. To this end, many countries, including China, have made unwavering efforts in this regard.

We have actively adjusted economic structure and intensified our efforts in energy conservation and emission reduction. We have endeavored to reduce energy consumption and emission in industrial, transport and construction areas as well as the areas concerning people's livelihood. In the energy-intensive industries such as power, iron and steel, cement and electrolytic aluminum, we have shut down a substantial amount of backward production facilities and introduced new ones. Over the past 5 years, we have shut down small coal-fired power plants with a total generating capacity of 80 million kilowatts, equivalent to the total installed capacity of a medium-sized European country. The government has provided these enterprises with due compensations and arranged new jobs for the over 600,000 laid-off workers. This was accomplished under the difficult circumstances caused by the international financial crisis. This step only can annually help China save 92 million tons of raw coal and cut 184 million tons of carbon dioxide emission. According to statistics, during 2005 to 2010, China's energy consumption per unit of GDP has decreased by nearly 20 per cent, equivalent to reducing CO_2 emission by 1.46 billion tons, demonstrating that China is making contribution to mitigating global climate change.

We have intensified policy support to promote the development of clean energy. By the end of 2011, the installed hydropower capacity has topped 200 million kilowatts, ranking the first in the world. With the installed capacities of 47 million kilowatts of wind power and 3 million kilowatts of solar power, China has become the world's fastest-growing region in these two areas. China's installed capacity of nuclear power has exceeded 10 million kilowatts and 27 units are under construction, which is the largest scale in the world. China's investment, speed and results in the area of clean energy have been widely recognized.

We have accelerated the upgrading of traditional industries to promote energy efficiency. We have advanced industrialization with information technology and applied advanced applicable technologies to upgrade traditional industries so as to greatly increase energy efficiency. In the past nearly five years, we have achieved prominent results in a variety of upgrading and energy conservation programs aiming at increase energy efficiency of furnace, electrical mechanic equipment, construction and lighting. For example, coal consumption for coal-fired power generation per kilowatt hour has been reduced by 37 grams, a decline of 10 per cent; energy consumption per ton of steel has been cut by 13 per cent; and the energy efficiency of some newly-launched programs such as non-ferrous metals, building materials and petrochemical has reached or approached the world's advanced level.

We have advocated low-carbon way of life and encourage green consumption. Although China's per capita energy consumption is much lower than that of other OECD countries, we encourage our public to reinforce the green consumption concept that is economical, civilized, proportionate and rational. In large and medium-sized cities, industrial parks and companies, we have extensively carried out our pilot projects of circular economy and low-carbon economy with the aim to promote clean production and comprehensive use of resources. We have reinforced strict energy-saving policies in national institutes and public buildings, that the indoor temperature should not be lower than 26-degree centigrade in summer and no higher than 20 in winter. Thanks to the example set by government, energy conservation and green consumption have more and more become a self-motivated practice of our citizens.

(4) 口译点津。

1) 在翻译一些中文的专有名时，若英文中无对应说法，或直接翻译较难理解，可以适量增译，令译文更易于接受。如"从薪柴时代到煤炭时代，再到油气时代",对比 era of wood, era of coal, and era of oil and gas 和 era of burning wood, era of burning coal, and era of burning oil and gas,孰优孰劣,一目了然。

2) 数字口译要精准,遇到数字不能慌乱,除了要记清楚数字本身,数字的所指以及单位也切忌漏掉。

3) 文章中对于中国方面作出的努力分成了四个点进行阐述,结构清晰。但是由于口译是用声音来传递,为了让听众能够更清晰地听到文章的层次,可以在开始阐述前先讲到会有 several aspects,在翻译过程中增加如 first, second 等词作为提示。

4) 中文中会出现很多无主语的句子,在译成英文时须添加主语。如文中"积极调整经济结构,加大节能减排力度"这类"口号"式的话语,在翻译时要适当根据意思,增加主语。这里应该是"我们已经做了……",因此可以翻译为"We have…"。

5) 此类专题性较强的文章,在做中译英口译时,英文的术语往往比较难记忆。除了在会前做足准备,熟练掌握术语之外,另可准备词汇表,放于口译现场,一旦遇到相关词语,可以及时查阅,减轻译员的记忆负担。

3.4.3 实战演练

1. 口译听解与表达

(1) 口译听辨。

Cooperation on clean energy is a _____ of where we can further our common interests and benefit not only our people but also many throughout the world for decades to come.

Our two countries have had some successes in this area. You'll hear about them through the day. The problem with those successes, which are often _____ in the context of a JCCT or an S&ED or some other _____, they don't necessarily _____ with average Americans or average Chinese. We have to _____. We have to make them real in ways that citizens on both sides better see the benefits of supporting a strong US China relationship. What does that mean? It means we can't just discuss these topics as _____ or _____ because they aren't. Ultimately we need to make clear that the US China relationship is one of the best opportunities we have to improve the quality of life for average American families and businesses, big and small, because the economic opportunities are increasingly very real. So when people ask me why we should cooperate with China on _____, I say it's very simple. We are _____ on a _____ in clean energy like the space program or electronics of the 20th Century that will dramatically expand high quality jobs, living standards, and our economy in the United States. We'll get better products, lower prices, and more jobs in both countries. I believe the possibilities in this particular area — clean energy, are unlimited.

(2) 复述练习。

Today, our world faces the major global environmental challenge of a changing climate. Our entire planet must address this problem because no nation, however large or small, wealthy or poor, can escape the impact of climate change. The United States can be a leader in reducing the dangerous pollution that causes global warming and can propel these advances by investing in the clean energy technologies, markets, and practices that will empower us to win the future.

While our changing climate requires international leadership, global action on clean energy and climate change must be joined with local action. Every American deserves the cleanest air, the safest water, and unpolluted land, and each person can take steps to protect those precious resources. When we reduce environmental hazards, especially in our most overburdened and polluted cities and neighborhoods, we prioritize the health of our families, and move towards building the clean energy economy of the 21st century.

To meet this responsibility, Federal and local programs will continue to ensure our Nation's clean air and water laws are effective, that our communities are protected from contaminated sites and other pollution, and that our children are safe from chemicals, toxins, and other environmental threats. Partnerships and community-driven strategies, like those highlighted by the America's Great Outdoors Initiative, are vital to building a future where children have access to outdoor places close to their homes; where our rural working lands and waters are conserved and restored; and our parks, forests, waters, and other natural areas are protected for future generations.

(3) 公众演讲。

以"首都变'雾都'——谁才是祸首?"为题,分别以英语及汉语作3～5分钟的演讲。

2. 单句口译

(1) 英汉口译。

1) It illustrates how we can work together to meet the challenges we face — sometimes in very big ways like working on agreements, but sometimes in smaller, equally significant ways like working through the Global Alliance on Cookstoves that China has just joined.

2) We live in an age where the world's population will have grown to 7 billion by

the end of this month and where more than half of them live in towns and cities.

3) Prevention should be addressed through better urban planning and building codes so that city residents, especially the poorest, are protected as far as possible against disaster.

4) This illustrates once again that the United States and China can and will work together in new ways and through many channels to address our common challenges on energy and the environment, two issues that transcend politics that we live with every single day in our homes, our businesses, and our communities.

5) Climate induced risks such as rising sea levels, tropical cyclones, heavy precipitation events and extreme weather conditions can disrupt the basic fabric and functioning of cities with widespread reverberations for the physical infrastructure, economy and society of cities.

(2) 汉英口译。

1) 很多城镇和城市，尤其是发展中国家的城镇和城市，依然在努力制定气候变化战略，研究如何争取国际气候变化资金，并学习走在前列的城市的经验。

2) 目前仍在继续的气候变化谈判表明，人们越来越清醒地认识到，减少森林的砍伐和退化，在我们应对气候变化、生物多样性丧失和土地退化等问题的共同威胁方面可以发挥重大作用。

3) 我们还承诺通过全面的能源与气候问题立法，创造工作机会，降低我国对外来石油的依赖性，同时减少碳污染。

4) 世界各地的民众、社区、企业和政府正在为了人类共同的未来而创造新的典范，在以可持续方式生活方面确立新的愿景，并为实现这一愿景而开发新的技术。

5) 过去的成就之所以成为可能，是因为符合美国普通百姓的要求，而应对今天的环境挑战将要求新的一代继承尚未完成的事业。

3. 段落口译

(1) 英汉口译。

Paragraph 1

Water challenges are most obvious in developing nations, but they affect every country on earth. Experts predict that by 2025, nearly two-thirds of the world's population will be water-stressed. Many sources of fresh water will be under additional strain from climate change and population growth. We need to work together to leverage the efforts of other nations, the international community, and partners in the nonprofit and private sectors. There are a number of areas where science and technological innovation can make a huge impact. We need to make sure that the work we do on water issues is not just of the moment, but truly does stand the test of time. I am convinced that if we empower communities and countries to meet their own challenges, expand our diplomatic efforts, make sound investments, foster innovation and build effective partnerships, we can make real progress together and seize this historic opportunity.

Paragraph 2

The benefits of forests are far-reaching. Forests catch and store water, stabilize soils, harbour biodiversity and make an important contribution to regulating climate and the greenhouse gases that are causing climate change. They generate profits for international businesses and provide essential income and resources for hundreds of millions of the world's poorest people. Yet, despite our growing understanding and appreciation of just how much we reap from forests, they are still disappearing at an alarming rate. This year's International Day for Biological Diversity is devoted to highlighting the need for urgent action. As the ongoing climate change negotiations demonstrate, awareness is growing that reducing deforestation and forest degradation can play a large part in our response to the combined threat of climate change, biodiversity loss and land degradation. I commend this renewed emphasis on the importance of forests to sustainable development.

（2）汉英口译。

段落1

节约能源，既是一场技术革命，也是一场社会变革。厉行节约、反对浪费，是各民族共有的传统美德。节约能源是化解能源供需矛盾的必然选择。不论能源富集国还是能源相对短缺的国家，都应当推动建立节约型生产方式、生活方式和消费模式。当然，节约能源不是简单地减少使用，也不是要降低人们的生活质量。要通过采用先进科技提高能效，建设低投入、高产出、低消耗、少排放、能循环、可持续的国民经济体系，以尽可能少的能源资源支撑经济社会的可持续发展。

段落2

可再生能源资源丰富，分布地域广，开发潜力大，环境影响小，大都可以永续利用，是开拓未来能源的重要方向。但是，除水能外，大部分可再生能源的经济性和稳定性还不够理想，推广普及的难度较大。各国应加强政策扶持，扩大应用规模，逐步降低成本，越来越多地替代化石能源。核电是安全可靠、技术成熟的清洁能源。安全高效地发展核电，是解决未来能源供应的战略选择。化石能源在今后很长一个时期内仍然是世界能源消费的主体。它的开发利用，一要清洁，二要高效,逐步实现高碳能源的低碳化利用。

4. 对话口译

A: 罗杰斯先生,首先感谢您接受我们的采访。

B: It's my pleasure to be here.

A: 罗杰斯先生,请问"地球日"什么时候开始从美国走向世界各地?

B: Earth Day has been global since its inception but became truly global on its 20th anniversary in 1990.

A: 您可以给我们介绍一些你们主办的主要国际性项目和活动吗?

B: First, let me say that the State Department has been absolutely essential in helping Earth Day Network plan our programs abroad. Some of the biggest Earth Day events this year are taking place in India and China, where we are collaborating directly with the US embassies in Delhi and Beijing and with four or five consulates in each country. In India, the American Cultural Centers across the country will host Earth Day events, and in China the State Department is using materials from our Education Department to teach university students about environmental issues and the history of Earth Day.

We have also partnered with the Kingdom of Morocco to organize events surrounding the presentation of their National Charter for Environment and Sustainable Development. Morocco is the first African, Muslim and Arab nation to commit, at the highest levels of government, to carry out a national event in honor of the 40th anniversary of Earth Day.

We also have events planned with partners in Buenos Aires, Kolkata, Barcelona and Tokyo, to name a few. Earth Day remains truly global!

A: 那么,"地球日网络"下一步的计划是什么?

B: Earth Day Network plans to build on the connections we have made this year, to deepen and broaden the scope of our activities and the mission of Earth Day. For instance, our Global Day of Conversation program has strengthened our relationship with 290 mayors and locally elected officials in more than 39 countries. We are working with more than 1,500 NGOs worldwide on climate change issues and building partnerships in many countries to create green schools. We are finishing up plans for a global conference on women and climate to be held in Washington. We are also planting 1 million trees around the world in partnership with James Cameron's film Avatar and Twentieth Century Fox Home Entertainment, and this vast undertaking will endure well after Earth Day. Domestically, we will continue to push for comprehensive legislation to confront climate change and to lay the foundation for a green economy.

We are extremely excited to see what we can all accomplish in the next 40 years.

("地球日网络"总裁罗杰斯访谈,节选)

5. 篇章口译
(1) 英汉口译。

China's Environmental Challenges

What does China want? Of all the large questions of our time, few are more compelling than those surrounding the rise of this economic superpower. Will the new generation of Chinese leaders, to be chosen later this year, harbour urges to overturn the US-led international order that has prevailed since the end of the second world war? Or is this a paranoid western delusion about a nation fixated on the extensive challenges it faces at home?

In the space of a few short years, China has become the world's biggest maker of solar panels and wind turbines. Its leaders have brought in a spate of pollution controls; shut down some of the filthiest coal plants; announced plans for pilot carbon markets, and spoken of building an "ecological civilisation" based on sustainable growth. But does this amount to meaningful change? Or is China still at heart a growth-at-all-costs vandal, ready to choke its rivers with vast mega-projects and allow industrial pollution devastating enough to poison its water, food and air? The answer is complex — and far more relevant to the rest of us than widely thought.

Judith Shapiro, a US academic who was one of the first Americans to live in China after relations with the US were normalized in 1979, explains many of the reasons why in this concise and illuminating book. For one thing, trying to clarify China's environmental policy is as fraught as trying to establish such a thing in the US — a country capable of approving both Arctic oil drilling and some of the world's toughest pollution rules. There are bureaucrats in Beijing eager to tackle the environmental destruction that makes the air in the capital itself a menace. But they face rivals who see no reason why China should not follow the "pollute first; mitigate later" model on which industrialised nations built their wealth.

Here lies the central conundrum facing not just China but the world: morally, it is impossible to argue that the Chinese people should be denied the right to the economic prosperity long enjoyed by the developed world. Environmentally, however, it is impossible to say that they should, for this is a country whose ecological impact is spreading far beyond its borders. From climate change to Californian air quality, the influence of the world's factory is immense. That makes China vital to any effort to stop global temperatures rising by more than 2C from pre-industrial levels — the threshold scientists say should not be crossed if the world is to avoid potentially dangerous climate change.

And it is not just China's carbon pollution that affects the rest of us. When Chinese dust storms are at their most violent, scientists say they blow contaminants as far as California and other western US states. China's appetite for everything from shark fins to tropical hardwoods and minerals has added to pressure on fish stocks, forests and African farmlands. Its hunger for coal and other fossil fuels spurs environmentally contentious exploration for such energy sources worldwide, from Canadian tar sands to Nigerian oilfields.

(*Excerpted from the article by Pilita Clark, Financial Times*)

(2) 汉英口译。

当前，世界政治经济格局正在发生大调整、大变革，各种全球性挑战日益增多。太平洋岛国自然和地理条件特殊，应对气候变化、防灾减灾、保护海洋环境、维护粮食安全面临的挑战更多，困难更大，需要国际社会给予充分的理解、支持和帮助。中国与太平洋岛国的人民有过相似的历史遭遇，面临振兴经济、摆脱贫困的共同使命。中方理解岛国的特殊处境和诉求，愿与各岛国同舟共济、精诚合作，共同应对各种挑战和风险，缔造南南合作的典范。

——我们的合作是平等的。我们一贯主张，国家不分大小、贫富、强弱，都是世界大家庭的平等成员。中方尊重并支持岛国选择适合本国国情的发展道路，支持岛国维护国家主权与发展权益，支持岛国平等参与国际和地区事务。

——我们的合作是真诚的。我们为岛国经济社会发展取得的成就感到由衷高兴，对岛国发展中遇到的困难感同身受。中方对岛国提供的帮助真诚无私，不附加任何条件。凡是我们答应的事情都会竭尽全力去完成，保质保量，善始善终。

——我们的合作是务实的。中方始终把促进岛国经济发展和民生改善，作为双方合作的出发点和落脚点。我们坚持优势互补、取长补短，把岛国的需求和中方的实际能力结合起来，把有限资金用在刀刃上，帮助岛国解决最现实、最迫切的困难，注重合作的实际效果和长远影响，增强合作的可持续性。

应对气候变化、拯救地球家园，是全人类的共同挑战，也是各岛国的重大关切。中国把应对气候变化作为重要战略任务，采取了一系列强有力的政策措施。中国是最早制订实施《应对气候变化国家方案》的发展中国家，是近年来节能减排力度最大的国家，是新能源和可再生能源增长速度最快的国家，是世界上人工造林面积最大的国家。中国将坚定不移地实行节约资源和保护环境的基本国策，着力推进绿色发展、循环发展、低碳发展，实现2020年单位国内生产总值二氧化碳排放比2005年下降40%～45%的目标，既为中国人民创造良好的生产生活环境，也为全球生态安全作出自己的贡献。我们在本届中－太合作论坛期间，同时举办2013中国国际绿色创新技术产品展，目的就是宣传绿色发展理念，促进低碳产业的交流与合作。我们愿意与岛国全面加强绿色发展合作，欢迎来自岛国的企业积极参展，寻求合作商机，共同推动绿色发展。

（2013年11月8日国务院副总理汪洋在第二届中国－太平洋岛国经济发展合作论坛暨2013中国国际绿色创新技术产品展开幕式上的演讲）

3.4.4 词语拓展

保障自然资源的合理利用	ensure the rational use of natural resources
濒危物种	endangered species
城市绿带	green belt
臭氧层	ozone layer
臭氧层损耗	ozone layer depletion
大气污染	atmosphere pollution
短期利益	immediate interest
恶化	deterioration
二氧化碳	carbon dioxide
防风林	windbreak
高级环境保护技术	sophisticated technologies for environmental protection
环保主义者	environmentalist
减排	emission abatement
节能	energy conservation
节约	economization
降解	decompose
经济发展应与环境保护齐头并进	Economic development should go hand in hand with environmental protection.
可再生能源	renewable sources of energy
可生物降解的物质	biodegradable substance
枯竭	exhaustion
灭绝	extinction
能源危机	energy crisis
气候变化	climate change
全球变暖	global warming

沙尘暴	dust storm
食物链	food chain
生态	ecology
生态平衡	ecological balance
生态系统	ecosystem
生物多样性	biodiversity
实现经济效益、社会效益、环境效益相统一	integrate economic, social and environmental benefits
使环境保护与各项建设事业统筹兼顾，协调发展	facilitate coordinated development of environmental protection and other undertakings
酸雨	acid rain
温室气体	green-house gas
温室效应	green-house effect
污染物	pollutant
消耗	consumption
循环利用	recycle
稀有物种	rare breeds
烟雾	smog
一氧化碳	carbon monoxide
雨林	rain forest
预防为主，防治结合	putting prevention first and combining prevention with control
植树造林	afforestation
资源节约型、环境友好型社会	a resource-conserving and environment-friendly society

3.4.5 厚积薄发

接到口译任务后，"临时抱佛脚"是至关重要的。短时间内译员要让自己成为该会议领域的专家，才能从容应对各种专题知识。但是口译涉及的领域多种多样，即便是专业性很强的会议，也不能保证完全不涉及其他领域的知识，这也要求译员必须是一个具有丰富生活经验和掌握百科知识的杂家。

做到以上两点都非常困难，无论多么充分的准备，总有无法预测的内容，那么在口译任务中遇到实在无法解决的问题时该怎么办？这就要求译员不耻下问。交传的现场与同传不同，译员是完全有机会跟发言人和听众进行及时的沟通和交流。一般在口译现场，发言人和听众并非完全不懂英文（或中文），即便不懂，他们大多是该会议主题的专家，对于中文（或英文）的专业知识了如指掌。因此，译员在遇到困难时可以得到他们及时的帮助。

跟发言人的及时沟通很有必要。有时，译员没有听清楚，或者听不明白，可以要求发言人再说一遍，或者换一种方式进行阐述。如果是因为发言人的说话习惯造成翻译难度增大，也可以及时跟发言人进行沟通。一般发言人也希望自己的讲话内容可以完全得到传达，所以不会觉得译员不够专业，反而会觉得译员很敬业，在尽心尽力地完成自己的任务。

有时候，译员还可以进行现场求助，让台下的听众帮忙。例如，发言人用英文描述一个物品，译员听懂了描述，却不知道该物品对应的中文术语名称。此时，译员完全可以将该物品的解释翻译出来，台下的听众或许就能知道该物品的中文名称，译员便可从困境中解脱出来。

译员要摆正自己的心态，切忌觉得求助是一件丢脸的事，而情愿胡编乱造蒙混过关。一名专业的译员很清楚自己的定位，口译不是作秀的地方，译员不是主角，译员应该是竭尽全力让语言文化不通的双方能够顺利地进行交流。"不耻下问"更显示出译员的认真负责。

3.5 体坛聚焦

3.5.1 背景阅读

The history of the Olympic Movement may be divided into the ancient and modern periods. The ancient period covered at least 12 centuries from 776 BC when the first Olympic Games was held in Greece to AD 339 when the Roman emperor Theodosius the Great prohibited the Olympic Games as a pagan activity. Then came a lull of some 15 centuries in which no Olympic Games were held, though the ancient Olympic ideals had not perished from the mind of many a great thinker. The modern period has covered less than one century, starting from 1896 when the first modern Olympic Games was held — on an international rather than national scale.

Chronologically, the ancient period of the Olympic Movement corresponded in Chinese history to the period from the Eastern Zhou Dynasty (770 – 256 BC) to the Jin

Dynasty (265 – 240 AD), while the modern period corresponded to the period from the latter part of the region of Guang Xu (1875 – 1909) of the Qing Dynasty to the present-day People's Republic of China. In the ancient period, China had no relations with Greece in the field of sport, although there was the Silk Road serving as a channel of trade and cultural exchanges between the East and West from the second century BC. In the modern period, however, China has been associated very early with the Olympic Movement. Such a relationship is more or less rooted in the common origin and features shared by ancient China and Greece in the field of sport, which forms part of national culture and is inseparable from socio-political life—for all social communities at all times.

So when was China invited for the first time to the Olympics? According to historical records, Chinese diplomat Wang Zhengting was elected into the IOC in 1922. It was then that the sports organization in China was formally recognized by the IOC. And it is stipulated in the Olympic Charter that only an organization recognized by the IOC may enter competitors in the Olympic Games. It was not until 1932 when the 10th Olympic Games were held in Los Angeles that China was invited for the first time to send athletes for competition.

Since 1979 Chinese athletes have taken part in seven Olympic Summer Games, taking a total of 163 golds, 117 silvers and 106 bronzes and making valuable contributions to the global Olympic Movement. Through the Games Chinese athletes have won medals, friends and experience and displayed China's strength to the rest of the world. In China's first full-scale participation in the Olympics in 1984, sharpshooter Xu Haifeng won China's first Olympic gold medal, which was described as "a break through zero".

During 1991 and 2001, Beijing, the Chinese capital city, made two Olympic bids, one for 2000 and the other for 2008. In its first bid Beijing lost to Sydney by a narrow margin of two votes, and in its second bid Beijing beat other nine cities to win the right to host the 29th Olympic Summer Games in 2008, thanks to its great potential of economic growth and the remarkable achievements in sport made by China over the previous decade. Beijing's renewed efforts to bid for the Olympic Games and its final success in the bid not only have the significance for sharing the Olympic spirit, celebrating humanity and expanding exchanges between the East and the West, but also help provide a good opportunity of showing the current state of economic, cultural, social and political development in China in a comprehensive way. While showing to the world a new, vigorous image of an open, modernized, civilized and well-developed metropolis in the lead-up to the 2008 Olympics, Beijing is ready to become a truly international city and make every effort to deliver a "Green Olympics", a "Hi-Tech Olympics", a "People's Olympics" and, to top it all, an unprecedented Olympics that would leave, as an IOC Evaluation Commission report believes, a unique legacy for both China and sport as a whole.

While China excels in many Olympic sports, more non-Olympic sports have developed in this country. Among them the most characteristic is wushu, which has always been closely associated with China and enjoys increasing popularity overseas. Chess and weiqi are also popular with a large number of followers. With an improved economic environment, sports like auto racing, billiards, sepaktakraw, rugby and bowling are fast finding a foothold in China.

China has a wealth of traditional sporting events and folk games, many stretching back over a long period of time and featured in traditional fairs, holidays and celebrations. They include dragon dance, kite flying, dragon boat racing, crossbow, and folk-style wrestling. Over the years the National Ethnic Games have been held on a regular basis, and many of the events have developed and gained popularity among people in different countries and regions.

(http://en.olympic.cn/)

3.5.2 口译精讲

1. 英汉口译

(1) 词语必备。

Paralympic Games	残疾人奥林匹克运动会
IOC	国际奥林匹克委员会
anchored	固定的
Olympic Truce Resolution	《奥林匹克休战决议》

(2) 口译课文。

Mr Chairman,

Members of the General Assembly,

I stand before you today as someone who has dedicated his life to sport and the Olympic Movement —as an Olympic athlete and now as Chairman of the London Organising Committee of the Olympic Games and the Paralympic Games. It is a real honour to be with you to introduce the draft resolution on "Building a peaceful and better world through sport and the Olympic ideal", also known as the Olympic Truce Resolution.

On behalf of the people of the United Kingdom, the British Government, the Mayor of the Host City, London, and the British Olympic Association, I would like to express our sincere gratitude for the support which the members of this General Assembly have already provided for this resolution.

Mr. Chairman, sport is one of those forces which can still offer real hope — both collective and individual. And, for over a century, the modern Olympic Movement has given voice to the positive values of humanity, not merely reflecting change but also driving it. The Olympic Movement forges links well beyond traditional social and diplomatic structures and geographic boundaries.

Mr. Chairman, it has never been more important to support this General Assembly resolution by actions, not just through words. Between now and the Games, the UK Government will lead a wide range of activities to promote peaceful development.

It has committed about $36 million to deliver an innovative global sports programme called International Inspiration. Aimed at young people from all backgrounds, it goes to the heart and soul of our vision for the London 2012 Games and the Olympic Truce.

Closer to home, our Olympic and Paralympic education programme, Get Set, is bringing alive in British schools and communities the Olympic and Paralympic values of friendship, respect, excellence, courage and determination. It is promoting social inclusion, health and physical activity, and tackling bullying and gang culture.

Mr. Chairman, I am also very proud that this resolution strongly highlights how sport enhances the lives of those who live with disabilities, and how much they contribute to the world of sport. The passion and determination of Paralympic athletes is an inspiration to us all.

Mr. Chairman, we look forward to working with the IOC and other member states on further activities to promote the Truce. These will be designed to help find local solutions to local challenges and contribute to long-term peace and stability.

Mr. Chairman, The UK had the honour of hosting the Olympic Games in 1948, when the world had been shattered by global conflict and still simmered with tension and hostility. Today, we cannot ignore the continuing spectre of conflict around the world. Through this resolution, anchored in the original spirit of de Coubertin's vision, we can, together, take active steps to ensure that the Olympics continue to serve the cause of peace.

Mr. Chairman, I can't think of a more appropriate way to conclude this introduction of the resolution, or to highlight the importance of your support for the Truce, than to quote one of the iconic figures of our time, Nelson Mandela, a long time friend of the Olympic Movement, and supporter of the Games in London next year. "Sport", he said, "has the power to change the world…sport can create hope…it is an instrument for peace".

Thank you.

(*Excerpted from the speech by the Chairman of the London Organising Committee of the Olympic Games and Paralympic Games Sebastian Coe on October 17, 2011*)

(3) 参考译文。

尊敬的主席先生、联合国大会的各位成员：

作为一个为体育事业和奥林匹克运动奉献一生的人、一个曾经的奥运选手、如今的伦敦奥运会及残奥会组委会主席，今天，我非常荣幸地站在这里向各位介绍题为"通过体育运动和奥林匹克理想创造美好世界"的决议草案，即《奥林匹克休战决议》。

在此，我谨代表英国人民、英国政府、奥运会主办城市——伦敦市的市长以及英国奥委会，向联合国大会成员对此提案给予的支持表示最诚挚的感谢。

主席先生，无论是集体项目还是单人项目，体育运动都能够带来真正的希望。在过去的一个世纪里，现代奥林匹克运动展现了人性积极的一面，它不仅反映了变化，而且推动革新。奥林匹克运动超越了传统的社会与外交结构以及地域边界的限制，建立起沟通与联系。

主席先生，用实际行动来促成这个决议的通过是当务之急，仅仅通过语言的支持是远远不够的。因此，从现在起至奥运会期间，英国政府将开展一系形式多样、内容丰富的活动，来促进世界的和平与发展。

英国政府承诺投资约3600万美元用于开展一个全新的国际体育项目——"国际激励"。活动受众是所有来自不同背景的年轻人，它体现了2012伦敦奥运会以及"休战协议"的精髓所在。

在英国国内，我们的奥运会及残奥会的教育项目"预备开始"在英国校园和社区里宣扬了奥运会及残奥会推崇友谊、尊重、卓越、勇气和决心的价值观。这个项目不仅促进了社会融合，推动了健康与体育活动的开展，同时也减少了欺凌现象以及削弱了帮派文化。

主席先生，令我感到万分骄傲的是，这项提案凸显了体育运动如何改善残障人士的生活，以及残疾人运动员对体育事业所作出的贡献。他们的激情和决心对我们所有人而言都是莫大鼓舞。

主席先生，我们期望与国际奥委会以及其他成员国建立更多的合作来推广奥林匹克休战活动。通过合作，我们能够因地制宜地解决局部问题，从而维持长期的和平与稳定。

主席先生，1948年，当整个世界深陷战乱的泥沼时，英国有幸承办了奥林匹克运动会。当今，全球范围内的冲突矛盾仍不容忽视。《奥林匹克休战决议》与顾拜旦先生创建奥运会的初衷不谋而合，我们应当携起手来，采取积极的措施，确保奥运会赛事将继续为和平事业的发展作出贡献。

主席先生，我想以纳尔逊·曼德拉先生的话来结束今天我对提案的介绍，或是强调您对"休战协定"的支持的重要性是再合适不过了。他是我们这个时代的标志性人物，是奥林匹克运动的老朋友，也是伦敦奥运会的支持者。"体育"，他说，"可以改变世界，缔造希望，带来和平"。

谢谢。

（4）口译点津。

1）The Paralympic Games

残疾人奥运会。第一次和第二次世界大战后，全球出现了不少残障军民，为了减少因为肢体伤残所带来的影响，复健治疗渐渐被重视，这些残障者开始接受体能训练，从运动中帮助复健以及恢复自信。1948年，一位医生在英格兰为第二次大战时的脊髓损伤军人组织了一个运动竞赛团体，4年之后，荷兰开始有残联者加入这项运动会。从此开启了残奥会的传承。

2）International Inspiration

即"国际激励"，是由伦敦奥组委和其他合作伙伴共同成立的首个国际体育遗产项目。该项目为全世界包括英国、巴西、南非等20多个国家和地区的1200多万少年儿童提供运动和学习的机会。

3）It has never been more important to support this General Assembly resolution by actions, not just through words.

…never…more important 意为"没有……比……更重要"，强调某事物的重要性，也可翻译为"……是最重要的"。

译文：用实际行动来促成这个决议通过是当务之急，仅仅通过语言的支持是远远不够的。

4）For over a century, the modern Olympic Movement has given voice to the positive values of humanity, not merely reflecting change but also driving it.

has given voice to 译为"表达"、"吐露"或"显示"。

译文：在过去的一个世纪里，现代奥林匹克运动展现了人性积极的一面，它不仅反映了变化，而且推动革新。

5）…when the world had been shattered by global conflict and still simmered with tension and hostility…

短语 simmer with 意为"内心充满"。全句可译为"……当全世界充斥着战乱的紧张和敌意"，或者意译为"……当整个世界深陷战乱的泥沼"。

2. 汉英口译

(1) 词汇必备。

职业生涯	professional career
退役	retire
应力性骨折	stress fracture
传承	inherit

(2) 口译课文。

各位领导，各位来宾，新闻界的朋友们，大家好，谢谢大家今天的光临。

今天对我来说是个重要的日子，无论是对我以及我以往的篮球职业生涯，还是未来个人发展，都具有特殊的意义。

去年年底，我的左脚第三次应力性骨折，我不得不离开赛场。半年多来，和很多关心我的朋友一样，我也是在漫长的期待中度过的。在那段时间里，我内心十分纠结，经过反复思考，我今天要宣布一个个人的决定：作为篮球运动员，我将结束自己的运动生涯，正式退役。

此时此刻，回顾过去，展望未来，我的内心充满感激。我首先要感谢的是篮球，这项伟大的运动为无数人带来了快乐，包括我自己。我4岁的时候有了第一个篮球，9岁进入上海市徐汇区业余体校，14岁进入上海训练队，16岁背上我父亲当年的号码，代表上海队比赛。篮球使我延续了家庭的传承，每当看到父母欣慰的眼神，我都感到无比的自豪；也非常荣幸能够和上海大鲨鱼队的队友们一起为上海赢得了2002年的CBA冠军，使我们和身后这座城市联系在了一起。同一年在进入NBA之后，篮球引领我进入一个更宽广的舞台，使我可以尽情地展现自己；更要感谢能有机会为中国国家队奋战10年，那是无数青年人的梦想。同时因为篮球，与心爱的人结缘，建立美满的家庭，获得一生的幸福。所有这些都是我无比热爱的篮球带给我的，我要感谢篮球。

今天提到的和没提到的，你们每个人都在我心里。总而言之，我感谢所有的亲人和朋友多年来的陪伴，我会继续做好我自己，不会离开大家！姚明和朋友们永远在一起，谢谢大家！

最后我要感谢这个伟大进步的时代，使我有机会去实现自己的梦想和价值。我曾经说过，有一天我的职业篮球生涯结束了，我希望它只是个逗号，不是个句号。今天这一天终于到来了，但我没有离开心爱的篮球，我的生活还在继续，我还是姚明。我还有很多事情可以做，远远没有达到画上句号的那一天，祝朋友们健康快乐，祝福我的家乡上海，第二故乡休斯敦，我们伟大的祖国，让我们热爱的篮球运动拥有更加美好的明天。谢谢大家！

(2011年姚明在宣布退役的新闻发布会上的讲话，节选)

(3) 参考译文。

Distinguished Leaders, Guests, and Friends of the Press, thank you for coming.

Today is an important day for me. It has a special meaning for myself, my basketball career and my personal development in the future.

As I had a stress fracture in my left foot for a third time at the end of last year, I had to leave the basketball court, and waited for more than half a year, just as many of those who care about me. During that period, I experienced a long-time puzzle and thought a lot. As a result, today, I am ready to announce a personal decision: I am going to end my athletic career and officially retire.

At this very moment, looking back on the past and right into the future, my heart is full of gratitude. Firstly, I'd like to thank basketball. The great sport has brought joy to countless people, including me. I had my first basketball when I was four years old. I entered the Amateur Sports School in Xuhui District in Shanghai when I was nine and later, entered the Shanghai Basketball Youth Team at fourteen. In my sixteen, I put on my father's number and joined the Shanghai Basketball Team. Playing basketball is the tradition I inherited from my family. In the eyes of my parents, I can feel that they are delighted of me, which makes me so proud. Further, I feel very honoured to win the CBA Championship with my Shanghai Shark team members for Shanghai in 2002; basketball has linked us to the city behind me. In the same year, basketball led me onto a greater stage since I entered NBA, where I could exhibit my abilities. What's more, I feel thankful that I had the opportunity to play for the national team for ten years, which is a dream for many young people. Thanks to basketball, I met and married my beloved woman. We made a happy family and obtained the happiness of my life. All of what I have are brought by my love, basketball. Thus, I want to thank the game of basketball.

All of you, whether I have mentioned or those I have not, you are all in my heart. All in all, I want to say thank you to my family and friends who have accompanied me in these years. I will continue to do the best and will continue to be with you all. Yao Ming will always be with friends, thank you all!

Finally, I want to express my gratitude to the great and progressive era, in which I have the opportunity to realize my dream and prove myself. Once I said that when I retired from my professional career one day, I hoped it was a temporary cessation rather than a permanent stop. Now the day comes, I do not leave basketball indeed. My life is continuing and I am still myself, Yao Ming. There are many things I wish to accomplish and it is far too early to say goodbye. Lastly, I wish you all a healthy and happy life. I wish the best blessings for my hometown Shanghai, my second home Huston and our great motherland. I wish our beloved basketball a brighter future. Thank you very much!

(4) 口译点津。

1) CBA。全称 China Basketball Association，中国篮球协会，或中国男子篮球职业联赛。中国男子篮球职业联赛是由中国篮球协会主办的跨年度主客场制篮球联赛，是中国最高等级的篮球比赛，中文媒体上多用 CBA 来称呼这些联赛。2005 年以后，联赛正式更名为如今的中国男子篮球职业联赛。

2) NBA。全称 National Basketball Association，是美国第一大职业篮球赛事，代表了世界篮球的最高水平，其中产生了姚明、迈克尔·乔丹、科比·布莱恩特、勒布朗·詹姆斯等世界巨星。该协会一共拥有 30 支球队，分属东部联盟和西部联盟；而每个联盟各由 3 个赛区组成，每个赛区有 5 支球队。30 支球队当中有 29 支位于美国本土，另外一支来自加拿大的多伦多。NBA 标志里的人物原型是杰里·韦斯特（Jerry West）。

3) 此时此刻，回顾过去，展望未来，我的内心充满感激。

"回顾过去，展望未来"是演讲常用语，可套用固定格式：Reviewing the past and looking into the future，或者 Looking back on the past and right into the future，等等。

4) 我希望它只是个逗号，不是个句号。

此句采用了比喻的修辞手法。既可直译为：It would be a comma rather than a full stop. 也可意译为：I hope it is a temporary cessation rather than a permanent stop.

5) 同时因为篮球，与心爱的人结缘。

"与……结缘"可译为 fall in love with，根据本文实际情况，译为 met and married。全句可译为：Thanks to basketball, I met and married my beloved woman.

3.5.3　实战演练

1. 口译听解与表达

(1) 口译听辨。

Have the Olympic Games ever been held in your country? Have the Olympic Games ever been held in your city? _____, people who live in London are getting ready for the 2012 Olympics next year. London has already _____ the Olympics twice before and this will make it the first city in history to have held three _____.

New at these Olympics was the _____ where athletes paraded with their teams behind their flag. Only 22 countries took part and the _____ were just over £ 21,000!

Because of the _____, the 1944 Olympics were cancelled. Four years later the war was over and London _____ hold the Games in 1948. Things were very different in London during these Olympic Games and many years of war had left the UK poor and hungry. People called them the _____. But there was still some great sport and some exciting events!

The Games next year are going to be bigger, better and more exciting than ever before. There will be more than 10,000 athletes from 204 countries _____!

London wants to _____ that the benefits of the Olympics don't just last for a few weeks in summer but go on much longer. The buildings have been made so that they can be used for different things when the Games are over.

(2) 复述练习。

We all look forward to the first Olympic Games in China next August. We all look forward to sharing the unique celebration that China and Beijing will stage for "One World, One Dream".

I should like to pay tribute to the new initiative of *Civilization Magazine* in publishing, not only in English and French, but also for the first time in Chinese, the manuscript of the "Olympic Manifesto" by Pierre de Coubertin, thus reminding us what the Olympic Games are all about and disseminating the Olympic ideals and values of friendship, peace and universality among the Chinese people and the people from all over the world.

I would like once again to congratulate *Civilization Magazine* for this commendable project and an authentic document of great value, thus illustrating the essence of the Olympic Games: a universal meeting of young people from throughout the world, with the same goal and the same enthusiasm.

As Coubertin said: "Humanity must draw from the heritage of the past all the strengths that can be used to build the future. Olympism is one of those."

(3) 公众演讲。

以"体育举国体制的利与弊"为题，分别以英语及汉语作 3～5 分钟的演讲。

2. 单句口译

(1) 英汉口译。

1) He is one of the best goalkeepers in the football history and his fantastic performance led the team to three champions in 1999.

2) Volleyball has now reached great heights of popularity in the United States and Brazil, largely thanks to the discipline of beach volleyball.

3) The women's marathon became an Olympic event only in 1984 — 56 years after Olympic doctors claimed that women who ran even 800 meters would "become old too soon".

4) An ancient sport as old as mankind, embodying the most direct manifestation of human strength, weightlifting has not only flourished, but also developed into a modern sporting discipline for the 21st century.

5) We have witnessed the continued growth, not only of the Olympic Tennis Event, but also of the international reach of our sport since tennis returned to the Olympic Games in 1988.

(2) 汉英口译。

1) 中国将作为主办国承办第 16 届亚运会。

2) 来自中国的网球运动员在第三轮女子双打中失利。

3) 任何事情都不能取代我对比赛的热爱,然而现在我将开始一个新的冒险。

4) 大学生运动会是大型国际体育盛会,半个多世纪以来蓬勃发展、贡献卓著、影响广泛。

5) 我们精心修建比赛场馆,训练运作团队,寻求科技支持,创造安全条件,也不断使这座城市的功能与形象得到提升。

3. 段落口译

(1) 英汉口译。

Paragraph 1

A dragon boat is a very long and narrow human-powered boat now used in the team paddling sport of dragon boat racing which originated in China in pre-Christian times. While competition has taken place annually for more than 20 centuries as part of folk ritual, it emerged in modern times as an international "sport" in Hong Kong in 1976. Like running, horse racing and marksmanship, the racing of dragon boats is among mankind's oldest organized competitions. For competition events, dragon boats are generally rigged with decorative Chinese dragon heads and tails. At other times the decorative regalia are usually removed, although the drum often remains aboard for training purposes. In some areas of China, the boats are raced without dragon adornments.

Paragraph 2

Football is a global language. It can bridge social, cultural and religious divides. It enhances personal development and growth, teaches us teamwork and fair play, builds self-esteem and opens doors to new opportunities. This, in turn, can contribute to the well-being of whole communities and countries. That is why the United Nations is using football as a tool in our work to reach the Millennium Development Goals — the set of powerful, people-centred objectives adopted by all countries as a blueprint for building a better world in the 21st century. And it is why the United Nations is turning to football in our efforts to heal the emotional wounds of war among young people in refugee camps, and in countries recovering from armed conflict. At the World Summit last year, all of the world's Governments declared that "sports can foster peace and development, and can contribute to an atmosphere of tolerance and understanding". Over the next few weeks, as billions of people worldwide focus on the FIFA World Cup, we appeal to players and fans everywhere to support to us in our mission. Let us harness the magic of football in our quest for development and peace.

(2) 汉英口译。

段落1

世界大学生运动会（以下简称"大运会"）自1959年创办以来，秉承"发展大学生体育运动、促进国际团结合作"的宗旨，为各国各地区大学生运动员同场竞技、展示英姿搭建了平台，为世界各国各地区青年加深互相了解、增进友好感情架起了桥梁，有力推动了国际青年体育事业发展。半个世纪以来，各国各地区大学生运动员在赛场上奋力拼搏、勇创佳绩，展现了朝气蓬勃、昂扬向上的青春风采。不同国家、不同民族、不同宗教信仰的青年学子在大运会上友好交流、积极互动，多彩文化在这里交融，友谊种子在这里播撒，合作信念在这里凝聚。这是大运会的魅力和真谛所在。

段落2

我始终记得，在1984年洛杉矶奥运会上给中国运动员许海峰颁发该届奥运会第一块金牌的情形。这也是中国历史上首次赢得奥运会金牌。从那以后，中国运动员在世界各地都取得了辉煌的成绩。他们曾经面临众多的挑战，为中国和全世界的下一代运动员作出了榜样。他们鼓励青少年积极参加体育活动，最重要的是激发他们参加奥运会的梦想。让我们期盼着2008年第29届北京奥运会，我深信中国人民和运动员一定会为这场盛会增色添彩！

4. 对话口译

A：我知道，虽然篮球对你来说非常重要，但它并不是你的全部。

B: That's exactly right, because playing basketball—it's fun—I love to do it, but you also have the opportunity to help others. So you have to take the advantage of that opportunity.

A：1996年4月29日，当时17岁的你告诉包括70多名媒体记者在内的所有人，你将放弃读大学，高中毕业后直接进入 NBA 打球，这是个艰难的决定吧。

B: Well, I looked at it as an opportunity to learn from the best of the best. That's how I looked at it. I said, "Well, I have this opportunity here, ahead of myself. Am I ready for the NBA? I don't know, but I know I'll do the work try to make myself ready." But it was a great chance to come into the NBA at a young age and learn from the best players on the planet.

A: 1996 年 11 月 3 日，当时你刚满 18 岁，就参加了职业生涯的第一场 NBA 比赛。还记得当时的情景吗？

B: That was nerve-racking. I was very nervous. You're thinking about everything, about doing it right, about doing it wrong, and it's all these things going in your head. It's funny, because when you think about it, you think of like all of the worst things that could possibly happen. And then you go out and you perform and it's not nearly as bad as you made it out to be in your own head. I think that's the first step toward gaining that confidence.

A: 当时你是 NBA 最年轻的球员，身上的压力很大，所以说那一定是一个艰难的时期。

B: Yeah, it could have been, but for me it was just, "Gosh, I just love playing basketball." It wasn't the pressure from media, from other people's expectations; it was the pressure that I had in myself. I really want to do well. And from that point forward I just continued to work and work and try to get better.

A: 2000 年，你第一次尝到了得冠军的滋味。

B: Yeah, very lucky. I was 21 years old, and there're a lot of players who don't get to the NBA finals in a lifetime, let alone win one, and in 2000 we did it.

A: 那次夺冠对你来说意味着什么？

B: Well, it was really about resiliency for us because the previous years we had enough talent to win the NBA championship. But for me, I had a chance to observe that talent alone isn't going to win a championship. You have to have togetherness; you have to have hard work; players get along and work as a team. For me, to observe that at an early age was a great lesson.

（2009 年 7 月 27 日，篮球运动员科比在北京接受央视主持人水均益专访，节选）

5. 篇章口译
（1）英汉口译。

Your Excellency Hu Jintao, Madame Liu Yongqing,
Athletes, Officials, Distinguished Guests,
Paralympic Sports fans from all over the world:

Good evening and welcome!

We are here tonight to celebrate the Opening Ceremony of the Beijing 2008 Paralympic Games. These Games will have more athletes, more competing nations, and more sporting events than ever before.

As we embrace these milestones in Paralympic history, our hearts go out to the millions of Chinese people who have been affected by successive national disasters in the first half of this year.

Despite these tragedies, China and the Beijing Organizing Committee and its President Liu Qi were able to continue preparations for marvellous Olympic Games and what we are sure will be stupendous Paralympic Games.

I would like to thank you all for this great work and hope that our collaboration over the past seven years has been of a cordial, frank, constructive, temperate and deferential nature.

I would also like to recognize the support of the International Olympic Committee, its President Jacques Rogge and His Excellency Juan Antonio Samaranch who is with us this evening.

Over the next 11 days, the heroines and heroes will undoubtedly be the athletes.

Paralympians, you have invested many years of your lives to be here. Ensure that you perform at your very best, and that you respect fair play. You never know, you may even exceed your wildest dreams.

You are also here to have fun, make new friends, and create memories in the cities of Beijing, Qingdao and Hong Kong. This is not about hope, but about vision and what you represent. We want to experience your confidence and self-determination, ranging from elite performance on the field of play, to voicing your opinions in the IPC Athletes' Council elections.

I want to take a moment with you all to recognize this marvellous stadium. The "Bird's Nest" is a shining example of China's commitment to a modern world.

We all can see its monumental structure of steel, concrete, glass and other Hi-tech materials, but this architecturally beautiful stadium truly comes to life when inhabited and animated by people like you, the spectators, performers, and athletes here tonight.

When combined with the Team and Games Officials, the media and the sponsors, and China's incomparable volunteers, you all create this unique Paralympic experience.

Starting tomorrow, we will see drama, we will see winning, and we will see disappointment. But above all, when we come together, we will be part of the creation of an almost touchable and definitely breathable distinctive energy source, which is at the heart of the Paralympic Movement, and it is what we call the Paralympic spirit. Once it gets hold, you can never let it go. It will last you a lifetime!

During the 12 days of the Beijing 2008 Paralympic Games, you will realize that the differences that you might have thought existed in the world are in fact, far less apparent.

You will see that we are all people of one world!

Thank you!

(*Excerpted from the speech by the Chairman of the International Paralympic Committee Philip Craven in Beijing Paralympic Game's opening ceremony on September 6, 2008*)

(2) 汉英口译。

尊敬的王乃坤副团长，

伦敦残奥会中国体育代表团的运动员、教练员和工作人员：

很高兴在伦敦迎接各位的到来。首先，我代表中国驻英国大使馆向大家表示最热烈的欢迎和最良好的祝愿！

第14届残疾人奥林匹克运动会将于5天后在伦敦举行。据我所知，这将是迄今规模最大的一届残奥会，共有来自166个国家和地区的4200名运动员参赛。这次我国派出了阵容强大的残奥代表团，总人数414人，其中运动员282人，这也是历史上我国在境外参加残奥会参赛人数最多的一届。

在不久前的伦敦夏季奥运会上，中国体育健儿顽强拼搏，奋勇争先，创造了我国境外参加奥运会的最好成绩。希望你们继续频传捷报、连奏凯歌，为祖国和人民赢得更多荣誉。

这里，我想说，比成绩更重要的是精神。每个残疾人运动员身后都有艰难的拼搏历程和感人的自强故事。你们来到伦敦的赛场，证明每个人都已经战胜了自己，站到了生活的最高领奖台上。希望你们在比赛中激发自身最大潜力，以优异的成绩和良好的风貌，展示中国残疾人自尊、自信、自强、自立的拼搏精神，展示中国残疾人事业的进步和成就，展示中华民族的优秀传统和文明大国形象。希望你们加强与各国残疾人运动员的交流，增进友谊，分享欢乐，为促进残疾人体育事业的发展、推动世界残疾人事业的进步作出积极贡献。

最后，我还想说，中国大使馆是你们在伦敦的家，我们将为你们全力提供各项保障支持，我们还将与在英华侨华人、留学生、中资机构人员一道为你们加油助威。

谢谢大家！

(2012年驻英国大使刘晓明在看望伦敦残奥会中国体育代表团时的讲话，节选)

3.5.4 词语拓展

《奥林匹克圣歌》（奥运会会歌）	Olympic Hymn/Olympic Anthem
奥林匹克五环（奥运会会徽）	Olympic Rings
《奥林匹克宪章》	Olympic Charter
《奥林匹克休战决议》	Olympic Truce Resolution
颁奖仪式	medal presentation
裁判	referee
冬季运动	winter sports
帆船	sailing
橄榄球	rugby
花样滑冰	figure skating
划船	rowing
滑旱冰	roller skating
滑翔运动	gliding; sailplaning
滑雪	skiing
滑雪板	ski
火炬	torch
火炬接力/火炬传递	torch relay
吉祥物	mascot
箭术	archery
接力	relay race; relay
奖牌	medal
竞走	walking; walking race
举重	weightlifting
跨栏比赛	hurdles; hurdle race
篮球职业生涯	basketball career
垒球	softball
马球	polo
皮划艇	kayak
骑马	equestrian

气功	qigong; breathing exercises
曲棍球	hockey
柔道	judo
山地车	mountain bike
手球	handball
速降滑雪赛，滑降	downhill race
跆拳道	taekwondo
体操	gymnastics
铁人三项	triathlon
退役	retire
网球	tennis
现代五项运动	modern pentathlon
兴奋剂	stimulant
运动员	athlete
业余爱好者（体育等方面）	amateur
主办城市	host city

3.5.5 厚积薄发

1928年7月28日，在荷兰阿姆斯特丹举办的第九届奥林匹克运动会上，中国首次派出代表前往观摩。在贵宾席上，中华全国体育协进会名誉干事宋如海深深地为现场的气氛所感动。他一边用心观看每一个入场细节，一边叨念着："Olympiade，Olympiade，奥林匹亚，'我能比呀'！"

1930年，宋如海根据在这届奥运会上的所见所闻以及考察感想，出版了《我能比呀·世界运动会丛录》一书，其中解释了"我能比呀"的来历："Olympiade"原系古希腊运动会之名称，世界运动大会仍沿用之。"我能比呀"虽系译音，亦含有重大意义。盖所以示吾人均能参与此项之比赛。但凡各事皆需要决心、毅勇，便能与人竞争。

更早的时候，奥林匹克还曾经被音译为"厄灵辟克"，比较而言，直白的"我能比呀"十分传神地表达了当时中国人对奥运的向往之情。

3.6 信息科技

3.6.1 背景阅读

Electronic Information Industry

Since 1978, China's electronic information industry has been advancing at a high speed, having far-reaching and favourable influence on other branches of the national economy. Computers, software and telecommunications are the three major parts of China's information industry. By 1999, the total scale of the information industry was at the top international level. The output of colour TV sets, sound equipment and telephones had leaped to first place in the world; the total sales income of the electronic information industry had reached 430 billion yuan, with 39 billion US dollars in export value. Chinese computer groups represented by Legend and Founder of Beijing University are not only the leaders in the domestic market, their products have also entered markets in Southeast Asia and Japan. At the same time, with remarkable market potential, computer software Chinese computer groups represented by Legend and Founder of Beijing University are not only the leaders in the domestic market, their products have also entered markets in Southeast Asia and Japan. At the same time, with remarkable market potential, computer software development and information services are also developing well in recent years. Currently, finance, posts and telecommunications, science and technology, education, business activities and government institutions in China all have their own network systems and data bases connected with the Internet. So far, China has 8.9 million Internet users. In 1999, Beijing opened a 45-megampere international exit, which made the total bandwidth of international exit of China's electronic information 130 megamperes. As the industry developed most rapidly since the reform and opening to the outside world, telecommunications manufacturing kept an over-30-percent development speed during the Eighth Five-Year Plan period. China has completed various public telecommunication networks throughout the country and linked with the rest of the world, including optical-fibre, digital microwave, satellite communication, program-controlled exchange, and mobile and data communication.

Posts and Telecommunications

Since 1978, the development of posts and telecommunications has entered a new historical stage. The scale and volume of the telephone network, and the level of technology and services have all realized qualitative leaps. China has built up its public telecommunications network to cover the whole nation and link it up with the rest of the world. The public postal network now boasts complete services and multiple transportation means. Many advanced methods are used, including optical cables, digital microwave networks, satellites, program-controlled exchanges, mobile telecommunications and data telecommunications. By the end of 1999, the nation's total mobile telephone exchange capacity had reached 160 million circuits, and the number of mobile telephone users had reached 43.24 million, making China the third-largest market for mobile phones in the world. The total number of telephone users in China reached 110 million in 1999, accounting for 13 percent of the nation's population, while the percentage in 1978 was 0.38 percent; and in urban areas, the percentage in 1999 was 28.4 percent, while in 1978 it was only 1.9 percent. In rural areas, 79.8 percent of the administrative villages now have telephones. China has 102,000 post offices nationwide, and the total length of postal routes and rural mail delivery routes reaches 6.215 million km. All large and medium-sized cities provide international express mail service, and have developed international automatic telex, data transmission, express fax, and TV program transmission services. Besides, various services via the Internet, including e-mail and e-commerce, are now available.

(http://www.fmprc.gov.cn/eng/ljzg/zgjk/)

3.6.2 口译精讲

1. 英汉口译

（1）词语必备。

juggernaut	世界主宰
replica	复制品
proliferate	激增
micropayment	小额支付
speculation	推测

（2）口译课文。

Chinese universities graduate more than 600,000 engineering students a year. China has consistently placed at or near the top of programming competitions. And while we have not seen China become a leader in information technology and computing, I expect that this will change in the coming decade.

Since the Internet revolution of the late 1990s, many successful companies have been built by taking American ideas and localizing them for China. These companies may have "copied" from the United States at first, but they acted swiftly, focused on their customers and developed their products, adding more and more local innovations.

For example, Tencent, one of China's three Internet juggernauts, started with an instant-messaging product named QQ, which was a replica of the same system on which Yahoo Messenger and MSN Messenger were based. But today, QQ has evolved to become a very different product — a combination of instant messaging, social networking, universal ID and gaming center. QQ has built the world's largest online community (about 700 million active accounts), while its American counterparts continue to build instant messaging as loss leaders.

I expect this type of innovation to proliferate, for three reasons.

First, we are entering the age of open platforms, mobile computing, pad devices, open-source and cloud computing. These will create many opportunities for talented Chinese I.T. professionals.

Second, development costs are the lowest in history. On the open platforms, four or five good engineers can build an application and validate it in just a few months.

Finally, the Chinese market is growing very rapidly, and more innovations will come out of such large markets. We expect the country to have 500 million mobile Internet users by 2012, and perhaps twice that in five years. Great innovative mobile companies are sure to follow.

An ancient Western adage — necessity is the mother of invention — is appropriate here. The Year of the Dragon begins on Jan. 23, and hundreds of millions of people will want to watch the New Year's gala on their computers. That has provided the impetus for inventing P2P, or person-to-person, technologies to handle the surge.

Chinese users have never had the habit of paying for software or digital content, but Chinese companies have come up with many clever micropayment strategies. For example, a Chinese e-book is free at first, but once you read half of it and get hooked, you have to pay a nominal charge per thousand words.

Traditional Chinese media have limited information, so sites like Sina Weibo have emerged, combining the viral propagation of Twitter and the rich media of Facebook.

What else might we look forward to? Chinese parents care deeply about education, yet schools in poorer cities are inadequate. Can China invent effective distance-learning solutions? There are more than 160 cities in China with more than a million people. These urban environments are the perfect places to develop "solomo" (social, local, mobile) applications: for example, finding a fast-food restaurant offering a discount within walking distance. Most Chinese people don't have credit cards. Can Chinese phones leapfrog those in the United States and become our electronic wallets?

Which of these speculations will come true in China first? I'm not sure, but I am sure that I have missed many other "killer applications" from China. In a country full of energy, desire, talent and ideas, there is no doubt that China will become a world leader in information technology.

(*Excerpted from the essay "China is Poised for an I. T. Golden Age" by the former head of Google China and the founder of Innovation Works Kai-Fu Lee in New York Times on December 5, 2011*)

(3) 参考译文。

在中国的大学毕业生中，每年有60万工科生。在各种程序设计比赛中，中国参赛者总是名列前茅。但中国并未在信息技术和计算机工程领域崭露头角，我盼望着这样的情况会在接下来的10年内有所好转。

自上世纪90年代末的互联网革命以来，许多中国企业成功地借鉴了美国的理念并在中国实现本地化运用。这些企业起初只是"复制"美国的成功例子，但他们很快将重心集中于客户以及产品的发展，进而增加了越来越多的本土特色。

例如，中国互联网三大巨头之一腾讯公司就是一个成功的案例。腾讯公司从一个即时通讯产品QQ起家，QQ复制了雅虎通和微软即时通讯软件的运行系统，但如今已经成长为一个完全不同的产品：它将即时通讯、社交网络、通用账号和游戏中心集于一体，形成了全球最大的在线社区（拥有超过7亿的活跃用户），而与此同时，美国的即时通讯产品却仍在亏损经营。

我期待看到这种形式的革新能大幅增加，原因有三点：

首先，我们正进入一个有开放平台、移动计算、平板装置、开放源代码和云计算的时代。这些领域为有天赋的中国IT从业者提供了更多的机会。

其次，现在的开发成本达到了历史最低点。就开放平台领域而言，四五个优秀的工程师在几个月内就能完成应用程序的编写和验证。

最后，中国市场发展尤为迅速，在这样一个大环境里能激发更多的创新潜能。到2012年，中国的手机上网用户预计将达到5亿人，这一数据有望在5年内翻一番。优秀且创新的手机公司也将应运而生。

有一句古老的西方谚语用在这里再合适不过了：需求是创造之母。龙年将在1月23日开始，届时将有数以亿计的观众通过电脑观看春节联欢晚会，因此，运用点对点技术来应对庞大的人数问题是大势所趋。

中国的用户从未形成对软件或者数字内容付费的习惯，对此，中国的企业想出了许多绝妙的小额支付策略应对这个难题。例如，在中国，电子书一开始是供读者免费阅读的，但当你读到一半并被书中内容牢牢吸引住的时候，你需要为剩下的内容以千字为单位支付小额的费用。

传统的中国媒体只提供有限的信息资源，所以像新浪微博这样的网站纷纷涌现，这类网站兼具推特网病毒式传播信息的特点和脸谱网丰富的媒体资源。

除此之外还有什么值得我们期待呢？中国家长一直以来十分关注孩子的教育问题，但在较为贫穷落后的地区，教学资源相对匮乏。中国是否能找出有效的远程学习方案来解决这一问题？在中国，已有160多个城市拥有超过百万的人口，这些城市是开发"社交本地移动"程序的理想地点，如帮助人们在步行距离范围内找到打折的快餐店。大多数中国人都不使用信用卡，中国的手机是否可以超越美国的手机成为我们的电子钱包？

以上这些猜想哪一项能在中国率先实现？我无法确定，但我很确定的是我已经错过了中国很多其他的"杀手级应用程序"（即绝大部分用户会用到的程序）。作为一个充满活力、需求、才能和创意的国家，中国无疑将成为发展世界信息技术方面的领军者。

（4）口译点津。

1) QQ has built the world's largest online community (about 700 million active accounts), while its American counterparts continue to build instant messaging as loss leaders.

此句中 its American counterparts 意为"它在美国的相对物"，即"美国的即时通讯产品"；loss leaders 意为"亏本商品"。

译文：QQ 形成了全球最大的在线社区（拥有超过7亿的活跃用户），而美国的即时通讯产品却仍在亏损经营。

2) An ancient Western adage — necessity is the mother of invention — is appropriate here.

necessity is the mother of invention 为同位语，可根据中文表达习惯译在中间或者调至最后。

译文：有一句古老的西方谚语：需求是创造之母，用在这里非常合适。

或者：有一句古老的西方谚语用在这里再合适不过了：需求是创造之母。

3) That has provided the impetus for inventing P2P, or person-to-person, technologies to handle the surge.

此句中 impetus 意为"促进、动力"，P2P 意为"点对点服务"，handle the surge 可译为"应对需求的剧增"。

译文：这为点对点技术的发展提供了动力，这一技术能应对需求的剧增。

或译为：运用点对点技术来应对庞大的人数问题是大势所趋。

4) Sina Weibo, 新浪微博, 是一个由新浪网推出的、提供微型博客服务的类

Twitter 网站。用户可以通过网页、WAP 页面、手机等发布消息或上传图片。可以把微博理解为"微型博客"或者"一句话博客"。

5)"solomo" application 是指"社交本地移动"应用程序，是社交（social）、本地（local）及移动媒体（mobile）相互结合的体现，是移动设备所独具的一个功能。

2. 汉英口译

(1) 词汇必备。

宽带用户	broadband users
微博	microblog
透明化	transparency
物联网	Internet of Things
云计算	cloud computing

(2) 口译课文。

近两年来中国网民规模急剧扩大，网络基础设施日益完善，互联网普及率不断提高。截至目前，中国网民规模达到 4.4 亿人，互联网普及率攀升到 33%，宽带网民规模 3.6 亿人，使用电脑上网的群体中宽带普及率达到 98%。特别值得一提的是，中国手机网民的规模达到 2.77 亿人，其中只使用手机上网的网民占整体网民的比例提升到了 11.7%。

手机网民快速增长的一个重要驱动力是移动互联网的快速发展，3G 的普及，基于 3G 的使用丰富多彩：阅读、音乐、互动社区、支付、应用程序商店等各种应用争奇斗艳，日新月异，吸引着越来越多的手机上网用户。

微博的流行也使无线网迅速流行，国内以新浪微博为代表的一批微博发展壮大，开始了中国微博时代。如何利用好微博等新媒体手段，进一步服务经济发展和促进公共事务透明化，是我们将要深入探讨和研究的问题之一。

电子商务服务业的作用也将随着电子商务应用的日益广泛和深入而显得更加突出，在与电子商务相关的信用、支付、物流、IT、金融等领域，涌现出越来越多的服务商和服务模式，为电子商务活动提供多样化的服务。

政府对互联网技术的发展与创新也非常重视，近年来一直积极推进和加快下一代互联网、物联网以及云计算等关键技术的研发和产业化，引领产业快速发展。

尽管近年来中国互联网的发展取得了一定成绩，但仍然需要继续努力和积极推动。此外，中国互联网行业的整体创新能力不够，在对互联网的理解利用程度和深度上，仍与国际同行存在一定差距。由于国家所处的发展阶段技术水平及文化方面的差异，中美两国互联网产业在发展过程中体现出不同的特点和情况，同时也存在着许多共同的话题和关注点，因此双方需要进一步加强相互理解、交流和合作。

本届论坛,为双方提供了一个良好的交流互动平台,在接下来的会议过程中希望来自中美两国互联网企业和专家代表们畅所欲言,各抒己见,特别希望中国互联网界的代表们,珍惜本次宝贵的机会,认真借鉴和学习美国同仁在互联网创新当中的成功经验和有效做法。

(2010年11月8日胡启恒理事长在第四届中美互联网论坛开幕式上的讲话,节选)

(3) 参考译文

During the past two years, the population of Chinese Internet users has grown rapidly. With the improvement of the network infrastructures, Internet penetration rate has increased continually. Up to now, the number of Chinese Internet users has reached 440 million and the Internet penetration rate has climbed to 33%. China has 360 million broadband users; 98% of the Internet users who surf the Internet on computers access to broadband networks. In particular, there are 277 million people surf the Internet on mobile phones and 11.7% of them only get access to mobile Internet.

The rapid development of the mobile Internet is an important driving force of the rapid growth of mobile Internet users. As the 3G networks expand, the services based on the 3G networks, such as reading, music, interactive communities, online-payment and application program stores are full of varieties and rapid changes, attracting more and more mobile Internet users.

The popularity of microblog promotes the development of Internet industry. In China, microblogging services, represented by Sina Microblog, have developed quickly, opening the microblogging era in China. How to make good use of new media means like microblog, to better serve economic development and promote transparency of public affairs, is one of the issues we are going to further discuss and research.

As the expansion of electronic commerce, the role of e-commerce services becomes more prominent. There are more and more service providers and service modes springing up in relevant credit, payment, logistics, IT, finance and other fields, providing various services for e-commerce activities.

The government also attaches great importance to the development and innovation of Internet technology. For the past few years, research and industrialization have been promoted and accelerated in some core technique areas, such as the next generation Internet, the Internet of Things and cloud computing, in order to speeding up industrial development.

In recent years, although China's Internet industry has some achievements, there is still room for improvements. In addition, China's general innovation in Internet industry lags behind international counterparts, which makes backward situation in understanding and utility of the Internet. Due to differences on development phases, technique levels and cultural backgrounds, there are different characteristics and situations between the Internet industries of China and the USA, also many common concerns being shared. In consequence, both countries should further strengthen mutual understanding, communication and cooperation.

This forum provides a good platform for communication and interaction for the two countries. In the following sessions, I hope the experts and delegates from Chinese and US Internet enterprises can feel free to air your opinions. Particularly, I hope delegates from China's Internet industry can cherish this precious opportunity to learn from successful experiences and effective practices of American counterparts on Internet innovation.

(4) 口译点津。

1) 基于3G的使用丰富多彩：阅读、音乐、互动社区、支付、应用程序商店等各种应用争奇斗艳，日新月异，吸引着越来越多的手机上网用户。

"争奇斗艳，日新月异"的译法是难点。若把"争奇斗艳"直译为 contend in beauty and fascination，把"日新月异"译为 change with each passing day 在此处略显勉强。根据上下文可知，"争奇斗艳"指的是3G应用的多样化，"日新月异"则强调手机应用发展之快。基于此种理解，原文可译为 full of varieties and rapid changes。

译文：the services based on the 3G networks, such as reading, music, interactive communities, online-payment and application program stores are full of varieties and rapid changes, attracting more and more mobile Internet users.

2) 如何利用好微博等新媒体手段，进一步服务经济发展和促进公共事务透明化，是我们将要深入探讨和研究的问题之一。

"公共事务透明化"可译为 promote transparency of public affairs。

译文：How to make good use of new media means like microblog, to better serve economic development and promote transparency of public affairs, is one of the issues we are going to further discuss and research.

3) 在与电子商务相关的信用、支付、物流、IT、金融等领域涌现出越来越多的服务商和服务模式……

此句中列举的几种服务商和服务模式分别译为 credit, payment, logistics, IT, finance；"涌现"可翻译为 spring up, come forth, emerge in large numbers，等等。

译文：There are more and more service providers and service modes springing up in relevant credit, payment, logistics, IT, finance and other fields, providing various services for e-commerce activities.

4) 近年来一直积极推进和加快下一代互联网、物联网以及云计算等关键技术的研发和产业化。

"下一代互联网"指不同于现在互联网的新一代互联网，它将解决现有互联网 IP 地址不足等缺点，可译为 the next generation Internet；"物联网"指将物体联接起来的网络，通过物联网可实现人与物体的沟通和对话，也可以实现物体与物体互相间的沟通和对话，可译为 the Internet of Things；"云计算"指一种基于互联网的计算方式，通过这种方式共享的软硬件资源和信息可以按需提供给计算机和其他设备，可译为 cloud computing。

译文：For the past few years, research and industrialization have been promoted and accelerated in some core technique areas, such as the next generation Internet, the Internet of Things and cloud computing.

5) 在接下来的会议过程中希望来自中美两国互联网企业和专家代表们畅所欲言，各抒己见。

"畅所欲言"可译为 speak one's mind freely, air one's views freely, assert without any restraint 或 state one's views unreservedly, 等等。"各抒己见"可译为 each one expresses his own view, everyone sets forth his own view, 等等。

译文：In the following sessions, I hope the experts and delegates from Chinese and US Internet enterprises can feel free to air your opinions.

3.6.3 实战演练

1. 口译听解与表达

(1) 口译听辨。

ITU is the United Nations _____ agency for information and communication technologies — ICTs. We allocate global radio spectrum and satellite orbits, develop the technical standards that ensure networks and technologies seamlessly _____, and strive to improve access to ICTs to underserved communities worldwide. Donwload ITU's brochure ITU _____ connecting the entire world's people — wherever they live. Through our work, we protect and support everyone's fundamental right to communicate. Today, ICTs underpin everything we do. They help manage and control _____, water supplies, power networks and food distribution chains. They support health care, education, government services, financial markets, _____ and environmental management. And they allow people to communicate with _____, friends and family anytime, and almost anywhere. With the help of our _____, ITU brings the benefits of modern communication technologies to people everywhere in an efficient, safe, easy and _____ manner. ITU membership reads like a Who's Who of the ICT sector. We're unique among UN agencies in having both public and private sector membership. So in addition to our 193 Member States, ITU membership includes ICT _____, leading academic institutions and some 700 private companies. In an increasingly interconnected world, ITU is the single global organization _____ all players in this dynamic and fast-growing sector.

(2) 复述练习。

In today's world, telecommunications are more than just a basic service — they are a means to promote development, improve society and save lives. This will be all the more true in the world of tomorrow.

The importance of telecommunications was on display in the wake of the earthquake which devastated Haiti earlier this year. Communications technologies were used to coordinate aid, optimize resources and provide desperately sought information about the victims. The International Telecommunications Union (ITU) and its commercial partners contributed scores of satellite terminals and helped to provide wireless communications to help disaster relief and clean-up efforts.

I welcome those efforts and, more broadly, the work of ITU and others to promote broadband access in rural and remote areas around the world.

Greater access can mean faster progress toward the Millennium Development Goals (MDGs). The Internet drives trade, commerce and even education. Telemedicine is improving health care. Earth monitoring satellites are being used to address climate change. And green technologies are promoting cleaner cities.

As these innovations grow in importance, so, too, does the need to bridge the digital divide.

The United Nations is committed to ensuring that people everywhere have equitable access to information and communication technologies. On this International Day, let us resolve to fully harness the great potential of the digital revolution in the service of life-saving relief operations, sustainable development and lasting peace.

(3) 公众演讲。

以"可穿戴电子设备给人类生活带来的改变"为题，分别以英语和汉语作3～5分钟演讲。

2. 单句口译

(1) 英汉口译。

1) With the explosion of information technology and the Internet, you can now have a virtual classroom right on your desktop.

2) Our team of information technology, web-design and communication experts guarantees optimal functionality of the Gateway.

3) He said students are returning to computer science because they like the field and not because it can necessarily make them rich.

4) Information technology professionals have to be kept up to date with new developments: other staffs need to be trained to operate unfamiliar, often complicated, machinery.

5) It's harder to switch roles if you come from certain fields like information technology or human resources, but that only means you have to try harder.

(2) 汉英口译。

1) 它告诉你一台计算机如何从另一台计算机获取信息。

2) 近1/4 的硅谷信息技术公司由中国人和印度人建立。

3) 据统计, 即时通讯、社区等平台已经成为近半数网民的首选入口。

4) 信息技术的特点之一是节约劳动力——这是国内现象, 与外包或全球经济无关, 但却伤害了一些工薪阶层。

5) 无论是门户网站还是其他网络服务平台都表现出了令人赞叹的活力与创新, 让中国网民真正实现了广义上的网络生活。

3. 段落口译

(1) 英汉口译。

Paragraph 1

Well first let me introduce a little bit about Alibaba Group. Alibaba was founded in 1999, 18 founders in my apartment. And we just have an idea we believe Internet is going to change China. Internet is going to boom. So nobody believed us. Everybody say, well, you know, how can you do Internet in China because Chinese government censorship is decent. There's no reason for us to survive. And today people say, Jack, you're visionary; how could you tell e-commerce Internet 10 years ago. And I said… I think we're like a blind man riding on the back of blind tigers. Just by accident. We focused, we make the thing happen and from 18 people now today we have more than 20,000 people. And we grow from one company to 5 companies right now.

Paragraph 2

As a Ph. D. student, I actually had three projects I wanted to work on. Thank goodness my advisor said, "Why don't you work on the web for a while?" Technology and especially the Internet can really help you be lazy. Lazy? What I mean is a group of three people can write software that then millions can use and enjoy. Can three people answer the phone a million times? Find the leverage in the world, so you can be truly lazy! Overall, I know it seems like the world is crumbling out there, but it is actually a great time in your life to get a little crazy, follow your curiosity, and be ambitious about it. Don't give up on your dream. The world needs you all!

(2) 汉英口译。

段落1

回顾中国接入国际互联网以来的16年，互联网对中国经济社会发展产生的影响是广泛的、深刻的。在今天的中国，越来越多的人通过互联网获取信息和知识，互联网已经成为人民生活不可或缺的重要组成部分，促进了人们生活质量的提高，丰富了人们精神文化生活。在今天的中国，越来越多的人通过互联网发表意见，互联网为人民享有知情权、参与权、表达权、监督权提供了前所未有的便利条件和直接渠道，为政府了解人民意愿、满足人民需求、维护人民利益发挥了日益重要的作用。

段落2

在中国，我们今天所谈论的门户与当初雅虎公司在美国初创时所说的门户已经有了很大不同。那个时候，提供搜索服务为主的网站成为网民进入互联网的"门户"。而在中国，门户的意义除此之外，还包含了"大而全"的资讯信息超市的含义。新浪、搜狐、百度等网站及其基本服务可以说是门户网站的基本形态。由于这些网站在中国互联网的发展过程中出现早、影响大，因而也为中国互联网深深地打下了"门户概念"的烙印。从这个意义上也可以解释，为什么今天我们会以"后门户"网站时代作为一个观察的视角。

4. 对话口译。

A：苹果公司计划在未来两年里将它在华的零售店数量翻倍。但与此同时，苹果在中国智能手机市场的份额已被三星超越。苹果在华面临了巨大的挑战，你认为苹果受到多大威胁，这又是怎样造成的？

B: I think Apple has a phenomenal brand in China, so I am generally bullish about Apple's future if it gets the execution right. Apple's brand is phenomenal: It demands a premium; it's the gift to give; and people, from kids to adults, love to have it, and they will pay more money for it. Now, at the same time, Apple is now so large locally, they need to really have a unified presence, in order to deal with the government and with public crises. Apple is one of the few companies that don't have a Head of China, and that's able to really communicate with the public and the government and very quickly get over the crises, which is a commonplace for multi-nationals in China. And its retail stores, I'm glad to see it's doubling but I think it should have doubled years ago. So I think if it gets the execution act together, there is a huge demand for the products.

A：蒂姆·库克本人已经多次去过中国，他最重要的议程之一就是达成与中国移动的合作，为何此事一直悬而未决？是因为苹果公司没有任命中国区总裁吗？

B: I think it is somewhat related, I mean the real, core reason, of course, is you have two giants that are not used to making compromises: China Mobile and Apple. I think it is unlikely China Mobile will compromise, so Apple will need to have a more flexible policy, which we've seen through its basically unprecedented apology with the rather small issue of warranty recently. I think it shows Apple's willing to be flexible, but if it had had the Head of China that is well connected in the government space, I think it could accelerate matters.

A：那么推出低价手机对苹果公司在规避风险上能有多大帮助？精明的中国消费者会青睐低价手机吗？

B: I am actually not a huge fan of the belief that a cheaper iPhone will really change things. Even the cheaper iPhone, the rumour price would be near 300 dollars, for the truly budget-conscious people, it's really still not competitive. So I think Apple will continue to really demand a premium based on its brand, and I am more bullish actually about the high end. I do think having a low-end iPhone will help, but it's really not a panacea.

（2013年李开复接受美国彭博电视台专访：谈苹果在中国未来的发展，节选）

5. 篇章口译
（1）英汉口译。

The first company is called Alibaba.com and it focuses on small and medium-sized companies. Helping small and medium-sized companies, we have all 37 or 38 million register SMEs in China using our services. Outside China we have more than 12 million SMEs using our services. So, well, our business model's very simple. One side is China side, is a domestic trading. Anything you want to buy, anything you want to sell, you can use the website in China. It's like a market place, like E-bay. But E-bay is C2C; we are B2B. The Alibaba B2B: one is China domestic trading; the other is import and export. It's a marketplace for global purchasing, global buying. It grows probably we listed 3 years ago in the HK market, and we were very lucky because the day we listed, the market was good. So our stock price grows from $13.5 to $40 without doing anything good. Just go up. And three months later, our stock from $40 to $3 without doing anything bad. Just, you know, just up and down. And there was the rock and roll. And now the company's stabilized, we still focus on e-commerce, still focus on SMEs. But except the company, the other 4 companies are private companies.

The other company which we own 100% is called Taobao. com which probably most Chinese people here have heard about it. It is much more influential than Alibaba. com in China. We have more than 300 million register users. It started with the C – C, but 95% is from B – C. And 6 years ago, we started to compete with E-bay. E-bay, a lot of money… At that time their market can be 80 billion dollars. They came to China, they said they would compete with Alibaba, and we started the business from zero and we got like 2% or 3% market share. Now we have 90% market share which E-bay have like 2% or 3% market share. So Taobao is a combination of Emerson, E-bay, and Google and Face book. It's a community on line and we have 43 million unique visitors visit the site shopping every day. And we finish 8 million transactions per day. And logistically last year the package delivery in the whole China is 2 billion packages' delivery on the road. We created 1.1 billion, so we have like 55% market share on this delivery. It's growing very fast and we already have like 100% growth in the past 7 years. And we will keep it 100% this year.

And the third company we have is called Alipays, like a PayPal. It's a very stupid model. 5 years ago, I found that it's so difficult to do transactions on line because people don't trust each other. The banking system is so bad. The infrastructure of finance is also bad. So I was worried about what I'm going to do. The bank has the license to do this. We know how to do business, but we don't have the license.

Today we have 400 million register users and we are the largest on-line third party payment without any business model. We just want to help people. That makes the banks very unhappy because we distract the business model. In the world, for a good bank, about 60% or 70% of the revenues are from the services. But in China, about 60% or 70% or 80% of revenues come from the loaning. So we go inside, go into the service.

The forth company is called Aliclub computing which we just founded 2 years ago. Because we have the data from small and medium-sized companies, because we have the data from Taobao consumers and we have the data from Alipays, the data we collected become so influential that we want all the consumers to share, to understand the data from SME and let the consumers understand SME data. So we've been focusing on clock computing.

(*Excerpted from the speech by the founder of Alibaba Ma Yun in Columbia Business School on September 21, 2010*)

(2) 汉英口译。

腾讯是为全国 4 亿网民提供高质量服务的企业，它提供从及时通讯、网络媒体、网络游戏、搜索引擎到电子商务完整的电子服务。今天，云计算的兴起使得为所有互联网用户提供更方便的应用成为了可能，也为我们互联网今后的发展提供了广阔的空间。

我们想结合我们的特点谈谈云计算，除了超级数据中心等的云计算平台以外，我想着重讲三方面的技术和挑战。

首先是信息安全。云计算就是相当于现在的银行，把现金存在银行里面，实际上比放在保险柜更安全又方便。首先是这个银行是有信用的，云计算能够得到普及和得到所有互联网用户的认可，关键在于互联网安全能否做好，另一方面使用户可以方便使用云端的服务，一方面是这些服务和隐私是得到保护的。我们知道便利性和安全性是矛盾的。

其次是通用和标准开放的平台。在标准化方面，微软和中国工业界正在制定统一的标准，云计算的目的之一是要将计算资源以最经济的方式提供给社会。由于它的规模巨大，不可能每一个企业和机构都发展自己的云计算平台，而是由主要的互联网公司提供给全社会。腾讯本着互通互利的原则，希望共同发展完善云计算的产业链，不仅让广大用户通过云计算平台共享信息和服务，也要让中小企业机构分享云计算的成果，基于云计算发展增值服务。

最后我想谈一下基于云计算的应用和服务。我们要在云计算的基础上整合各种已经有的 IT 服务，从通信、媒体、办公自动化、网络游戏、SNS、搜索引擎到电子商务等完整的各种各样的互联网应用，这样才能真正给用户带来好处。

刚才谈了三个挑战性问题，我们希望基于云计算平台为客户提供更多价值，通过开放和合作，为 IT 行业提供新的商机。

中美互联网论坛已经举行了 4 届，成为两国互联网业界最重要的交流和合作的机制，腾讯也在积极布局海外，向包括美国在内的其他市场的网络用户提供产品和服务，我们也希望通过中美互联网论坛这一平台，与两国的互联网企业加强交流，共同探讨互联网行业新的趋势、新技术和新的理念，为推动中美乃至全球互联网的繁荣与发展作出贡献！

(2010 年 11 月 8 日，腾讯首席执行官马化腾在第四届中美互联网论坛的演讲，节选)

3.6.4 词语拓展

半导体	semiconductor
保真度	fidelity
半双通通信	half-duplex communication

笔记本系统单元	notebook system unit
并行端口	parallel ports
标志检测	mark sensing
操纵杆	joystick
场效应管	field-effect transistor
磁道	track
磁头碰撞	head crash
插件程序	plug-in
超链接	hyperlink
程序控制语言	programming control language
单向通信	serial data transmission
电话学	telephony
电子数据表	spreadsheet
电子文稿程序	presentation graphics
非易失性存储	nonvolatile storage
分辨率	resolution
分时系统	time-sharing system
硅片	silicon chip
计时信息	instant messaging
开放式体系结构	open architecture
目标链接	object linking
识别	identification
视影通信	line of sight communication
数字化	digitization
数字传输	digital transmission
数字输入	numeric entry
图像获取设备	image capturing device
拓扑结构	topology
网页浏览器	web browser
微秒	microsecond
物理安全	physical security
无线革命	wireless revolution
协议	protocol
与门	AND gate
源文件	source file

振荡器	oscillator
真空管	vacuum tube
指令寄存器	instruction register
智能终端设备	intelligent terminal
主存	primary storage
纵向门户	vertical portal
直接传输	direct transmission

3.6.5 厚积薄发

科技英语词汇一般分为三类，即科学技术词汇（scientific and technical terms）、半技术词汇（semi-technical terms）以及非技术词汇（non-technical terms）。在科技类讲稿中，出现频率最多的并不是一长串复杂拗口的专业技术词，而是那些看似平淡无奇、常被我们忽略的普通英语词汇。这些普通词汇除了具有基本含义外，出现在不同的专业领域时又具有相应的专业词义，这类词汇就是所谓的"半技术词汇"。对于译员来讲，专业技术词汇可以在译前准备环节中进行归纳总结，但半技术词汇则需要平日的积累。

下面表格中列举的是一些较为典型的半技术词汇：

半技术词汇	普通词义	专业词义
actor	演员	作用物
bed	床	床层，床层
crane	鹤	起重机
current	流通	电流；几率流
cat	猫	吊锚
die	死亡	模具
flash	闪光	闪蒸；毛边
leg	腿	支腿，支架
pencil	铅笔	光线锥，光束
trip	旅行	跳闸

3.7 经贸往来

3.7.1 背景阅读

China's overall economic construction objectives were clearly stated in the Three Step Development Strategy set out in 1987: Step One — to double the 1980 GNP and ensure that the people have enough food and clothing — was attained by the end of the 1980s; Step Two — to quadruple the 1980 GNP by the end of the 20th century — was achieved in 1995 ahead of schedule; Step Three — to increase per-capita GNP to the level of the medium-developed countries by the mid-21st century — at which point, the Chinese people will be fairly well-off and modernization will be basically realized.

Economic restructure is one of the most crucial elements of China's reform and opening-up policy. For the first 30 years of the PRC, the government practiced a planned economy system, whereby industrial production, agricultural production, and the stocking and selling of goods in commercial departments were all controlled by state plan. The variety, quantity and prices in every sphere of the economy were fixed by state planners. While this contributed to the planned, focused and steady development of China's economy, it also sapped its vitality and limited its growth. Economic reforms began with the rural areas in 1978, and were extended to the cities in 1984. In 1992, after some 10 years of reform in the clear direction of the establishment of a socialist market economy, the government set out the main principles of economic restructuring: encouraging the development of diversified economic elements whilst retaining the dominance of the public sector; creation of a modern enterprise system to meet the requirements of the market economy; a unified and open market system across China, linking domestic and international markets, and promoting the optimization of resources; transformation of government economic management in order to establish a complete macro-control system; encouraging certain lead groups and areas to become rich first, enabling them to help others towards prosperity too; the formulation of a China-appropriate social security system for both urban and rural residents, so as to promote overall economic development and ensure social stability. In 1997, the government stressed the importance of the non-public sector to China's national economy, in which profitability is encouraged for such essential factors of production as capital and technology, so as to further progress economic reforms.

The "West-to-East Electricity Transmission," the "West-to-East Gas Transmission," and the "South-to-North Water Diversion" are the government's three key strategic projects, aimed at realigning overall economic development and achieving rational distribution of national resources across China.

A socialist market economic system has now taken shape, and the basic role played by the market has been improved in the sphere of resource allocation. At the same time, the macro-control system continues to be perfected. The pattern has basically been formed in which the public sector plays the main role alongside non-public sectors such as individual and private companies to achieve common development. According to the plan, China is forecast to have a relatively complete socialist market economy in place by 2010 and this will become comparatively mature by 2020.

3.7.2 口译精讲

1. 英汉口译

（1）词语必备。

convene	召开，召集
financial crisis	金融危机
strategic and economic dialogue	战略经济对话
intellectual property	知识产权
prone to	倾向于
IMF	国际货币基金组织
World Bank	世界银行
G-20	20国集团
Financial Stability Board	金融稳定委员会

（2）口译课文。

We convened the first Strategic & Economic Dialogue three years ago in the depth of the most serious threat to the global economy and financial system in decades. We worked together to put out the fires of the global financial crisis, and today the world is better for it. We have worked to address the inevitable problems in our economic relationship in a constructive manner and with mutual respect. And both of our nations are better for it.

The diversity of the economic issues we address in this Dialogue reflects the breadth and importance of our relationship. We don't always agree, but we share strong common interests, and we recognize that promoting these common interests requires cooperation and commitment from both sides.

As two of the world's largest trading nations, we both depend on an open global trading system in which workers and companies compete on a level playing field. We have a common interest in promoting productivity growth through research and innovation, by protecting intellectual property and open markets. We have a mutual interest in building a global financial system that is more stable and less prone to crisis.

Because of the size and importance of our two economies, we also have a shared responsibility for the global economy. As we have worked to promote economic reforms in the United States and China, we have worked together to strengthen and reform the IMF and the World Bank and to mobilize more resources to support development in the world's poorest countries.

We have worked together to support Europe's efforts to better manage its financial crisis. We have worked to build new mechanisms for cooperation on international economic and financial issues in the G-20 and the Financial Stability Board.

We meet at a time of risk and challenge in the global economy, and we both face considerable economic challenges at home.

In the United States, we are making progress in repairing the damage from the financial crisis and putting in place a stronger foundation for future economic growth. We are putting in place a comprehensive program of economic reforms to improve education, increase investments in scientific research and innovation, improve incentives for private investment, and reform the financial system. And we are working to legislate a comprehensive program of reforms to restore fiscal sustainability, building on tough, 10-year spending cuts we put in place last summer. While there is still a long way to go to recover from the financial crisis, the economic expansion in the United States is now more broad based and resilient, and we are significantly more advanced than are the other major developed economies in addressing the imbalances that helped cause our crisis.

In China, you are in the process of exploring the next frontier of economic reforms, recognizing as your predecessors did more than 30 years ago, that future economic growth will require another fundamental shift in economic policy. These new reforms recognize the new reality that China must rely more on domestic consumption rather than exports, and more on innovation by private companies rather than capacity expansion by state owned enterprises, with an economy more open to competition from foreign firms, and with a more modern financial system.

(*Excerpted from remarks by Scretary Geithner at the Opening Ceremony of the 2012*

Strategic and Economic Dialogue on May 3, 2012)

(3) 参考译文。

3年前，当全球经济和金融体系正面临几十年来最严重的威胁，我们举行了第一次战略与经济对话。我们齐心协力，扑灭了全球金融危机的大火，如今世界才能变得如此美好。我们共同合作，本着相互尊重的精神，以建设性的方式，解决两国经济关系中诸多不可避免的问题，我们两国的发展才能变得如此顺利。

我们在对话中要解决的经济问题多种多样，这反映了两国的合作很广泛，并且这种关系很重要。我们并非总能达成共识，但我们有很多共同利益，我们意识到，获得这些共同利益需要双方的合作与承诺。

作为世界上两个最大的贸易国家，我们两国都依赖于开放的全球贸易体系，在该体系中，工人与企业能够开展公平竞争。我们进行科研和创新、保护知识产权，还有开放市场，以此促进生产力增长，在这些方面我们有着共同的利益。我们想建立一个更加稳定、不易遭遇危机的全球金融体系，在这方面我们也有共同的利益。

由于我们两大经济体的规模巨大，且极具重要性，我们还担负着对全球经济的共同责任。我们努力促进美中两国的经济改革，巩固国际货币基金组织和世界银行，推动其改革，调动更多的资源支持世界贫穷国家的发展。

我们还合作支援欧洲，帮助其更好地解决金融危机。我们协力在20国集团和金融稳定委员会内建立国际经济与金融问题相关的新合作机制。

美中两国共同应对全球经济带来的风险与挑战，也同样面临着严峻的国内经济挑战。

在美国，我们正努力修复金融危机造成的破坏，同时为未来经济发展建立更坚实的基础，并已取得进展。我们制订了全面的经济改革计划，以改进教育，增加科研创新投资，鼓励私人投资，我们还改革金融体系。我们在努力通过立法，制订改革计划，以恢复财政稳定。去年夏天我们开始大刀阔斧地削减支出，实施10年削减赤字计划，在此基础上我们会继续努力。尽管要从金融危机中复苏还有很长的路，但美国的经济扩张已有了更广阔的基础，并具备了更强的适应能力。导致危机的原因之一就是不平衡，在面对这个问题上，我们远远领先于其他主要发达经济体。

在中国，你们正在探索下一个经济改革的道路，如同你们的前人在30多年前得出的结论一样，你们认识到，想要保持未来的经济增长需要在经济政策方面作出根本性的转变。这些新的改革是基于新的国情：中国必须更多地依赖国内消费，而非出口；更多地依赖民营企业的创新，而非国有企业扩大产能；中国的经济应当对外国企业的竞争更加开放，金融体系也应更加现代化。

(4) 口译点津。

1) 在遇到此类讲话时，应当注意一些专有名词和术语的翻译。这些词汇在经贸类的口译中会反复出现，译员在日常生活中需多积累。如 financial crisis 是经济危机，IMF 是国际货币基金组织，World Bank 是世界银行，等等。

2) 第一段出现了两次 better for it。it 所指并不明确，此时若联系上下文的意思，可以推断出其是指经历了磨难之后，一切"变得更好"。在发言人指代不明确、译员又无条件询问时，可根据上下文进行合理的推测和补充。

3) The diversity of the economic issues we address in this Dialogue reflects the breadth and importance of our relationship.

在口译当中，为能让目标语更易理解，可对词性进行转换。例如，本句未必处理为"我们在这一对话中所要解决的经济问题的多样性反映了两国关系的广度和重要性"，可考虑译成"我们在对话中需要解决的经济问题多种多样，这反映了两国的合作很广泛，并且这种关系很重要"。

4) We have a mutual interest in building a global financial system that is more stable and less prone to crisis.

这句话中的状语中包含了一个定语从句，若处理为"我们在建立一个更加稳定、不易遭遇危机的全球金融体系方面有着共同的利益"，并不符合中文表达习惯。遇到此类句子，若勉强依据英文的形式翻译为一句话，译文听起来会拗口，若句子再长一些，很可能听众听完后半句又忘记了前半句，因此有必要进行恰当地断句，可考虑翻译为"我们要建立一个更加稳定、不易遭受危机的全球金融体系，在这方面我们有着共同的利益"。

5) 在口译过程中，译者虽然无法事先获知接下来的内容，但应时刻保持对语篇整体的把握，抓住主线逻辑，进行合理的猜测，会有助于更好地理解和产出。例如，在听到 We meet at a time of risk and challenge in the global economy, and we both face considerable economic challenges at home 时，回顾已经翻译过的内容，是描述两国如何共同应对危机，此时可以把握到讲者接下来是对两个各自面临的经济危机进行描述。这是一个过渡性的句子，在翻译中我们要保持对此类句子和短语的敏感度，以更好地把握全文。

2. 汉英口译

(1) 词汇必备。

立足亚洲、面向世界	based in Asia yet with a global perspective
开放包容	open and inclusive
可持续发展	sustainable development
后发优势	late-development advantages
宏观调控	macro-economic management

稳中求进　　　　　　　　　　　seek progress while maintaining stability
立足当前　　　　　　　　　　　address the immediate needs

(2) 口译课文。

尊敬的各位贵宾，

女士们、先生们，朋友们：

很高兴参加博鳌亚洲论坛2012年年会，与来自世界各国的朋友们见面。我们开会的地方——博鳌，10多年前还是一个鲜为人知的小渔村，现在已成为可以共商亚洲发展之计的大平台。博鳌是在中国和亚洲开放发展中快速成长起来的，它的开放与变化表明了中国与亚洲、亚洲与世界的联系日益密切。可以说，身在博鳌能够"博览天下"、"博采众长"，博鳌论坛是一个立足亚洲、面向世界、开放包容的大平台。本次年会"以变革的世界为背景，谋求亚洲健康与可持续发展"，很有意义。在此，我谨代表中国政府，对年会的召开表示热烈祝贺！对各位远道而来的嘉宾表示诚挚欢迎！

博鳌论坛诞生于亚洲金融危机之后。10多年来，亚洲国家在应对风险过程中提高了自身免疫力，在调整变革中促进了经济健康发展。这次国际金融危机中，亚洲经济率先复苏，呈现出比较好的基本面。目前，亚洲经济总量已占世界的30%以上，亚洲经济增长对世界的贡献率超过30%。亚洲成为全球新兴经济体最为集中的地区，后发优势和发展潜能进一步展现。

中国是亚洲大家庭的一员，中国经济与亚洲经济密不可分。中国坚持走经济社会全面协调可持续的科学发展之路，也将为亚洲健康与可持续发展贡献力量。近年来，中国经济继续朝着宏观调控的预期方向发展，实现了经济平稳较快增长和民生不断改善。中国经济的基本面是好的，发展的态势没有改变，有条件保持经济长期平稳较快发展。

我们也认识到，中国仍然是世界上最大的发展中国家，发展中不平衡、不协调、不可持续问题依然突出，一些结构性矛盾凸显，需要逐步解决。当前，我们将按照推动科学发展、加快转变经济发展方式的要求，把握稳中求进的总基调，既立足当前，稳增长、控物价、促和谐；又着眼长远，在调结构、惠民生、抓改革等方面取得新进展，继续促进中国经济社会全面协调可持续发展。

我们相信，广袤的亚洲大地一定能为各国发展提供广阔的空间。面对变革的世界，亚洲人民完全有能力把握机遇、携手前行，实现亚洲健康与可持续发展，共建人类美好未来！

最后，祝博鳌亚洲论坛2012年年会圆满成功！

谢谢大家！

(国务院副总理李克强在博鳌亚洲论坛2012年年会开幕式上的演讲，节选)

(3) 参考译文。

Honorable Guests,
Ladies and Gentlemen,
Dear Friends,

It is my great pleasure to attend the Boao Forum for Asia Annual Conference 2012 and meet with friends from the world. More than a decade ago, Boao was still a small fishing village little known to the outside world. But now it has become a premier platform for people to discuss issues pertinent to Asia's development. Boao enjoys rapid growth through the opening-up and development of Asia and China. Its opening-up and changes have shown the increasingly close relations between China and Asia, and between Asia and the world. It can be said that this conference in Boao gives us a good opportunity to look at our world and learn from each other. Based in Asia yet with a global perspective, the Boao Forum is an open and inclusive platform. This year's theme is quite meaningful — "Asia in the Changing World: Moving Toward Sound and Sustainable Development". Here, on behalf of the Chinese government, I would like to avail of this opportunity to extend our warmest congratulations on the opening of the conference and our sincere welcome to all the participants coming from afar.

This Forum was founded in the wake of the Asian financial crisis. In the past ten years and more, Asian countries have improved their immunizing power, thus are more resilient in dealing with risks and promoting sound economic development through adjustment and reform. In this international financial crisis, Asian economy has taken the lead in recovery and displayed quite solid fundamentals. At present, Asia takes up more than 30 percent of global GDP. Asia's economic contribution to global growth also surpasses 30 percent. This region has the biggest number of emerging economies in the world, and its late-development advantages and development potential are getting more and more apparent.

As a member of the Asian family, China is highly connected with Asia economically. China's commitment to scientific development, which is comprehensive, coordinated and sustainable in economy and society, will contribute to Asia's sound and sustainable development. In recent years, China's economy has grown towards the prospective trend of macro-economic management, having realized fairly fast and steady growth in economy and improvement in people's lives. With sound fundamentals of China's economy and unchanged course of development, China is capable of maintaining long-term, steady and fairly fast development.

We should also recognize that China is still the largest developing country in the world. The development remains seriously unbalanced, uncoordinated and unsustainable, and some outstanding structural problems need to be dealt with step by step. At present, we will seek progress while maintaining stability as we endeavor to promote scientific development and move faster in changing the economic growth model. We will address the immediate needs by ensuring steady growth, controlling price level and promoting harmony while keeping an eye on the future development by ensuring fresh progress in structural adjustment, improvement in people's livelihood and continued reforms, keeping promoting a comprehensive, coordinated and sustainable economic and social development in China.

We are convinced that the vast land of Asia will definitely provide ample space for the development of all countries. Facing an ever-changing world, the Asians are fully capable of seizing the opportunities and moving ahead hand in hand with other countries, achieving Asia's sound and sustainable development and creating a better future for mankind!

Lastly, I wish the Boao Forum for Asia Annual Conference 2012 great success! Thank you!

(4) 口译点津。

1）博鳌亚洲论坛。Boao Forum for Asia，缩写 BFA，或称为亚洲论坛、亚洲博鳌论坛，是一个非政府、非营利性的国际组织，目前已成为亚洲以及其他大洲有关国家政府、工商界和学术界领袖就亚洲以及全球重要事务进行对话的高层次平台。博鳌亚洲论坛致力于通过区域经济的进一步整合，推进亚洲国家实现发展目标。

2）我们开会的地方——博鳌，10多年前还是一个鲜为人知的小渔村，现在已成为可以共商亚洲发展之计的大平台。

这句话中的"我们开会的地方"这个信息点不是很重要，即使省略也不会妨碍听众理解，因此在翻译中只要中心词"博鳌"译出来即可。"共商亚洲发展大计"这个短语的译法比较灵活，可考虑译为 discuss issues pertinent to Asia's development，也可以译为 compare notes on issues important to Asia's development 等，只要意思正确即可。

3）10多年来，亚洲国家在应对风险过程中提高了自身免疫力，在调整变革中促进了经济健康发展。

翻译"提高免疫力"时可以采用直译加解释的方法，也可不拘泥于字面的意思，采用释意法。

译文：Asian countries have improved their immunizing power, thus are more resilient in dealing with risks. 也可译为：Asian countries have acquired greater resilience in dealing with risks.

4) 中国坚持走经济社会全面协调可持续的科学发展之路，也将为亚洲健康与可持续发展贡献力量。

这句话中的前半句"经济社会全面协调可持续的科学发展之路"，如果按照原文顺序翻译会比较困难，也不符合英语的语言表达习惯，翻译时要注意拆分句子结构，分清各成分之间的关系。因为"经济社会全面协调可持续"是修饰"科学发展之路"的，在翻译的时候可考虑采用定语从句，译为 China's commitment to scientific development, which is comprehensive, coordinated and sustainable in economy and society, will contribute to Asia's sound and sustainable development, 这样会使句子间的逻辑更清晰，减轻听众的负担。

5) 我们也认识到，中国仍然是世界上最大的发展中国家，发展中不平衡、不协调、不可持续问题依然突出，一些结构性矛盾凸显，需要逐步解决。

这句话的后半句是难点，在翻译前首先要在正确理解句子的同时理清各成分间的关系。很明显，"发展中不平衡、不协调、不可持续问题依然突出"和后面的"一些结构性矛盾凸显，需要逐步解决"这两部分是并列的关系，所以在翻译中要体现出这种并列关系。可以考虑译为：There is a serious lack of balance, coordination and sustainability in its development, and some outstanding structural problems need to be addressed gradually。也可以译为：The development remains seriously unbalanced, uncoordinated and unsustainable, and some outstanding structural problems need to be dealt with step by step.

3.7.3 实战演练

1. 口译听解与表达

(1) 口译听辨

China's economy will probably grow by less than 8 per cent this year due to weak international demand and a _____ domestic real estate market. Now the talk among China-watchers is that it is approaching a breaking point on its path of growth: the _____ of high growth is over and the country is heading towards a path in the _____ of 6 - 7 per cent.

This mood is strong inside China. When Justin Yifu Lin, who just returned to China from his position as chief economist of the World Bank, announced China would keep growing by 8 per cent before 2030, the Chinese media _____ his claim as "shooting a satellite" — a phrase referring to the widespread _____ of output _____ in the "Great Leap-forward" of 1958. There are good reasons to believe China's _____ is permanent. The growth of China's _____ has been falling since

2010 and by 2020 its stock will start to decline. In accordance, wages are increasing fast; China's episode of _____ is approaching its end. However, an international comparison gives hope that China may be able to maintain an 8 per cent growth rate for at least another decade. China's _____ GDP is about the level of Japan's in 1962 and the level of Korea's in 1982. Both countries grew by 9.7 per cent in the following 10 years after they reached China's per-capita income of today.

（2）复述练习。

President Obama,

Dear Colleagues,

I am glad to meet you here in Hawaii. As this beautiful place connects the two sides of the Pacific, it is of special significance for us to come here and explore ways to promote economic development and deepen cooperation in the Asia-Pacific region. We live in a world where economic globalization is gaining momentum, countries are becoming increasingly interdependent economically, and new changes are underway in global economic governance. At the same time, the global economic environment remains complex and volatile. Some major economies are experiencing economic slowdown, and some countries are facing acute sovereign debt problems. Volatility in the international financial markets persists. Rising inflationary pressure confronts emerging markets. Protectionism in various forms is on a notable increase. As a result, the global economic recovery encounters greater instability and uncertainty. In addition, the continuous international and regional hotspot issues as well as acute global issues such as food security, energy security, climate change and major natural disasters all add to the grave challenges confronting the global economy.

（3）公众演讲。

假设你是一位经济学专家，请就上海自贸区的建设与发展提出意见和建议，分别以英语及汉语作3～5分钟的演讲。

2. 单句口译

（1）英汉口译。

1) The European Union has reacted promptly and firmly, devoting very large amounts of money to restore the confidence of the public, protect deposits and reestablish the flows of interbank loans.

2) The European Union has also taken a leading role on the world stage by calling for stronger international cooperation and setting an example and showing to the world what concrete actions can be taken.

3) I want to reaffirm our commitment to continue to work closely with China to

build a stronger economic relationship and to build a stronger framework for cooperation on global economic issues.

4) China and the United States are both now sources of strength for the global economy, and we are moving toward the more balanced, and complementary growth strategies that are so important for the world.

5) We need to work together, in a spirit of reciprocity, to eliminate obstacles preventing the access, in many sectors, of European goods and services to the Chinese market.

(2) 汉英口译。

1) 亚洲许多国家发展水平总体较低，区域内各国发展差距仍然很大，资源环境制约日益加剧，地区安全稳定存在挑战，发展的道路并非平坦。

2) 新的形势下，需要各国继续加强磋商与合作，推动全球贸易自由化、投资便利化，反对各种形式的保护主义。

3) 从战略高度考虑彼此关系，求同存异，寻求利益最大交汇点，是各方根本利益和长远利益所在。

4) 加快转变经济发展方式是中国"十二五"发展的主线，经济结构战略性调整是转方式的主攻方向，扩大内需是结构调整的首要任务，城镇化是中国内需最大的潜力所在。

5) 我们坚持实行更加积极主动的开放战略，实行出口和进口并重，利用外资和对外投资并举，有重点地扩大进口、促进对外贸易平衡发展，努力提高开放型经济发展水平。

3. 段落口译

(1) 英汉口译。

Paragraph 1

In the last month we have witnessed a financial crisis on a scale not seen for many decades. We have seen stock-markets plummet and banks taken over by national governments. Hard-earned savings have disappeared; well-known institutions have ceased to exist overnight. The financial crisis has shown how interdependent we have become. What began as a seemingly isolated issue with sub-prime loans in the United States a year ago gradually spread, showing once again that in the world economy of today, markets and investments know no boundaries. The handling of the crisis has demonstrated that we need more and better long term coordination to ensure transparency and confidence in the market. In order to cushion the impact of the financial crisis on the real economy, we also need to sustain domestic demand and to further promote international trade. Here China's contribution to world economic activity is crucial. We believe that this crisis was not only about the problems of some financial institutions. The crisis also shows the risks of some macroeconomic imbalances and point to problems with the fundamentals of the global economy.

Paragraph 2

This greater interdependence is not limited to the financial sector. The new challenges of today are global in nature and therefore, they demand a global response. This applies to issues such as climate change, energy security, terrorism prevention, trafficking and organized crime. We can no longer meet these challenges by closing the door and simply looking after our own house. Instead, we must reach out and seek cooperation, wherever cooperation is more effective. The world is currently witnessing the broadest and deepest wave of globalization ever producing great opportunities but also some risks. Globalization has helped hundreds of millions from poverty and provided businesses with the possibility to invest and expand abroad. But those same businesses know that they can no longer live on past achievements. Workers around the world fear for their jobs. Globalization increases competition and exposes weaknesses and poor commercial decisions.

(2) 汉英口译。

段落1

我们高兴地看到，在两国政府和工商界共同努力下，中爱双边经贸合作一直保持良好发展势头。据中方统计，2011年双边贸易额达到58.7亿美元，比上年增长8.6%。中国已连续5年成为爱尔兰在亚洲的第一大贸易伙伴，爱尔兰对华贸易已连续3年保持顺差，2011年顺差额超过15亿美元。截至2011年底，爱尔兰在中国投资项目累计已达241个，实际投资6.41亿美元。中国对爱尔兰投资虽然起步稍晚，但发展势头迅猛，目前实际投资已达1.48亿美元。不断扩大的双边经贸合作，给两国和两国人民带来了实实在在的利益，也增进了双方交流，加深了彼此友谊。

段落2

中美经济相互依存，高度互补，拥有广泛的共同利益。虽然两国国情各异，发展阶段不同，软硬实力差距很大，但均面临转方式、调结构的艰巨任务。中国正在实施"十二五"规划，坚持科学发展，努力实现速度与结构、质量、效益相统一。美国也在加快结构性改革，实施出口倍增计划和"选择美国倡议"。双方应当充分发挥经济对话的平台作用，加强经贸、投资、金融、旅游、科技、基础设施、清洁能源等各领域合作，推动两国地方、企业等各层面合作全面发展。

4. 对话口译

A: 骆大使，首先，感谢您接受我们的采访，我们也借此机会欢迎您再次来到中国。

B: Thank you! I am honored to be here today with all my good friends at the American Chamber of Commerce in South China. And I am delighted to be back here in my new role as US Ambassador to China and I look forward to coming back often.

A: 广州美领馆一直与华美商会保持良好的合作关系,您怎么看待两者之间的合作?

B: Consul General Brian Goldbeck has told me about the robust, cooperative partnership the Consulate enjoys with AmCham South China. And I know that AmCham South China's support and partnership have been a critical component in making the Consulate's Foreign Commercial office No. 1 globally in generating export successes for US firms. And we hope that you will also visit us in Beijing whenever possible: to offer your ideas and your perspectives on trade and investment initiatives, and how we can move the US-China relationship forward.

A: 那么,您如何看待中美之间的经贸关系呢?

B: As I said last month in Beijing, the US-China economic and trade relationship is of immense importance to both countries and indeed to the entire world. Three years after the financial crisis, the global economy has yet to return to full strength. And too many people back home in America are still looking for jobs. It's times like these when leadership really matters — and as the two largest economies in the world, the United States and China must step up.

A: 众所周知,您的祖父于19世纪90年代离开台山前往美国,几年后,他回到台山成家立业,后来他回到华盛顿州工作,寄钱回中国养家,直至把家人接到美国。所以此行对您应该有特别的意义吧?

B: Yes, when I was elected governor of Washington State, I moved into the Governor's residence, which was only one mile away from where my grandfather used to work washing dishes and sweeping floors. We joked that it took the Locke family one hundred years to move that one single mile. Though I am here to represent the United States and the American people, I have always been proud of my Chinese heritage. I feel doubly fortunate to say both those things.

A: 非常感谢您接受我们的采访。谢谢!

B: Thank you!

(美国驻华大使骆家辉专访,节选)

5. 篇章口译

(1) 英汉口译。

During the same period, the world has witnessed China's spectacular development.

Hundreds of millions have been lifted from the infernal cycle of poverty and underdevelopment, and today China can look to her future with confidence and pride.

Since its beginnings, the EU has actively supported China's opening up and reform policy. We have opened European markets and our companies helped your economic revitalization and employment in China, as well as by transferring technology and know-how through our investments. We have an active and vibrant European business community in China.

We have developed cooperation in all fields: from scientific research to education, from energy to the environment, from transportation to tourism, and in many other areas. We have supported China's accession to the WTO and have welcomed China's increasingly important role in various international organizations. In other words, we have demonstrated through our policies and actions, our interest in and support for your stability, prosperity and success. We will continue to engage in China's development, just as we wish for China itself to become more and more engaged in global affairs, in a way that reflects China's growing global position.

Our bilateral dialogue on human rights serves the same purpose. In this important year when we celebrate the 60th anniversary of the UN Universal Declaration of Human Rights, it is imperative to redouble our efforts in ensuring that all human beings are born free and equal in dignity and rights. Human rights are universal; they belong to each and every individual around the world. I hope you — the people of the great nation of China — will join us in celebrating the 60th anniversary and contribute to the spreading and consolidation of human rights.

The trend towards a more multi-lateral world is getting clearer. It is positive that other nations are ready and willing to take on global responsibilities.

The case for increased cooperation between China and EU is stronger than ever. Together, the EU and China can contribute to solving the problems the world is facing.

Relations between China and the EU are good and dynamic. Together, we have developed a strategic partnership in which we cooperate on numerous issues. We are currently elaborating a partnership and cooperation agreement, to better reflect how our relations have developed and to boost those relations for the future.

People-to-people exchanges have increased. Our bilateral trade has grown. Today China is the most important source of imports for the EU, and the EU is China's largest trading partner. Our political, economic and people-to-people contacts have increased exponentially over the last decade.

(*Excerpted from the speech by EU Commission President Jose Manuel Barroso at*

China National School of Administration on October 23, 2008)

(2) 汉英口译。

尊敬的默克尔总理，

女士们，先生们：

今天有机会同中德工商界朋友相聚，共商经贸合作大计，我感到很高兴。我对峰会的召开表示热烈祝贺，对致力于中德友好合作的各界人士表示崇高敬意！

今年是中德建交40周年，这是值得纪念的大事。建交之前，笼罩世界的"冷战"阴霾阻隔了中德之间的正常交往，双方的接触要通过第三方进行，人员往来也要绕道香港，那时开展经贸合作的困难是当代人难以想象的。1972年，中德领导人顺应时代潮流和人民意愿，跨越"冷战"鸿沟，排除各种干扰，开启了长期封闭的中德关系大门，成功架起了一座通往友谊与合作的桥梁。

40年来，在双方的共同努力下，中德关系经受住了国际风云变幻的考验，总体保持顺利发展，逐步进入成熟、健康、稳定发展的轨道。目前，双方的合作正处于最广泛、最活跃、最富有成果的时期。

政治上，两国高层互访频繁，政治互信加深。2010年，两国关系提升为战略伙伴关系。去年6月，我率10多位部长访问德国，参加首轮中德政府磋商。这是中国第一次同外国政府建立类似机制，是中德关系史上的一个里程碑。

经济上，中德是重要合作伙伴。双方经贸合作无论在广度还是深度上，都走在中欧合作的前列。建交之初，中德贸易额仅有2.7亿美元，2011年达到1691亿美元，占中国与欧盟贸易总额的三成。德国在中国设立企业7500多家，累计投资185亿美元。德国是中国自欧洲引进技术最多的国家，合作金额超过500亿美元。

人文上，双方在科技、教育、文化、旅游等领域的合作硕果累累。德国是中国最重要的远程客源市场之一，也是欧盟首个中国公民组团出境旅游目的地，2011年双方互访游客都超过50万人次。两国共有69对友好城市，有500多所高校建立了校际联系。

回首过去，中德两国携手走过了40年不平凡的历程，留下了光辉的足迹。展望未来，我们将更加坚定地站在一起，做南北对话和共同发展的典范。我相信，有见识、有作为的两国工商界人士，一定会抢抓机遇，乘势而上，奋力开创中德战略伙伴关系新局面，共同开辟一条大国之间互利共赢的光明之路！

谢谢大家！

（2012年4月23日，国务院总理温家宝在中德工商峰会上的致辞，节选）

3.7.4 词语拓展

产值　　　　　　　　　　　　　　output value

道琼斯工业平均指数	the Dow Jones industrial average
改善经济环境	improve economic environment
股息，红利	dividend, bonus stock
股本	capital stock
股东	stockholders
鼓励	give incentive to
国有股减持	state stock reduction
国民生产总值	GNP (Gross National Product)
恒生指数	the Hang Seng index
宏观控制	exercise macro-control
积极的财政政策	proactive fiscal measures
技术密集型经济	technology-intensive economy
解放生产力	liberate/unshackle/release the productive forces
举措	move
控股	become the majority shareholder/take a controlling stake
扩大内需	expand domestic demand
劳动密集型经济	labour-intensive economy
贸易管制	restraint of trade
贸易逆差	trade deficit
贸易顺差	trade surplus
牛市	bull market
期货市场	futures market
企业个体	business entity
人均国民生产总值	per capita GNP
实行股份制	enforce stockholding system
实在的	tangible
输入活力	bring vigor into
所得税	income tax
通货紧缩	deflation
通货膨涨	inflation
投入	input
外汇储备	foreign exchange reservers
稳健的货币政策	steady monetary policies
熊市	bear market

询盘	inquiry
优化经济结构	optimize the economic structure
预调微调	preset and fine-tune
与去年同期数字相比的	year-on-year
增值税	value-added tax
债权人	creditor
整顿市场秩序	rectify the market order
证券交易委员会	Securities and Exchange Commission
知识经济	knowledge-based economy
最低生活保障系统	a minimum living standard system

3.7.5 厚积薄发

学习口译的同学在遇到经贸商务这种需要较多专题知识的话题时，一般是不求甚解，译前准备的内容往往是一些专业术语，而对于术语的真正所指却不甚了了。

仅仅具备专业词汇，而不去考究专题知识，这样的做法在口译当中会让译员处于相当被动的地位。当说话人试图解释某一术语时，若译员此时早已具备相关的专业知识，那么承受的压力自然会小很多，因为说话人所解释的内容在译员脑中早有储备，只需稍微加工即可产出。若仅记住了术语对应的译文，那么译员则只能聚精会神地听讲话人说出的每一个单词，重新组织后才能产出。这对于原本已经绷紧的神经，无疑是雪上加霜。

对专题知识的深刻了解不仅能减轻译员的负担，同时也能让译员应对更加灵活，口头表达更多样化，且能说出"行话"。例如在经济危机爆发时，几乎每场与经济相关的活动都会提到"Financial Crisis"，在一些稍微专业的会议中，译员会发现行家的用语不仅仅局限于单一词汇，他们会用上诸如"Subprime Mortgage Crisis"，"economic downturn"或"depression"等专业词汇，也会使用如"financial tsunami"或"tornado"等形象生动的词汇。对于专题知识有深刻了解的译员，便能理解这些"花样繁多"的表达所指的其实都是经济危机。译员在翻译时若在自己的产出中也使用这类行家们熟悉的词汇，便能让他们更快地理解自己的翻译，何乐而不为。

值得注意的是，专题知识的积累并不能完全依靠临时抱佛脚。短期记忆固然重要，但是长期记忆也不容忽视。在日常生活中遇到相关的术语，不能不求甚解，应刨根问底，并注重平日的累积。

3.8 政治外交

3.8.1 背景阅读

China's Foreign Policy

Since the inauguration of the PRC on October 1, 1949, the Chinese government has been ready to establish diplomatic relations with all foreign governments which are willing to observe the principles of equality, mutual benefit and respect for each other's territorial integrity and sovereignty. But any country seeking to establish diplomatic relations with China must show its readiness to sever all diplomatic relations with the Taiwan authorities and recognize the government of the PRC as the sole legal government of China.

China pursues an independent and peaceful foreign policy directed toward peace, which has the following major components:

— Adhering to independence. In international affairs, China shall decide its own stand according to the rights and wrongs of an affair, shall never yield to pressure from any big countries, and shall not form alliances with any major power or group of nations.

— Safeguarding world peace. China shall neither take part in any arms race, nor engage in military expansion. China shall adhere to opposing hegemonism, power politics and aggressive expansion in any form; and adhere to opposing the infringement by any country on other countries' sovereignty and territorial integrity or interfering in other countries' internal affairs on the excuse of ethnic, religious or human rights issues.

— Establishing friendly and cooperative relations. China is willing to establish and develop friendly and cooperative relations with all countries on the basis of the following five principles: mutual respect for sovereignty and territorial integrity, mutual non-aggression, non-interference in each other's internal affairs, equality and mutual benefit, and peaceful coexistence.

— Developing good-neighborly relations. China actively develops friendly relations with its surrounding countries, safeguards the peace and stability of the region, and promotes economic cooperation at the regional level. China maintains that the disputes concerning borders, territory and territorial waters left over by history be solved through dialogues and talks so as to seek fair and reasonable solutions. If a dispute cannot be solved right away, it may be put aside for the time being, and common ground be sought while reserving differences. An unsolved dispute should not affect normal relations between the relevant countries

— Strengthening unity and cooperation with developing countries. China has consistently attached great importance to developing all-round friendly and cooperative relations with the Third World countries, actively seeking mutually complementary economic, trade, scientific and technological cooperative channels, strengthening consultation and cooperation with them on international issues, and jointly safeguarding the rights and interests of developing countries.

— Opening to the outside world. China opens to developed countries as well as to developing countries. On the basis of equality and mutual benefit, China actively conducts extensive international cooperation to promote common development.

Acting in accordance with the above-mentioned principles, China established diplomatic relations with 19 countries in the 19 months between October 1949 and May 1951. Japan, the United States and other Western countries joined a great number of Third World countries in establishing diplomatic relations with China, raising the total number of countries having diplomatic relations with China to 121 by the end of 1979. In the 1980s, even more countries in Asia, Africa, Latin America and Oceania established diplomatic relations with China. Since the beginning of the 1990s, China has established diplomatic relations with still more countries, such as Israel, the Republic of Korea and South Africa, as well as with the newly independent republics that emerged from the former Soviet Union. By the end of 1999, 161 countries had diplomatic relations with China.

(http：//www.fmprc.gov.cn/eng/ljzg/zgjk/3575/t17823.shtml)

3.8.2 口译精讲

1. 英汉口译
（1）词语必备。

Diaoyutai guest house	钓鱼台国宾馆
zero-sum competition	零和竞争
gunpowder	火药
realm	领域
ancestral	祖先的，祖传的

(2) 口译课文。

President Chen, faculty and students of Beijing Foreign Studies University:

Thank you for inviting me here today. It is truly an honor to be here, and I congratulate you on celebrating your 70th anniversary. The start of a school year marks a new beginning for students. And so it's fitting that I'm here to talk about a new beginning of my own. When I first attended college in 1968, a gathering like this would not have been possible — because America did not even have an ambassador in Beijing. For 40 years, our two countries have been increasing our cooperation and interconnectedness for a very simple reason: It is in our mutual interest. Millions of jobs are sustained in China and the United States by the trade we do with one another. Similarly, the United States and China share an interest in maintaining peace and prosperity around the world.

I recently visited the Diaoyutai guest house where four wood panels illustrate the Chinese contributions that defined the world for centuries: the compass, gunpowder, papermaking and the printing press. And in the United States, we take great pride in our contributions — such as the light bulb, the television, the personal computer, and the Internet, which has changed all of our lives so profoundly. From the flash of gunpowder to the light of electricity, from the printed page to a webpage, from navigating the waters of the globe to navigating the Internet, our two nations have contributed so much to the world of today. That's why I reject the notion that China and the United States are engaged in a zero-sum competition, where one side must fall for the other to rise. We can and must achieve security and prosperity together.

In the 1890s, my grandfather first left his ancestral village near Jiangmen City for America. A hundred years later, I was elected the Governor of Washington State, becoming the first Asian-American governor on the US mainland. I've sometimes asked myself: How did the Locke family go in just two generations from living in a small rural village in China to the governor's mansion? The answer is American openness. America was open to my grandfather and millions of other immigrants like him, coming to its shores to pursue a better life. And the America I was raised in was open to new ideas, where I was allowed to think what I wanted to think and say what I wanted to say…to join organizations that could question or challenge American government policy. Our family's story is the story of America.

I believe the economic and cultural opening that began with Deng Xiaoping has led to a China that is fairer, freer, and more prosperous, respected, and successful. I hope this opening will continue and accelerate. I hope the opening will continue in other realms of Chinese life as well.

By the very nature of your study of different languages and cultures, you're opening your minds to a world of possibilities. In the years ahead, as you become the leaders and entrepreneurs and artists who shape China, I hope you will stay open, and encourage the same sensibility among your countrymen and women. We know that a more open China will lead to a stronger China and a more prosperous China. And more transparency in the US-China relationship will help us further increase the US-China cooperation, improve mutual understanding, and deepen our relationship. I look forward to working with you, China's leaders and the Chinese people on finding new ways to cooperate and continuing to advance our relationship to meet the challenges not only of today, but of tomorrow as well.

Thank you.

(*Excerpted from the speech by the US Ambassador to China Gary Locke in Beijing Foreign Studies University on September 9, 2011*)

（3）参考译文。

陈校长，北京外国语大学的全校师生们：

感谢你们今天的邀请，我感到非常荣幸，同时我要对贵校70周年校庆表示祝贺。新学年的开始，对学生来说标志着一个新的起点，因此在这里谈一谈我自己的新开始也非常适合。1968年在我刚上大学的时候，这样的聚会是不可能的——因为当时美国甚至还没有驻北京大使。40年过去了，我们两国不断加强彼此的合作和联系，理由非常简单：我们拥有共同的利益。中美之间的贸易为两国创造了数百万份工作。同样的，在维护世界和平与繁荣方面，中美两国同样拥有共同利益。

最近我参观了钓鱼台国宾馆，那里有四幅木版画，展现了中国数百年来对世界发展作出的贡献：指南针、火药、造纸术及印刷术。在美国，我们为我们的贡献而感到自豪，比如电灯、电视、个人电脑以及深刻地改变了我们生活方方面面的互联网。从火药引爆的闪光到电力带来的光明，从印刷纸页到网页，从引领全球的航线到引领因特网的发展，我们两国为当今世界作出了巨大的贡献。正因为如此，我不同意这样的说法，即中美两国处于零和竞争，一方的崛起必然导致另一方的衰落。我们可以也必须共同实现安全和繁荣。

19世纪90年代，我的祖父离开他的家乡，江门市附近的一个小村庄，来到美国。100年后，我被选为华盛顿州州长，成为美国本土首位亚裔州长。有时我会问自己：骆家是如何在仅仅两代人的时间里，从中国的一个小村庄迁入美国州长官邸的呢？答案就是美国的开放。美国向我的祖父以及数以百万像他一样来到美国口岸、追求更好生活的移民开放。养育我的美国对新思想开放，我可以在这里想我所想，畅所欲言……甚至加入能够质疑和挑战美国政府政策的组织。我的家族史就是美国的发展史。

我相信邓小平所开创的经济文化开放带来了一个更公平、更自由、更繁荣、更受尊重和更成功的中国。我希望中国能够继续开放，并加快速度。我也希望开放能够渗入中国人民生活中的其他领域。

你们学习不同语言和不同文化，其实就是在向一个充满各种可能性的世界敞开心胸。在未来的岁月中，当你们成为影响中国的领导人、企业家或艺术家时，我希望你们保持这种开放性，并鼓励你们的同胞们这样做。我们知道，一个更加开放的中国将变得更加强大和繁荣。增加中美关系的透明度将有助于加强双方的合作，促进相互了解，深化两国关系。我期待与你们、中国领导人和中国人民团结协作，寻找新的合作途径，继续推进两国关系向前发展，以迎接今天还有未来的挑战。

谢谢！

（4）口译点津

1）Millions of jobs are sustained in China and the United States by the trade we do with one another.

在这句话的翻译中，…are sustained 被动句式宜转化为主动结构，符合中文表达习惯，使听众更加容易理解句子的含义。

译文：中美之间的贸易为两国创造了数百万份工作。

2）I recently visited the Diaoyutai guest house where four wood panels illustrate the Chinese contributions that defined the world for centuries.

在这句话的翻译中，译者易将 Diaoyutai guest house 误译为"钓鱼台宾馆"，而其官方说法是"钓鱼台国宾馆"，一字之差，即可看出平日是否重视专有名词的积累及是否对细节给予足够的重视。另外，defined the world for centuries，这里不需要拘泥于原文的结构，把意思译出来，达到"传意"的目的即可，可译为"展现了中国数百年来对世界发展作出的贡献"。

3）From the flash of gunpowder to the light of electricity, from the printed page to a webpage, from navigating the waters of the globe to navigating the Internet, our two nations have contributed so much to the world of today.

这句话的处理中，navigate 一词是难点。译员在翻译时要注意词语的正确搭配，如可把 navigate the waters of the globe 译为"畅游全球水域"，navigate the Internet 译为"畅游互联网"，也可译为"引领全球的航线"和"引领互联网的发展"。

4）That's why I reject the notion that China and the United States are engaged in a zero-sum competition, where one side must fall for the other to rise.

这句话较长，可以采用顺句驱动法。

zero-sum competition 零和博弈（zero game），是博弈论（game theory）中的

术语，意同汉语里的"此消彼长"，即处于竞争关系的双方，一方的增长、发展，必然导致另一方的损失、衰退。

译文：正因为如此，我不同意这样的说法，即中美两国处于零和竞争，一方崛起，另一方必定衰落。

5) I believe the economic and cultural opening that began with Deng Xiaoping has led to a China that is fairer, freer, and more prosperous, respected, and successful.

对于长句，可以灵活处理。既可以按照原文的语序，译为"我相信邓小平先生开创的经济及文化开放已经使中国更加公平，更加自由，更加繁荣，更受尊敬和更加成功"，也可根据中文表达习惯，调整句子结构，译为"我相信邓小平所开创的经济文化开放带来了一个更公平、更自由、更繁荣、更受尊重和更成功的中国"。

2．汉英口译

（1）词汇必备。

中国外交学院	China Foreign Affairs University
自焚	self-immolation
海啸	tsunami
核泄漏	nuclear leaks
包围	encircle
排挤	keep out
斗争和妥协	confrontation and compromise
末日	doomsday
党的"十八大"	the 18th CPC National Congress

（2）口译课文。

秦亚青院长，各位专家学者和媒体朋友们，

大家上午好。

首先，感谢外交学院邀请我出席此次研讨会。

在这里，我想重点就如何看待和理解中国外交谈几点个人看法。

第一，要看到中国外交成就来之不易。今年初，谁也没有想到，一个突尼斯青年自焚，引发西亚、北非这么大的动荡。3月11日，日本发生地震，谁也没想到引发这么大的海啸和核泄漏，到现在影响还未彻底消除。纵观全年，世界出现这么大的动荡，这么复杂的局面，恐怕任何有远见的人都未曾想到。在这种情况下，中国能够保持总体稳定，经济实现较快发展，国际地位显著提高，国际影响进一步扩大，这些成绩来之不易，应该珍惜。

第二，要看到中国外交顺应了世界人民求和平、谋发展、促合作的大势。前几天我听联想老总柳传志说，中国刚刚加入WTO时，大家都很担心，认为"狼来了"。结果我们"入世"10年,"与狼共舞"越舞越好。我们要有自信,只要中国坚持和平发展、开放合作,把自己的事情办好,就没有人能包围我们,排挤我们。

第三,不能简单地用"软"和"硬"来界定中国外交。斗争和妥协都不是外交的目的,也不是评判外交好坏的标准,而只是实现外交目标的方式和选项。这就要求我们该斗争的斗争,该合作的合作,该周旋的周旋。

第四,要看到新形势下做好外交工作并不容易。我们的 GDP 总量已经是世界第二了,但同美欧日相比,中国经济的"蛋糕"还不够大,质量也不够好。中国国情的复杂性导致中国人对本国的认识不一样,对外交的诉求不一样,给外界留下的印象也不一样。何况,我们在外交上还不断遇到许多新情况新问题。

展望明年,世界恐怕不会像电影《2012》描绘的那样进入末日,但国际形势的变化肯定还会很大。中国外交要做好准备,应对好外部经济环境变化和各种风险挑战,为党的"十八大"顺利召开营造良好的外部环境。

最后,感谢各位专家学者、媒体朋友们长期以来对外交工作的支持。我相信,只要我们坚持不懈,共同努力,我国的外交一定会有更大发展,中国的国际地位和影响一定会有更大提高。

祝大家新年好。

(2011年12月18日,外交部部长助理乐玉成在2011年中国外交回顾与展望研讨会上的讲话,节选)

(3)参考译文。

President Qin Yaqing, Ladies and Gentlemen, Friends from the media,

Good morning.

First of all, I would like to extend my gratitude to China Foreign Affairs University for inviting me to this seminar.

I wish to share with you some of my personal views and understanding of China's diplomacy.

Firstly, we must know that the achievements of China's diplomacy are hard-earned. At the beginning of this year, no one would have imagined that the self-immolation of a Tunisian youth would have caused such large scale unrest in West Asia and North Africa. No one would have expected that the earthquake that struck Japan on March 11 would have triggered such a massive tsunami and nuclear leaks, whose impact has not been completely removed up till now. Even far-sighted people would not have anticipated such serious turbulences and complex situations in the year. However, under these circumstances, China was still able to maintain its overall stability, achieve relatively rapid economic growth, and significantly enhance its international standing and influence. These achievements have not come by easily and should be cherished.

Secondly, we must recognize that China's diplomacy is consistent with people's wish for peace, development and cooperation. Several days ago, Mr. Liu Chuanzhi, chairman of Lenovo, told me that people were really worried when China first joined the WTO and they thought there came the wolf. But ten years have passed, and we have got better and better at "dancing with the wolf". We must be confident that as long as China pursues peaceful development, adheres to opening up and cooperation, and attends our own affairs well, nobody can encircle us or push us out.

Thirdly, China's diplomacy cannot be simply labeled as "soft" or "hardline". Confrontation and compromise are not the objectives of diplomacy, nor are they the yardstick for our diplomatic work. They are just means to achieve our diplomatic goals or options we can choose from. This means we must know when to fight, when to cooperate, and when to avoid direct confrontation.

Fourthly, we must be well aware of the difficulties in our diplomatic work in the new world situation. Our GDP has ranked the second largest in the world, but compared with the US, European countries and Japan, the "pie" of the Chinese economy is still not big enough, and its quality needs improvement. China's complicated national conditions lead to people's different understandings and ideas about our country and our diplomacy, therefore leaving different impressions on the rest of the world. Moreover, we have to cope with many new situations and new problems in our diplomatic work.

As for next year, I don't think it will be doomsday for the world as depicted in the movie 2012, but the international situation will undergo great changes. Therefore, we must get ready to properly address changes in the external economic environment and various risks to create a favorable external environment for the 18th CPC National Congress.

Lastly, I wish to thank you, our experts, scholars and friends from the press, for your continued support for our diplomatic work. I believe that as long as we make unremitting efforts together, China's diplomacy will enjoy greater development and China's international standing and influence will witness a further enhancement.

I wish every one of you a happy new year!

(4) 口译点津。

1) 要看到中国外交成就来之不易。

此句中的"来之不易"与"这些成绩来之不易"中的"来之不易"可以译为"hard-won","hard-earned"或"have not come by easily"。译员在平日学习中，要注意积累同一种表达的不同说法，增加口译表达的多样性。

2）日本发生地震，没想到引发这么大的海啸和核泄漏。

动词"引发"在翻译时对应词语的选用有 cause, trigger, initiate, incite, instigate 等。

3）要看到中国外交顺应了世界人民求和平、谋发展、促合作的大势。

文中的第一、二、四点都是以"要看到"的句式开头。语篇中的重复有加强语气的作用，所以翻译时要重现原文结构，建议处理为"we must..."这样的句式。

4）中国刚刚加入WTO时，大家都很担心，认为"狼来了"。结果我们"入世"10年，"与狼共舞"越舞越好。

由于狼在中西方文化中都有"凶残暴虐，易造成威胁、伤害"之意，"狼来了"和"与狼共舞"中的"狼"此处采取直译策略，不仅易于理解，又可以保留原文的生动比喻，因此可译为"there came the wolf"和"dancing with the wolf"。

5）这就要求我们该斗争的斗争，该合作的合作，该周旋的周旋。

这句话的实际含义是"我们要知道什么时候该斗争，什么时候该合作，什么时候该周旋"。所以可以译为：We must know when to fight, when to cooperate, and when to avoid direct confrontation. 其中，"周旋"可用反面着笔法译为"avoid direct confrontation"。

3.8.3 实战演练

1. 口译听解与表达

（1）口译听辨。

Forty years ago, President Nixon paid a historic visit to China, during which our two countries issued the _____ Shanghai Communiqué. With extraordinary strategic vision and political wisdom, the Chinese and American leaders _____ between China and the United States and opened a new chapter in our bilateral relations. I was in my early 20s and was about to go to Britain to study when I heard the news. And I was very excited. That historic event has changed so many things, _____. Forty years have passed since President Nixon's visit to China. Thanks to _____ of both sides, China-US relations have kept moving forward despite some ups and downs over these years. With strong vitality and great potential, our relationship has grown into one of the most important bilateral ties in the world today. _____ and _____ have become a regular feature of the bilateral ties. Over the past 40 years and particularly the past few years, our leaders have maintained close contacts through _____. These high-level contacts have played an irreplaceable part in _____ of our bilateral ties. There are now over 60 bilateral dialogue and consultation mechanisms, including the Strategic and Economic Dialogues and the High-Level Consultation on People-to-People

Exchange. These mechanisms cover _____ and many other fields. Indeed, few other two countries can claim to have so many _____ that cover such diverse fields.

（2）复述练习。

The Russian Prime Minister Vladimir Putin is heading for a comeback as the country's new president after Sunday's elections. Mr Putin claimed victory in front of tens of thousands of cheering supporters outside the Kremlin.

"Dear friends, first, I want to thank all citizens of Russia who took part in today's election for the president of the Russian Federation. Special thanks of course to those who've gathered here today in Moscow and to all those who support us in every corner of our vast homeland. Thanks to all who said yes to a great Russia. I once asked you 'Will we win?' We have won. We won in an open and honest fight."

Partial results suggest his share of the vote was about 60%. Counting is still going on. But an opposition activist said there had been fraud on a vast scale despite the presence of thousands of independent observers and web cameras at polling stations. The Communist Party leader Gennady Zyuganov accused Mr Putin's party of using the might of the state to ensure victory.

"In honest elections, the huge state machine works according to strict observation of the law to ensure a level playing field for all of the candidates. In this case, the whole of our enormous criminal corrupt state machine worked only for one candidate."

（3）公众演讲。

以"中美关系——'零和'？'双赢'？"为题，分别以英语及汉语作3～5分钟的演讲。

2. 单句口译

（1）英汉口译。

1) Every year, the comprehensive Strategic and Economic Dialogue brings together policymakers from across both governments to discuss topics ranging from breaking down trade barriers to economic cooperation to collaborating on pressing regional and global issues.

2) In discussing this issue, with China or any other country, we start from the premise that all people are entitled to the protections contained in the Universal Declaration of Human Rights.

3) Fair competition prompts companies to be more efficient with lower cost goods and helps spur new innovations and products.

4) I will seek to further the economic and commercial ties between the US and China by building our trade relationship in a mutually beneficial manner that reduces

barriers to trade and increases jobs in both our countries.

5) From property rights, to food safety to environmental protection, Chinese citizens are increasingly engaging in a national dialogue that has led to meaningful advances improving the lives of all the people of this country.

(2) 汉英口译。

1) 今年,在党中央、国务院的领导下,我们的全方位外交取得显著成就,进一步提升了我国国际地位和影响。

2) 当前,我国的经济总量已经位居世界第二,在国际事务中的地位和作用举足轻重,各方包括国内民众对中国外交的关注、期待和要求越来越高,外界对中国的发展还存在一些疑虑和误解。

3) 我们坚持不干涉内政原则,尊重地区国家人民的意愿和选择,妥善处理联合国安理会有关决议,同有关国家关系平稳过渡。

4) 希腊发生债务危机,希腊的 GDP 只占欧洲的 2%,本来对于富足发达的欧洲来说不算什么,但也引发了深刻的欧债危机,逆转了世界经济复苏走势。

5) 中国无意也无力在亚太排挤美国,希望美国在亚太发挥建设性作用,包括尊重中方的重大关切和核心利益。

3. 段落口译

(1) 英汉口译。

Paragraph 1

2012 marks the 40th anniversary of the establishment of diplomatic relations between China and Australia. In four decades, remarkable progress has been made in wide ranging exchanges and cooperation, in areas like political relations, economy and trade, science and technology and people-to-people links. China-Australia relations have grown more mature, and fruitful cooperation has brought noticeable benefits to our peoples. And now, I want to use this occasion to focus on development of defense and security relations between China and Australia. First, political mutual trust continues to deepen. China and Australia view each other as an important partner for cooperation. Frequent contacts and interactions have taken place between the two leaderships and foreign and defense departments. Second, strategic-level dialogue mechanisms continue to develop. The bilateral strategic dialogue, launched by the two foreign ministers, has seen three rounds of successful talks. Third, defense and security cooperation continues to expand. Our navy ships exchanged several visits, and Australia is the first western country that carried out live-fire naval exercises with China.

Paragraph 2

Ladies and gentlemen, in 2010, we had the pleasure of welcoming President Hu on his official visit to Canada. In the past two days in Beijing, we had the opportunity to renew our acquaintance, as well as to talk with Premier Wen, Chairman Wu and Vice Premier Li. I am encouraged by our discussions, encouraged that in this time of both great opportunity and risk in the global economy, our two great countries can cooperate for the mutual benefit of our peoples. Now some will observe that, despite all that has been accomplished, much work remains to be done if we are to truly maximize the real potential of this relationship. That is true, and it is why we are here, but I will also say this: the future of our relationship is laden with promise.

(2) 汉英口译。

段落1

巴基斯坦山河壮美，资源丰富，文化底蕴深厚。这片古老而神奇的土地孕育了灿烂的文明。巴基斯坦人民善良淳朴、勤劳勇敢，有着坚忍不拔、自强不息的精神。建国60多年来，巴基斯坦政府和人民克服重重困难，主要依靠自己的力量，在建设国家和发展经济的道路上取得了显著成就。当前，巴基斯坦正处于一个关键时期，面临不少困难和挑战。巴基斯坦政府和人民没有退却。英雄的巴基斯坦人民一定能够渡过难关，迎来希望，实现新的发展。我对此深信不疑。中国政府和人民将坚定地与你们站在一起，同舟共济，共克时艰！

段落2

中非友谊源远流长。进入新世纪，中非关系全面、快速、深入发展。中非合作论坛、中非新型战略伙伴关系的建立和发展，极大地推动了双方在政治、经贸、人文等各领域的交流与合作。中非政治互信更加牢固，利益联系更加紧密，人民友谊更加深厚。中国始终是非洲的好朋友、好伙伴、好兄弟，不断巩固和加强中非团结合作，促进共同进步发展，是中国对外政策的重要基石，也是中方长期、坚定的战略选择。展望未来，中方将一如既往地与非方并肩携手，为非洲和世界的和平与发展事业作出更大贡献。

4. 对话口译

A: Vice President Xi, thank you for receiving this interview. As you will be on an official visit for Ireland tomorrow, could you tell me your purpose of this visit?

B: 这次我应肯尼总理邀请对爱尔兰进行正式访问，主要是同爱尔兰领导人就中爱关系深入交换意见，进一步加深两国友谊，推动务实合作，使两国关系向更高水平迈进。

A: So how do you think of the China-Ireland relations and the future development of bilaterall cooperation?

B: 中爱建交30多年来，始终坚持相互尊重、平等相待。中爱在制度上、文化上都有一些差异，但这些差异并没有影响到我们的交往与合作。中爱在经贸上互利共赢。中爱在人文等领域的交流合作也取得丰硕成果。中方看好中爱合作前景，我们期待着同爱尔兰在携手发展过程中继续相互支持、彼此借鉴、共同进步。

A: Recently, some think that the EU has become less important because of its sovereign debt crisis. What do you think?

B: 目前欧盟虽然遇到一些困难和挑战，但欧盟在克服困难、战胜危机、维护和推进欧洲一体化成果方面有着高度的政治共识。我们相信，欧洲的困难是暂时的，欧盟和欧洲各国政府和人民有能力、有智慧、有办法解决主权债务问题，实现经济复苏和增长。

A: So do you think China's development will provide more opportunities to the world?

B: 中国的发展仍处于重要战略机遇期，在较长时期内继续保持经济平稳较快发展仍具备不少有利条件。特别是未来5年，中国进口总额将达8万亿美元，每年对外投资将超过1000亿美元。这将给世界带来更大的市场、更多的机遇和更广阔的合作空间。中国是包括爱尔兰在内的欧洲各国应对危机、实现复苏可以借重的力量，是在国际多边事务中可以信赖的合作伙伴。

A: Thank you for receiving our interview. Thanks very much.

B: 谢谢。

（2012年2月18日，国家副主席习近平接受《爱尔兰时报》采访，节选）

5. 篇章口译

（1）英汉口译。

Distinguished Guests,

Ladies and Gentlemen,

It is my great pleasure to join you at this gracious dinner hosted by the 48 Group Club to celebrate the Chinese New Year and the Lantern Festival.

According to Chinese tradition, the Lantern Festival is the last day of the Chinese New Year celebration. As we ring out the Year of the Tiger and ring in the Year of the Rabbit, let me share with you my thoughts about 2010 and hopes for 2011.

2010 was a memorable year, or "exceptional" as the Chinese leaders put it. As I saw it, 2010 was about momentous successes, tough challenges and joyous moments. For China, the biggest success was that we not only weathered the impact of the international financial crisis, but continued steady and fast economic growth. We took major steps to restructure our economy and have now become the second largest in the world. We made active efforts to improve people's living standards and social services. We withstood the tests of the Yushu earthquake in Qinghai Province and the mudslide in Zhouqu, Gansu Province. Our joy came from the success of the Shanghai World Expo and the Guangzhou Asian Games. Both events have presented a confident, open, inclusive and modern China to the world.

The Lantern Festival is also a special day for me, because I arrived in London as the new Chinese Ambassador on the Lantern Festival last year. This has been quite a year for me. I am truly glad and grateful that China-UK relations are in such a good shape today. This wouldn't have been possible without your support and the support of other friends in the UK.

We have seen closer political ties. These included Prime Minister Cameron's successful visit to China with a senior delegation, including Mr Huhne. Our leaders worked closely together at the G20 summits. The recent visit by Vice Premier Li Keqiang to Britain was another success, keeping up the good momentum for the growth of our relations.

We have seen fruitful cooperation across the board. Our trade in goods hit a record of over 50 billion US dollars in 2010, and a goal was set to double this figure in the next 5 years. Britain's spectacular performance at the Shanghai World Expo has enabled the Chinese public to see and experience what Britain is like today. I am also pleased to find that there is an emerging "mandarin fever" here. More and more people started to learn mandarin, whether as college students, primary school children or adults wanting to learn for business or just pleasure. Of course there is a huge potential to tap, if you look at the number of Chinese learning English — 400 million. Cultural exchanges have been robust. Just 10 days ago, half a million people enthusiastically attended the Trafalgar Square Chinese New Year Celebrations. I also had the pleasure of witnessing the signing of an agreement on joint research, which will soon bring two lovely giant pandas to Edinburgh Zoo.

An ever growing China-UK relationship counts on the support of people from all sectors. I take this opportunity to express my heartfelt thanks and deep appreciation to the 48 Group Club for its outstanding contribution to this relationship. I wish the 48 Group Club continued success in the Year of the Rabbit, under Stephen's leadership.

Thank you.

(*Excerpted from the keynote speech by H. E. Ambassador Liu Xiaoming at the Icebreakers Chinese New Year Dinner on February 17, 2011*)

(2) 汉英口译

苏西洛总统，各位同事：

我很高兴再次来到美丽的巴厘岛，与东盟及日、韩领导人共商东亚合作发展大计。

这些年，东盟一体化取得重要进展。东亚国家加强合作，共谋发展，成功应对国际金融危机，保持了经济较快增长和金融稳定，地区经济融合进一步加深。东盟与中日韩10+3合作为此发挥了重要作用。在外部环境不利的情况下，我们要采取更加有力的措施，增强凝聚力和发展动力，通过进一步深化合作提高抵御风险的能力和整体竞争力，在世界格局的变化中占据主动位置。

下面，我谈几点意见：

第一，加快推进本地区贸易自由化和便利化。今年8月，中日共同提出加速推进东亚自贸区和东亚全面经济伙伴关系建设的倡议。中方愿在充分尊重东盟中心地位、循序渐进、兼顾各方关切的基础上，务实推进，希望得到各方支持。

第二，进一步提升区域财金合作水平。10+3财金合作取得显著成果，前景广阔。建议下一阶段着力提高《清迈倡议》多边化协议有效性，在危机救助功能基础上拓展危机防范功能；推动储备库资金由当前分散管理实现实际汇集，更好发挥储备库资金作用；增强10+3宏观经济研究办公室的经济监测能力；积极推动亚洲债券市场建设，促进本币债券发行，使亚洲储蓄更多投资于本地区，投资于实体经济，为东亚经济发展服务。

第三，加大对东亚互联互通建设的投入。中日韩三国要加强协调，形成合力，发挥在资金、技术和人力上的优势，更好地支持《东盟互联互通总体规划》的实施，促进东亚互联互通，为推进东亚一体化建设打下基础。

第四，促进地区经济发展方式转变和可持续发展。10+3机制要加强在科技、新能源、节能环保等领域合作，为各国特别是东亚发展中国家实现可持续发展提供支持和帮助。

各位同事，

东亚合作处于发展的关键阶段，坚持东盟主导，突出发展、互利、共赢的主题，继续以10+3为主渠道推进东亚一体化建设，符合各国的共同利益。明年是10+3合作进程启动15周年，我们要以15周年为契机，进一步坚定信心，团结协作，推动10+3合作达到更高水平。

谢谢。

(2011年11月18日，国务院总理温家宝在第十四次东盟与中日韩（10+3）领导人会议上的讲话，节选)

3.8.4　词语拓展

霸权	hegemony
不结盟	non-alignment
边境、领土争端	border or territorial disputes
重温旧情，结交新友	renew old friendship and establish new contacts

大使/大使馆	ambassador/embassy
地区动乱（冲突）	regional turmoil (conflicts)
独立自主的和平外交政策/独立自主原则	independent foreign policy of peace/principles of independence
多极世界	multipolar world
符合，与……一致	accord with, agree with, conform to, meet, correspond to…
复杂多变的国际形势	a complex and volatile international situation
干涉	intervene in/interfere in (interference)
高级官员	senior officials
各国人民的福祉	well-being of all nations
给……的历史增加了新的一页	add a new page to the history of…
和平共处	peaceful coexistence
互利合作伙伴	partners of mutual benefit and cooperation
回顾过去，展望未来	look back on the past and look into the future
建设性的战略合作伙伴关系	a constructive strategic partnership
扩大共识	expand the common ground
礼尚往来	reciprocity in courtesy, reciprocal (mutual) courtesy
两岸关系	cross-strait relations
民族、宗教矛盾	ethnic or religious contradictions
民不聊生	anguish in poverty and starvation
民间外交	people-to-people diplomacy
内忧外患	domestic disturbance and foreign invasion
排外主义	exclusivism
排除干扰与障碍	remove interferences and obstacles
起积极作用	make positive contribution to
求同存异	seek common ground while reserving/shelving/putting aside differences
权利顺利平稳过渡	smooth transition of power
认真履行国际义务	earnestly fulfill international obligations
深厚底蕴	profound richness
深切哀悼	convey one's profound condolence to
审时度势	size up the situation

坦诚深入的	candid and in-depth
条约，宣言，公告，协议	treaty, declaration, proclamation, agreement
推动睦邻友好关系	promote good-neighbor relationships between... and ...
外部封锁	external blockade
为大众谋利	seek a common good
文明古国	an ancient civilization
详细谈论	elaborate on
以史为鉴，面向未来	take history as guidance and look into the future
永不屈服	never yielding
种族隔离	apartheid/racial segregation
主权和领土完整	sovereignty and territorial integrity

3.8.5 厚积薄发

"押头韵"作为一种修辞手法，是指相邻或邻近词语的字头发音相同。由于特殊的语音构成，它的使用可以产生极强的节奏感和韵律感。

"押头韵"常出现于文学领域，较为典型的例子如 Pride and Prejudice（《傲慢与偏见》），The Prince and the Pauper（《王子与贫儿》）。在外交口译乃至普通口译中，适当运用此手法，也可为译文增色不少。以下为在外交口译中较常出现的运用"押头韵"的词组：

consultation and cooperation	协商与合作
first and foremost	首先
guts and glory	勇气与荣耀
peace and prosperity	和平与繁荣
public and private	公共与私人的
safe and sound	安然无恙
security and stability	安全与稳定
through thick and thin	同甘共苦
weal and (or) woe	福与（或）祸
with might and main	全力以赴

第4章 口译培训

本章主要介绍内地翻译专业硕士（MTI）院校、港台口译专业院校、国外口译教育机构及国内主要口译资格水平考试。

北京外国语大学高级翻译学院

北京外国语大学（以下简称"北外"）高级翻译学院成立于1994年，其前身为1979年设立的联合国译员训练部（班），为联合国组织和国内各机构共培养了500余名专业翻译人才。北外高级翻译学院在翻译人才培养方面具备优良传统和卓越成绩，在社会上享有广泛的声誉，同联合国机构和其他国际组织保持着密切关系。

学院每年招收硕士学位研究生。专业包括英汉同声传译、复语同声传译（法/德/俄/西/韩/泰+英汉）和MTI（翻译硕士）。高级翻译学院提供的口笔译培训课程享誉全球，一方面是因为其提供的教学保持着很高的质量；另一方面则因为该课程培养出来的学生在国内外就业市场均极具竞争力。高级翻译学院的课程包括会议口译（交替传译和同声传译）、笔译、视译和翻译研究，完成学业的学生授予硕士和博士学位。高级翻译学院开设的口笔译硕士学位课程包括中、英、德、法、俄五种语言，同时还开设了翻译和语言对比研究博士学位课程，其中硕士研究生课程学习年限为两年，博士研究生课程学习年限为3～4年。

详见：http://gsti.bfsu.edu.cn/

上海外国语大学高级翻译学院

上海外国语大学高级翻译学院于2003年4月18日在上海外国语大学成立。2003年12月，中国第一个翻译学学位点在上海外国语大学高级翻译学院设立，这是我国内地高等院校在外国语言文学专业下建立的第一个独立的翻译学学位点（二级学科），这也标志着我国内地高等院校在翻译学学科和学位点建设方面进入了一个新的阶段。

2005年11月，上海外国语大学高级翻译学院获得了国际会议口译员协会（AIIC）的最高评级；2007年，上海外国语大学高级翻译学院成为首批国务院学位委员会批准的15所翻译硕士专业学位（MTI）培养单位中少数能兼招笔译（MT）和口译（MI）的高等学院。2009年12月，上海外国语大学高级翻译学院正式成为国际高校翻译学院联合会（CIUTI）会员单位，其所设置的口译方面的硕士课程包括会议口译专业及翻译硕士专业学位口译方向。会议口译专业作为国家"十五"、"211"重点项目于 2003 年设立在上海外国语大学高级翻译学院，是全国唯一由教育部专项拨款建设的同声传译教学基地。翻译硕士专业口译方向旨在培养专业口译人员而建立的，培养具有国际水准的、能胜任各种重大国际交往场合的专业口译员。

详见：http：//giit.shisu.edu.cn/

广东外语外贸大学高级翻译学院

广东外语外贸大学高级翻译学院是一所旨在培养高层次翻译人才的研究型学院。高级翻译学院现设有"翻译实务"专业双学位、本科学位及翻译学硕士学位（设国际会议传译、口笔译研究等研究方向）。

高级翻译学院为全国的翻译从业人员及拟参加全国翻译专业资格证书考试的考生提供培训，特别是定期为本省各主要外事、外经贸单位提供团体翻译人才培训，定期为全国高校的翻译师资，特别是口译教学师资提供培训。

高级翻译学院是国家外文局翻译专业资格考试中心暨中国翻译工作者协会认证的"翻译专业资格考试"指定培训机构。高级翻译学院在读的硕士、博士研究生及本科生参加"全国翻译专业资格证书考试"相应等级的考试，毕业后直接取得由国家权威机构认证的从业资格。

详见：http：//www1.gdufs.edu.cn/sits/gfxy/

香港理工大学

香港理工大学翻译及传意文学硕士课程由香港理工大学中文及双语学系开设，采用两年兼读制或一年半年全日制。课程分研究型和授课型两大方向，研究型硕士为有志修读哲学硕士及博士学位的研究生，以及志愿从事翻译学研究人士提供全面培训；授课型硕士主要针对双语及翻译实务人士的需求而设。

详见：http：//www.cbs.polyu.edu.hk/

台湾辅仁大学

1988 年，台湾辅仁大学成立了台湾的第一个翻译研究所，该校开设的课程有基础视译、进阶视译、口译入门、基础同步口译、进阶同步口译、口笔译实习。通过演练、示范和现场指挥，使学生熟识经贸、科技、环保、国际政治等技术性会议的会前准备和接续口译技巧，培养学生小心求证、力求准确的习惯。

详见：http：//www.gitis.fju.edu.tw/

国立台湾师范大学

国立台湾师范大学翻译研究所是台湾第一所以翻译为研究对象的公立研究所,在翻译专业硕士课程方面,该所分口译、笔译两组,口译组的必修科目包括视译、连续传译、同声传译。除以上科目外,研究所还开设科技口译、经贸口译、政法口译及文史哲口译课程,不仅为学生打下坚实的口译技能基础,并提供丰富的背景知识,使得"术业有专攻",以利于学生平日习得的口译知识及技能能够更好地应用于将来的实践中。

详见:http://www.ntnu.edu.tw/tran/index.html

美国蒙特雷国际研究学院

蒙特雷国际研究学院始建于 1955 年,前身为蒙特雷外语学院。该校在语言和国际政策研究方面蜚声海内外。蒙特雷国际研究学院设有翻译硕士、翻译及本地化管理硕士、翻译及口译硕士及会议口译硕士,旨在培养翻译及口译、语言教学及国际商务方面的专业人才。该研究院是世界上最前沿的翻译和口译专家训练基地,培养最顶级的外交、贸易、科学及商业领域的翻译及口译人才。该学院与巴黎高等翻译学院和英国纽卡斯尔大学翻译学院并称为世界三大顶级翻译学院。

该院的会议口译硕士课程被瑞士日内瓦的国际会议口译员协会(Association Internationale des Interprès de Confénce, AIIC)列为全球最顶尖的 15 个研究生课程之一。

详见:http://www.miis.edu

法国巴黎第三大学高级口笔译学院

巴黎第三大学高级口笔译学院是欧洲历史最悠久的著名的翻译高校之一,是口笔译高等教育机构常设国际会议的创始成员。该院创建于 1957 年,首任校长为著名的口译专家和口语教育家、国际口译工作者的创始人之一、法国国家博士达妮卡·塞莱丝柯维奇(Danica Seleskovitch)教授。该院是巴黎新索邦第三大学下属的一个学院,在校笔译学生 300 人,口译 150 人。

详见:http://www.univ-paris3.fr/

英国巴斯大学

巴斯大学有口译与翻译硕士课程,提供有汉、日、法、德、西、意、俄等多种外语,学生可以选择汉语/英语双向口译和翻译。

巴斯大学口译与翻译硕士课程为有意从事专业口译和翻译的语言学人才而设计,课程已有超过 40 年历史,是欧洲最早提供翻译课程的学校之一,多年来已造就无数翻译专家,在翻译领域居翘楚地位。巴斯大学重视学生的翻译和口译实践，课程以实用为主，并非纯学术理论导向，学生有机会到联合国在欧洲举行的会议进行观摩，英国大学学校还会请来知名的翻译家和口译员进行讲座或者讲课。小班授课。毕业校友在各国从事与语言相关的工作。第一学期，所有学生依照核心课程学习专业翻译、同步口译、连续口译，第二学期可以有更多不同的课程选择，进一步提升专业能力。

详见：http://www.bath.ac.uk/

英国纽卡斯尔大学

纽卡斯尔大学现代语言学院的口译/翻译硕士课程，是英国大学中设有中英/英中翻译历史最悠久的课程。纽卡斯尔大学的现代语言学院是全世界唯一设有从高级文凭、硕士到博士学位课程的大学，为优秀学生提供在翻译及口译的领域内进修和研究的机会。纽卡斯尔的翻译课程为将来有意开拓翻译或口译事业的学生设计了一年或两年的中英/英中翻译/口译硕士学程。

两年课程的第一年是为期9个月的高级翻译文凭（Diploma），接下来是第二年为期12个月的硕士（MA）课程。MA课程中学生可依专长和兴趣选择以下四种不同的领域：MA Translating 翻译硕士、MA Interpreting 口译硕士、MA Translating & Interpreting 翻译及口译硕士，或者 MA Translation Studies 翻译学硕士。同时，在学习期间研究所每年会带队学生自费前往欧盟和联合国参观及学习国际会议口译。

详见：http://www.ncl.ac.uk/postgraduate/subjects/translation

翻译专业资格（水平）考试 CATTI

翻译专业资格（水平）考试（China Accreditation Test for Translators and Interpreters —CATTI）由国家人事部统一规划指导，中国外文局负责翻译专业资格（水平）考试实施管理，人事部人事考试中心负责各语种、各级别笔译考试考务；国家外国专家局培训中心承担各语种、各级别口译考试考务工作，国家外专局培训中心指定的考试单位具体承担口译考务工作全国翻译专业资格（水平）考试。考试共分为四个等级：资深翻译，一级口译、笔译翻译，二级口译、笔译翻译，三级口译、笔译翻译。各级别翻译专业资格（水平）考试均设英、日、俄、德、法、西、阿等语种。各语种、各级别均设口译和笔译考试。

各级别口译考试均设口译综合能力和口译实务两个科目，其中二级口译考试口译实务科目分设"交替传译"和"同声传译"两个专业类别。报名参加二级口译考试的人员，可根据本人情况，选择口译实务科目相应类别的考试。

详见：http://www.catti.cn/

全国外语翻译证书考试（NAETI）

全国外语翻译证书考试（NAETI）是由教育部考试中心与北京外国语大学合作举办、在全国实施的面向社会的非学历证书考试，主要测试应试者外语笔译和口译能力，并对应试者提供翻译资格的权威认证。该项考试参考了包括美国、加拿大、欧盟、英国、澳大利亚等国家和地区的翻译资格认证标准，是一项具有国际水准的认证考试。

全国外语翻译证书考试目前设英、日两个语种。日语包括三个级别，英语包括四个级别。两个语种的各个级别均包括笔译和口译两种证书，考试合格者可获得相应级别的笔译或口译证书。其中，英语四级翻译证书于2008年10月首次开考，从2010年下半年开始把笔译和口译分为两个独立的考试，分别颁发证书。

详见：http://sk.neea.edu.cn/wyfyzs/index.jsp

上海外语口译证书考试

上海外语口译证书考试是上海紧缺人才培训工程重要项目之一，由上海市高校浦东继续教育中心（PCEC）负责组织实施。自1995年6月开考以来，已有大批合格者获得由上海紧缺人才培训工程联席会议办公室颁发的《上海市外语口译岗位资格证书》，近千人获得由上海市外语口译岗位资格证书考试委员会颁发的《上海市英语口译基础能力合格证书》，为社会培养了大批外语人才。

上海外语口译证书考试包括英语中级口译证书考试、英语高级口译证书考试、日语中级口译证书考试、日语高级口译证书考试、英语口译基础能力证书考试及英语口译基础能力证书（B级）考试。

详见：http://web.shwyky.net/index.htm

第5章 口译职业

5.1 初识口译职业真面目

正如中国古代爵位分为公、侯、伯、子、男,有高低之别,市场中的口译员也可分成不同"阶层"。

最高层:皇亲国戚。代表:联合国译员。成为联合国译员估计是不少译员一生的梦想。这群人在职时见证历史,退休后亦可以借名气发挥余热(如到高校任教或自己成立翻译公司)。但是成为联合国译员难度系数之大不是一般人能想象的,需要经过层层选拔和考试,过关斩将。联合国每隔一段时间都面向全球招考中文类译员,但能通过考试的凤毛麟角。即便通过考试进入后备人员库,如果运气不好只能终其一生待在名单上,连 UN 的门都没机会进。

第二层:贵族阶级。代表:政府机关译员、高校口译教师。此类人群的共同特点是平日工作,闲时兼职,旱涝保收。进入这个阶层的难度虽略逊于联合国译员,但也需经过全国公务员考试或高校教师招考层层筛选(一般高校招聘门槛较高,需要博士学历、持教师证、若干年口译教学或实战经验等)。

并列第二:世外高人。代表:某些在特定领域做成权威、专家的译员或拥有固定高端客户群的资深翻译。这些人大多在翻译市场奋斗多年,口碑好、名气大,几乎与客户形成一对一联络关系,很少在市场上露面。需要时每年给特定领域或客户做上几场会议口译,一年的收入就到手了,活得非常惬意。不过他们的舒适不是凭空得来的,需要数十年的不懈努力和奋斗,个中艰辛恐怕不是后生晚辈所能了解的。

第三层:富贵闲人。代表:自由职业翻译中经验丰富、资源较多者。他们从不发愁无会可做,因为每天都有大量客户或会议主办方打电话找来,因此有充分的选择空间,即使拒绝某些会议也不怕断了财路。普通译员修炼到这个阶段大概需要 8~10 年。

第四层:小康阶级。代表:大部分市场上的自由职业译员(从业 5 年以上)和企业内部的专职翻译(in-house)。前者一般各个领域的会议都接(只要有时间),没有什么特殊偏好;后者则是因为"拿人钱财",必须为人"分忧"。这个阶层虽然不比"富贵闲人"们有钱有闲，但只要工作努力，收入尚可，衣食无忧。

第五层：工薪阶级。代表：翻译公司的译员和处在上升期的自由职业译员（入行3～5年）。前者辛辛苦苦工作还要被公司盘剥（这点不如自由职业译员），后者则为了闯出"牌子"迈向高端市场努力接活儿，不挑剔，忍气吞声（怕得罪客户），还不时面临"开不了张"的情况（比如某个月工作量会减少）。

第六层：低薪打工族。代表：刚入行的新手和兼职学生。因为没有经验或经验不足，这一类人群较易沦为廉价劳动力，被分配到的大多为最苦最累钱最少的活儿，付出与收获远远不成正比，有时还会被无良客户或翻译公司欺负。

5.2　口译新人入行锦囊

（1）问好价钱再接活儿，不要为了所谓"实践的机会"委屈自己。为了能早点进入口译圈站稳脚跟，很多译员几乎只要有口译机会，就不计价钱、不辞劳苦，什么活儿都敢接，什么活儿都想接。但是结果就是几乎成了廉价劳动力或"救火队员"的角色，在相当长一段时间里永远徘徊在低端陪同口译市场，和刚毕业甚至没毕业的学生站在一条起跑线上，连"口译圈"的门都摸不到。

（2）要想进入一个圈子，找到"圈中人"很重要。可以通过给各大翻译公司投简历而获得口译工作的机会（记住，一定要是有声誉的大翻译公司，不能饥不择食，见到翻译公司就投）。同时可以请求学长学姐帮助和引荐，这样便有机会逐渐踏入口译高端市场，例如同声传译。同传这个圈子非常小，从业者几乎都是同行举荐，因此找到"圈中人"比自己瞎折腾、碰运气要有效得多。

（3）苦练内功，提高实力。找到"圈中人"虽然很重要，但如果自己实力欠缺，每做一场口译都只能给举荐人和同行带来麻烦，长此以往，便没有人再愿意"带你玩"。有些新译员往往过于重视外界的东西而忽视自身能力的提高，当机会降临时，如果因为自身原因没有把握住是十分可惜的。因此新译员一定要注意，实力比机遇更重要，是金子终究会闪光的。

（4）注意细节，做好反馈。译员只要接下一个口译任务，就需要特别小心、极其认真。除了资料和内容方面的准备，还应该事前取得客户的联络方式，就细节进行沟通，任务结束后可以给客户一张反馈表，让其为自己的表现打分。

一名初出茅庐的口译新人要经过至少3～5年的打磨才能成长为成熟译员。希望新人们不要急于求成，要内外兼修，方能早日成为合格的译员。

参考文献

［1］ Gile, D. *Basic Concepts and Models for Interpreter and Translator Training*. Philadelphia: John Benjamins, 1995.
［2］ 鲍刚. 口译理论概述. 北京: 旅游教育出版社, 2000.
［3］ 蔡小红. 口译评估. 北京: 中国对外翻译出版公司, 2007.
［4］ 达尼尔·葛岱克. 职业翻译与翻译职业. 北京: 外语教学与研究出版社, 2011.
［5］ 胡庚申. 近年我国口译研究综述//杨自检, 刘学云. 翻译新论. 武汉: 湖北教育出版社, 1994.
［6］ 黎难秋. 中国口译史. 青岛: 青岛出版社, 2002.
［7］ 刘和平. 口译技巧——思维科学与口译推理教学法. 北京: 中国对外翻译出版公司, 2001.
［8］ 马祖毅, 等. 中国翻译通史（古代部分）. 武汉: 湖北教育出版社, 2006.
［9］ 塞莱斯科维奇, 勒代雷. 口译训练指南. 北京: 中国对外翻译出版公司, 2007.
［10］ 谢天振. 中西翻译简史. 北京: 外语教学与研究出版社, 2009.
［11］ 许建忠. 《联合国译员史》简介. 中国翻译, 2005（1）.
［12］ 张维为. 英汉同声传译. 北京: 中国对外翻译出版公司, 1999.